West German Foreign Policy, 1949–1963

West German Foreign Policy 1949-1963

International Pressure and Domestic Response

WOLFRAM F. HANRIEDER

1967
Stanford University Press
Stanford, California

Stanford University Press
Stanford, California

Printed in the United States of America
L.C. 67-13657

To Barbara

Acknowledgments

This study was completed with the help of financial support received from the University Research Fund and the Center of International Studies of Princeton University. For their generous counsel I am greatly indebted to Ernst B. Haas and to the members of the Center of International Studies. None, of course, bear any responsibility for my conclusions.

W. F. H.

Contents

Abbreviations

BDI	Federation of German Industry *Bundesverband der Deutschen Industrie*
BHE	Refugee Party
BP	Bavaria Party
CDU/CSU	Christian Democratic Union/Christian Social Union
DGB	German Trade Union Federation *Deutscher Gewerkschaftsbund*
DP	German Party
ECSC	European Coal and Steel Community
EDC	European Defense Community
EEC	European Economic Community (Common Market)
EFTA	European Free Trade Association
EPU	European Payments Union
FDP	Free Democratic Party
GATT	General Agreement on Tariffs and Trade
JEIA	Joint Export and Import Agency
KPD	German Communist Party
OECD	Organization for Economic Cooperation and Development
OEEC	Organization for European Economic Cooperation
SACEUR	Supreme Allied Commander, Europe
SACLANT	Supreme Allied Commander, Atlantic
SHAPE	Supreme Headquarters, Allied Powers, Europe
SPD	German Social Democratic Party
UNESCO	United Nations Educational, Scientific, and Cultural Organization
WAV	Economic Reconstruction Union *Wirtschaftliche Aufbau-Vereinigung*
WEU	Western European Union

West German Foreign Policy, 1949–1963

Introduction

The absence of viable alternatives is often regarded as the outstanding characteristic of West German foreign policy. There is much truth in this assessment. The political vacuum left by the defeat of the Nazi regime, the years of occupation, and the Cold War not only raised the major foreign policy issues that were to preoccupy the Bonn Government, but also apparently mapped, or foreclosed, the paths toward their resolution. Problem and solution, or problem and failure, seem to have been rigidly determined by historical circumstances over which the policy makers in Bonn had comparatively little control.

The relative intractability of the international environment is a problem for the foreign policy makers of all nations. Purpose and power are met by cross-purpose and countervailing power, and each country's foreign policy projects face external restraints that the makers of policy can neglect only at the risk of failure. Viewing foreign policy and statecraft from this perspective, however, implies a good deal of determinism. In its more extreme analytical manifestations, this viewpoint reduces the pursuit of foreign policy goals to a contest between statesman and environment that is already settled by the insurmountable obstacles of the international "system." Nations are regarded as "actors," implicitly delegated to play out the roles the international system has "assigned" them in order to maintain system stability or equilibrium. Domestic political variables are largely neglected in this analytical perspective. Foreign policy aspirations are assessed primarily in terms of whether a nation has adequately "internalized" system "rules"—that is to say, whether it has adjusted to the vagaries of the international system, which moves toward a preordained historical or analytical *telos.* The strictures of necessity, imposed by the international environment, take analytical precedence over considerations of preference and the possibility of choice.[1]

There is another analytical perspective for viewing foreign policy, which focuses on the *internal* political processes of the nation-state. This perspective stresses the motivational elements that shape a nation's foreign policy goals, and highlights the sociocultural predispositions and institutional processes that lead to their formulation and to the choice of a method for their implementation. Although this approach apparently stresses choice rather than necessity, it frequently imposes a teleology of its own. The international conduct of a nation tends to be regarded as either irreversibly determined by its historical past and "political culture" or decisively shaped by the personal idiosyncrasies of its decision makers. Analytical emphasis rests on the domestic political system as a "subsystem" of the enveloping international system; the contemporary strictures and opportunities of the international environment are relegated to the secondary analytical role of serving as "inputs" from the international system into the domestic system.[2]

There is nothing novel about either of these views of international politics and international statecraft. The advantages and shortcomings of either approach must be assessed in terms of its relevance to the kind of questions that are being raised. The choice of the "systemic" or "subsystemic" approach does not reflect caprice on the part of the analyst, but a legitimate and calculated decision that is determined by the analytical purpose of the inquiry. An analyst interested primarily in the *outcome* of foreign policy will necessarily focus on the *operational* environment of the nation-state in the historical circumstances of the international system. An analyst concerned with the *motivational* aspects of foreign policy making will necessarily concentrate on internal political processes and the *perception* of external conditions, which is the basis for choosing among alternatives of ends and means.[3]

Nonetheless, the analyst of foreign policy is on safe ground in arguing that a full consideration of a nation's foreign policy should focus both on the opportunities and strictures presented by the nation's external, operational environment, and on the internal, psychological environment of the national system. When both dimensions are covered, a wider range of variables is brought together, and a more comprehensive analysis becomes possible. Almost by definition, foreign policy goals are circumscribed both by internal-motivational-psychological phenomena and by external-operational ones. It is literally impossible to speak of foreign policy goals without thinking at once of a psychological-motivational "unit" and the contextual, operational environment in which the unit seeks to realize its goals.[4]

The processes of contemporary international politics lend a special urgency to this analytical question, for they challenge the utility of the traditional and comfortably neat separation between international and domestic politics and the corollary distinction between the external and internal dimensions of foreign policy projects. Although the nation-state may still be regarded as the major actor in world politics, both the nature of the nation-state and that of the political processes of the international system have changed to such an extent that the analytical formulation of these transformations is a question of immediate concern.[5]

In the first place, many contemporary nations find it increasingly difficult or meaningless to draw distinctions between foreign policy and domestic policy. This holds true not only for the developing new nations but also for the industrialized nations of the northern hemisphere, whose reallocations of resources and values are strongly affected by international contingencies. The postwar occupation regimes in Germany and Japan, the United States involvement in South Vietnam, the United Nations operations in the Congo, foreign aid grants with restrictions on their use—these are just a few examples of the way prevailing patterns of power and purpose in the international system can strongly affect the allocation of values in a national system. National decision makers have become very much aware of this process, and have begun to recognize that in many political issues external events have a direct impact on the allocation of values that traditionally took place largely within national institutional structures.[6]

Second, nowhere is this phenomenon more clearly visible and institutionalized than in the operations of regional international organizations that are endowed with some measure of supranational authority, however limited. How can one draw distinctions between the foreign and domestic policies of nations operating in the context of an institution whose actions have consequences that cannot be assessed in terms of either purely external or purely internal ramifications?[7] In fact, the whole phenomenon of regionalism—whether institutionalized or not—suggests that an intermediate level of analysis should be employed to avoid the traditional, sharp distinction between national and international systems.[8]

Third, the very nature of the nation-state has been subjected to far-reaching mutations. As John Herz has cogently argued, the previously existing "hard shell" of physical, legal, and psychological boundaries, which national systems have traditionally maintained against the external environment, is becoming increasingly "permeated," primarily because of developments in modern weapons technology and the application of economic and psychological warfare.[9]

All these examples—and they are by no means exhaustive—go beyond the mere fact that there is an increasing "interdependence" among national actors in the system; rather, they are examples of a process of interpenetration in which the traditional boundaries separating the nation-state from the environing international system are becoming increasingly obscured.[10]

It is not surprising, therefore, that the conceptual relationship between the external and internal dimensions of foreign policy, or between "international politics and foreign policy,"[11] has received increasing attention.[12] This reflects not so much an academic fashion as the saliency of this question in a historical period when the nature of international politics and the nation-state is apparently undergoing important transformations.

An examination of West German foreign policy can claim a special relevance to the question of which level of analysis produces the most profitable results. There are two major reasons why. First, there is considerable historical evidence that the restrictions and opportunities of the international operational environment provided the West German Government with a relatively narrow range of acceptable alternatives. This points to the utility of applying an analytical framework that highlights the operational contingencies of the international system, since they were apparently predominant. On the other hand, it is striking to what extent the makers and critics of Bonn's foreign policy viewed the outcome of foreign policy issues as determining the kind of society that would ultimately prevail in Germany. Foreign policy projects were consistently evaluated in terms of the limitations and opportunities they posed for creating the social order that the interested parties were committed to establishing. For example, Kurt Schumacher, the postwar leader of the German Social Democrats, noted that "the contest over foreign policy is at the same time the contest over internal policy and the social content of the political order. . . . Foreign policy sets the limits to the possibilities of our economic and social policy."[13] Similarly, Adenauer and his supporters expected that the results of foreign policy would help create the prerequisites for the sociopolitical and cultural values they hoped to instill in the German body politic. Thus, the internal political dimensions of West German foreign policy goals should not be slighted, but should be granted the same analytical relevance as external dimensions.

There is nothing unique about the realization that the external environment can be manipulated in ways that have a fundamental effect on the domestic political order. History—and especially German history since the middle of the nineteenth century—abounds with examples of deliberate attempts to bring about international conditions considered conducive to the establishment or perpetuation of a distinct domestic social order. In the early years of the American Republic, for example, the Jeffersonians' preoccupation with westward expansion called for a different foreign policy than the Hamiltonian conception of an "Atlantic-directed" American destiny that rested on the cultural and political values of the eastern seaboard.

An examination of historical periods when the makers and critics of a nation's foreign policy connect it directly with the content of the internal sociopolitical order seems to call for a treatment that specifically acknowledges this phenomenon in the analytical framework employed. It is important to consider both external and internal dimensions of foreign policy precisely because its makers and critics apparently find it meaningless or impossible to separate them. Yet there is a great advantage, for purposes of analysis, in separating them initially, not only because their subsequent correlation becomes sharper, but because the two dimensions of foreign policy goals reach into significantly different analytical environments—namely, the external-international-operational and the internal-domestic-motivational.

This poses a problem. Granted that it would be desirable to consider both the external and the internal dimensions of foreign policy projects, first separately and then together; still, propositions derived from these two different analytical environments, or levels of analysis, cannot be readily correlated because they are culled from different sets of empirical data and methodological assumptions. This is the old problem of adding pears and apples. Propositions that can be established for one or the other level of analysis are frequently regarded as noncumulative because they emerge from significantly different analytical contexts.* Consequently, if conceptual linkages are to be established between these two levels, they must be couched in terms sufficiently isomorphic to assuage critics who contend—for sound reasons—that concepts from one level cannot be automatically applied to the other.

There are two concepts which, I believe, permit a useful correlation of important external and internal dimensions of foreign policy aims, and which allow the analyst to view foreign policy

* J. D. Singer, for example, argues that such propositions, "representing different levels of analysis and couched in different frames of reference . . . would defy theoretical integration; one may well be a corollary of the other, but they are not immediately combinable. A prior translation from one level to another must take place." ("The Level-of-Analysis Problem in International Relations," *World Politics*, Oct. 1961, p. 91.)

as a continuous process that bridges the analytical barriers between the international and domestic political systems. The first is the concept of *compatibility,* which is intended to assess the degrees of feasibility of foreign policy goals, given the strictures and opportunities of the *international* system; the second is the concept of *consensus,* which assesses the measure of agreement on the ends and means of foreign policy on the *domestic* political scene. The analytical meaning of both terms derives from the respective conceptual context they are drawn from; hence, if one concept were to be applied indiscriminately to the analytical environment of the other, it would lose a good deal of its utility. Nonetheless, they share a common element of meaning that allows their analytical linkage and correlation. In essence both concepts describe the limits of what is politically possible; they may be regarded as standards of feasibility.

By compatibility between the conditions of the international system and foreign policy goals I mean that a particular objective has a reasonable chance of realization if implemented with a policy that an outside observer would deem appropriate. The degree of complementarity *among* goals—an interesting target for speculation—can be established by aggregating their respective individual compatibilities vis-à-vis the international system. If one goal is judged compatible with the conditions prevailing in the international system, and if the pursuit of this goal is seen to have a negative effect on another goal's chances of success, these two goals may be regarded as incompatible. That is, the respective degrees of compatibility between individual goals and the international system serve as the basis for evaluating the degree of complementarity among goals. The conditions of the international system provide the backdrop for both relationships.

Clearly, the concept of consensus lacks this kind of "operational" background. No standard of feasibility on the domestic political scene corresponds precisely to the one the operational contingencies of the international system provide for the external dimensions of foreign policy goals. The motivational-psychological determinants of foreign policy projects may be checked by ethical restraints, inadequate perception of opportunities, realistic perception of external strictures, and so on, but the range of political goals that the members of a political system can advocate and agree on is at least hypothetically without limits.

Still, the differences between the concepts of compatibility and consensus need not be exaggerated. Compatibility is a concept of feasibility by definition, and if consensus is defined as the existing measure of agreement on policy projects among the relevant elements of a national system's decision-making process, it necessarily imposes boundaries on the activities the political system can pursue without risking fragmentation. In that sense, consensus is in fact a standard of feasibility, especially in a democratic political system; it determines, in the long run, what foreign policy goals a government can pursue without losing popular support and office.

I shall therefore be concerned with three sets of relationships. The first is the one between foreign policy goals and the conditions of the external operational environment in which they are pursued. The key concept in that analytical operation is compatibility. Chapters 2 and 5 spell out the major attributes of the international system and present an account of how the Bonn Government sought to implement its foreign policy goals on the international scene. Chapters 3 and 6 are addressed more specifically to the question of the degrees of compatibility that existed between systemic conditions and West German foreign policy objectives, and the resulting measure of complementarity among them. For this purpose I shall regard elements of the international system as either restrictive, permissive, or irrelevant for the objectives pursued by the Bonn Government.*

* A useful working definition of the term "international system" is the one proposed by Stanley H. Hoffmann: "An international system is a pattern of relations between the basic units of world politics, which is characterized by the scope of the objectives pursued by those units and of the tasks performed among them, as well as by the means used in order to achieve those goals and perform those tasks. This pattern is largely determined by the structure of the world, the nature of the forces which operate across or within the major units, and the capabilities, pattern of power, and political culture of those units." (Hoffmann, "International Systems and International Law," *World Politics*, Oct. 1961, p. 207.)

The second set of relationships is the one between foreign policy goals and the internal motivational environment of approbation or contention. Here, the key concept is consensus. In Chapters 4 and 7, I shall attempt to trace the shifting and overlapping patterns and degrees of consensus that emerge from the expressed attitudes and conduct of political parties and relevant pressure groups. Particularly important in this context is, of course, the role of the governing coalitions and that of the Social Democratic Party as the major voice of organized opposition. It should go without saying, however, that these indicators of preferences can provide us with only an approximation of the degree of existing consensus on a particular issue.

The third set of relationships is a correlation of the first two sets, and an attempt to bridge them. In the concluding chapter, the external dimensions of foreign policy objectives, in terms of compatibility, will be specifically related to their internal dimensions, expressed in terms of consensus.*

The period covered in this study extends from the beginning of the Federal Republic in 1949 to roughly the end of the Adenauer regime in 1963. Mainly in order to stress the changes in the international system during that span of time, I considered it useful to divide the study into two halves. The first begins with the establishment of the Federal Republic in 1949—after a brief discussion of the postwar years in Chapter 1—and ends with Germany's access to NATO and the restoration of German sovereignty in 1955. The second covers the following years, up to the end of Adenauer's tenure as chancellor in 1963.

Even though they mark the end of a distinct phase in West German foreign policy, the historical events of 1955 cannot claim to represent a turning point in the international system. But it is a basic assumption of my argument that fundamental attributes of the international system were undergoing far-reaching changes in the middle 1950's, especially in light of the

* Because of the various external and internal perspectives presented in different chapters, this book could be read in any of the following chapter sequences to provide continuity for either compatibility or consensus discussions: Chapters 1 through 8; Chapters 1, 2, 5, 3, 6, 4, 7, 8; Chapters 1, 2, 3, 5, 6, 4, 7, 8; Chapters 1, 4, 7, 2, 3, 5, 6, 8; or Chapters 1, 4, 7, 2, 5, 3, 6, 8.

developing nuclear stalemate and the emergence of economic and political regionalism in Europe and elsewhere. Since the international system provides strictures and opportunities for the pursuit of a nation's foreign policy goals, we may expect that the major projects of West German foreign policy began to meet with different sets of restraints and possibilities after the middle 1950's; the compatibilities between foreign policy aims and the international system shift with transformations of the system.

Against the backdrop of this gradually changing international system, the main aspirations of West German foreign policy remained essentially the same even though their specific content changed as they met with success or failure. They can be conveniently and legitimately grouped under three major headings: security, recovery, and reunification. On a more specific level of content and implementation, these projects were designed to achieve, first, the physical integrity of West German territory against external threats; second, the restoration of sovereignty, the readmission of Germany to the society of free nations, internal political stability, and a thriving economy with its corollary social benefits; and third, the reunification of the separated entities of West Germany, East Germany, the so-called Eastern Territories, and the Saar, which, in their entirety, represent roughly the territorial expanse of Germany in 1937.

The conflicting interpretations of the content to be placed into these abstract goals, of their proper order of priority, and of the means of achieving them will be treated in the chapters on the patterns of consensus.

Part I: 1945-1955

1. *The Shaping of the Issues, 1945–1949*

When the Adenauer Government took office in the fall of 1949, it inherited a series of problems that would have been staggering even for a well-established and less constrained government. In part, the tasks to be confronted had emerged from the demise of the Nazi regime, and in part they were the result of the disagreements that developed among the victorious Allies during the immediate postwar period. Although a new government can seldom begin with a *tabula rasa,* the internal and external strictures imposed on West Germany's foreign relations were unusually extensive and severe. The very creation of the Federal Republic reflected the pressures and conflicts of the postwar international system.

The most striking attributes of power and purpose that characterized the international system from the end of World War II to the middle 1950's, and the strictures and opportunities they posed for West German foreign policy goals, will be treated in some detail in the next chapter. It is the purpose of this chapter to provide a brief summary of the events that led to the establishment of the Federal Republic, by way of discussing the background of the major foreign policy issues* that were to preoccupy the Bonn Government.[1]

* Strictly speaking, the goal of maintaining the security of the Federal Republic from external attack, which will be treated as a major goal category in subsequent chapters, has no specific "background" in the period from 1945 to 1949. The occupation and complete disarming of Germany after the war left the responsibility for maintaining the physical security and territorial integrity of Germany entirely in the hands of the four occupying powers. The security concerns that were to preoccupy the Bonn Government after the establishment of the Federal Republic evolved from the general context of the Cold War and from disagreements among the occupying powers over the political future of defeated Germany.

RECOVERY

Political Recovery

The contest over Germany, which became the major Cold War issue in the decade following World War II, was foreshadowed in the differing conceptions with which the occupying powers approached governing their zones of occupation immediately after the war, and in the diverging blueprints they entertained for the future of Germany. With the disintegration of the Nazi regime in 1945, the four occupying powers assumed "supreme authority with respect to Germany, including all the powers possessed by the German Government, the High Command, and any state, municipal, or local government or authority."[2] At the Potsdam Conference in the summer of 1945, it was decided that no central German government would be established for the time being, although it was agreed that the development of democratic parties should be encouraged throughout Germany, and that local self-government should be reestablished as quickly as was consistent with the purposes of military occupation.

The purposes of occupation were not entirely clear to the United States and Great Britain. During the war, when the future of a defeated Germany had been a frequent topic of discussion among Allied statesmen, punitive attitudes on the part of American and British decision makers were tempered by the recognition that for the sake of a stable order in postwar Europe the German people should be led toward an appreciation of a democratic way of life. But Washington, in particular, failed to provide its military authorities in occupied Germany with clear-cut directives spelling out fundamental objectives and the ways and means of implementing them. Throughout the earliest years of the occupation, American policy consisted essentially of a series of pragmatic, ad hoc responses to the challenges posed by Soviet manipulations and by the need to administer the American zone with some degree of efficiency and continuity.

The purposes of the occupation, and the larger political aims to be furthered by it, were much clearer in the minds of the decision makers of the Soviet Union and France. Both countries had suffered immense losses at the hands of Nazi Germany and were determined to be compensated for their material losses by territorial gains and German reparations. France was hoping to permanently weaken Germany and to wrest from it the control of the industrial complex of the Ruhr and Saar, if possible bringing them under French authority, if necessary under international administration. The Soviet attitude had been ambivalent throughout the war. On the one hand, the Russians had supported the various punitive proposals for the dismemberment of Germany, and had demanded an enormous amount of reparations. On the other hand, German Communist cadres had been kept in readiness in the Soviet Union and were apparently groomed to help extend Soviet control over central Europe, on the basis of a future Russo-German rapprochement if that should be necessary. These differing aspirations of the occupying powers contained the seeds of the divisive forces that were to rend the Allied Control Council and culminate in the split of Germany.

In the Western zones of occupation, German advisory councils, whose members were nominated by the occupation authorities, were set up during 1945 at the municipal and county level; later, similar councils were organized at the *Land* and zone level. In the summer of 1945, the formation of political parties was authorized in the three Western zones, and in November parties were permitted to organize on a Land basis in the American zone. The major parties recognized at that time were the Christian Democratic Union (CDU), the Free Democratic Party (FDP), the Social Democratic Party (SPD), and the Communist Party (KPD). In January 1946, elections were held in the smaller towns and villages in the American zone; and elections in the larger towns and the cities followed in April. In the fall of 1946, local elections were held in the British and French zones, and constitutions for the three Länder in the American zone were approved by the occupation authorities and subsequently endorsed by plebiscite.

In addition to establishing and furthering the institutional prerequisites for a democratic political order, the Western powers, especially the United States and Great Britain, realized the need to reorient German attitudes toward politics as such. An extensive program of political "reeducation" was undertaken in the American zone, and efforts were made to expurgate the remnants of Nazism and militarism by screening the entire population. This was done with questionnaires and interviews designed to categorize degrees of responsibility and guilt, and to serve as a basis for measuring out appropriate retribution. Much attacked because of the miscarriages of justice involved, in 1946 the general administration of the denazification program was turned over to German authorities under the supervision of the Western occupation powers.[3]

The Potsdam Agreement had envisaged the establishment of central German agencies in the fields of finance, transport, communications, foreign trade, and industry, to be headed by German state secretaries under the direction of the Allied Control Council. The tensions that developed among the occupation powers, however, were soon reflected in the Control Council and prevented the establishment of even provisional administrative departments. But the day-to-day requirements of governing the occupation zones soon made it seem desirable to the Western occupation authorities, except the French, to set up a more coordinated administrative organization, even if this would have to be accomplished without Soviet participation. On January 1, 1947, the American and British zones were fused into "Bizonia," and during 1947, after no agreement could be reached among the four occupying powers on more centralized German agencies, the Anglo-American occupation authorities established a German Bizonal Economic Administration early in 1948. Although the Germans were denied participation in a Four Power administrative apparatus, because one could not be established in light of the developing Cold War tensions, they gradually obtained a measure of influence in the deliberative councils of the Anglo-American occupation authorities.

By the spring of 1948, the Western powers had become seriously concerned about apparent Soviet designs on central Europe, and increasingly frustrated by the difficulties of dealing with the Russians in the Allied Control Council. Western policy already began to anticipate the need to confront the Soviet Union in central Europe with a more tightly structured defense organization, and in March, Great Britain, France, the Netherlands, Belgium, and Luxembourg entered into the Brussels Treaty Organization for mutual defense. At the Six Power Conference, which met in London from February until June 1948, and which was highlighted by the Communist coup in Czechoslovakia, the Western powers decided to stabilize the situation in Germany by creating a West German state, established the International Control Authority to supervise and administer the industrial complex of the Ruhr basin, and agreed on measures that would lead to some form of European economic integration. On July 1, a few days after the Berlin blockade had been imposed by the Soviets, the Allied Commanders-in-Chief issued letters to the minister-presidents of the eleven Länder in the Western zones, authorizing them to call a constituent assembly for the purpose of drawing up a federal constitution for Western Germany.

The German minister-presidents were very reluctant to accentuate the developing division between East and West Germany by setting up a West German political structure. After lengthy discussions, they agreed to call a constituent assembly, with the stipulation that the proposed West German state would be viewed as a merely provisional arrangement—a reservation later incorporated in the Basic Law. A committee of experts went to work on a preliminary draft of the Basic Law during the summer, and a Parliamentary Council of 65 members, elected by the Länder parliaments, met in Bonn in September under the chairmanship of Konrad Adenauer.

There was considerable tension between the CDU and SPD delegates on a number of points, primarily because the Socialists objected to a relatively loose federal system as being detrimental to the economic planning they advocated as a major function of the proposed West German state. In February 1949, a compromise draft of the Basic Law was sent to the military governors for their consideration. Here again centralization posed a problem, because the occupation authorities, especially the French but also the Americans, objected to the proposed status of Berlin as a member state of the Federal Republic, and to what they considered an undesirable concentration of power in the central government. Both issues were finally resolved in a compromise. The Parliamentary Council approved the Basic Law on May 8, 1949, and the military governors gave their consent on May 12. Bonn was chosen as the provisional capital, and in August the first elections took place for the Bundestag. Ballots were cast by 78.5 per cent of the eligible voters. Of the 402 Bundestag seats contested, the Christian Democrats (CDU/CSU) won 139, the Socialists (SPD) 131, the Free Democrats (FDP) 52, the German Party (DP) 17, the Bavaria Party (BP) 17, and the Communists (KPD) 15; 31 seats went to various other parties, such as the Center, the Economic Reconstruction Union (WAV), and rightist groups. Theodor Heuss was elected President of the Republic; and after barely being elected chancellor by the Bundestag—his own vote being the decisive one—Konrad Adenauer formed a coalition government that aligned his own CDU/CSU with the Free Democrats and the German Party. His Cabinet, which was sworn in on September 20, consisted of eight CDU/CSU members, three Free Democrats (including the vice-chancellor), and two members of the German Party. On September 21, the Western occupying powers officially recognized the Federal Republic of Germany.[4]

The degree of independence gained by the Federal Republic was extremely restricted and conditional. In their letter of July 1, 1948, the military governors had spelled out the general outlines that they wished to have govern the relationship between the German Government and the occupation authorities. In April 1949, the Occupation Statute had been approved by the three Western foreign ministers in Washington; it was proclaimed on May 12, and came into effect with the establishment of the new German state. The Occupation Statute imposed stringent limitations on the German Government and reserved the following matters to the control of the occupation authorities:

foreign affairs and foreign trade; disarmament and demilitarization; reparations; control of the Ruhr basin; displaced persons and refugees; the protection, prestige, and security of Allied soldiers and their dependents; respect for the Basic Law and the constitutions of the Länder; and control of German prisoners sentenced by Allied courts. Furthermore, the Allied powers reserved for themselves the right to resume full authority if this should appear necessary for reasons of security or for the continuation of democratic government. To symbolize the end of military government, three High Commissioners, forming an Allied High Commission, replaced the three military governors.[5]

In the meantime, a "German People's Congress for the Unity of Germany and a Just Peace" had been assembled in the Soviet zone at the end of 1947. In March 1948 and May 1949, two more such assemblies were called to elect a Volksrat of four hundred members. In October 1948 the Volksrat, calling itself the only legitimate representative body of the German people, promulgated the draft of a constitution for the German Democratic Republic. The population of the Soviet zone approved the constitutional draft by a bare majority, although a number of dubious election practices and pressures had been applied. The third Volkskongress, established on the basis of this plebiscite, ratified the constitution for the GDR on May 30, 1949; it also elected a new Volksrat, which assembled in October 1949. The popular elections provided for in the constitution were postponed until October 1950 because of a national "emergency," and the Volksrat transformed itself into a provisional Volkskammer, claiming the rights of that body provided by the constitution. The Volkskammer elected Otto Grotewohl minister-president and established a Chamber of Provinces, as a second house, through existing provincial assemblies. The two houses together elected Wilhelm Pieck President of the Republic.[6]

Economic Recovery

The Potsdam Agreement provided that Germany would be treated as an economic unit, and the four zones of occupation were expected to share their industrial and agricultural output.

Aside from the Soviet Union's interest in dismantling industrial plants for reparations, Allied economic policy at that stage was primarily designed to prevent the reactivation of Germany's industrial war machinery. This was to be accomplished through large-scale dismantling of German industry, decartelization, and deconcentration of banking. Germany was to be self-supporting, but on a very low level.

In March 1946, the four occupying powers agreed on a Level of Industry Plan, which called for the dismantling of those plant facilities that would bring German production above an established ceiling set at approximately 50 per cent of the 1938 level of heavy industrial production. When the Russians failed to contribute to the agreed-on interzonal exchange of commodities, the Western powers, to compensate, raised the permissible level of industrial capacity in their zones. At the same time, the economic policies of the American occupation authorities were being reappraised, in part as a result of apparent Russian designs on central Europe. Initially, the economic policies to be followed by the United States military authorities were defined in the Joint Chiefs of Staff Directive 1067 of April 1945, which was a modified version of the extremely punitive Morgenthau Plan. In this directive, American occupation authorities were instructed to take no steps toward the economic rehabilitation of Germany or to maintain or strengthen the German economy. However, these instructions were qualified by an important proviso: "except as may be necessary to carry out your basic objectives."

These "basic objectives" were rather ambiguous to begin with, and were soon reevaluated in light of the tensions developing between the Soviet Union and the West. Furthermore, the day-to-day necessities of effective military government, and the desire to prevent "disease and unrest," almost inevitably led to policies that did in fact maintain and strengthen the German economy. American and British authorities began the importation of food, helped in reconstructing the disrupted network of transportation and communication, and on the local level many area commanders helped the Germans to bring some order out of economic and social chaos.

As early as September 1946, Secretary of State James Byrnes stated in his Stuttgart speech that the United States had no desire "to deny the German people an opportunity to work their way out of their hardships as long as they respect human freedom,"[7] and in July 1947, a new Joint Chiefs directive (no. 1779) stressed a self-supporting German economy as the major goal of American economic policy. In the following month a Revised Level of Industry Plan raised the permissible ceiling from 50–55 per cent to 70–75 per cent of the 1938 level. (At that time, current production was still under the ceiling established in the first plan.) As mentioned previously, on January 1, 1947, the American and British occupation zones were fused, in large part because of economic considerations; and in May the Germans were granted a small measure of participation and responsibility through the establishment of a German Bizonal Economic Council. In mid-1948 an agreement was signed making Bizonia eligible for Marshall Plan aid, to be channeled through the military governors; and a special bizonal agency was established for its administration.[8]

Undoubtedly the major event of Germany's postwar economic reconstruction was the currency reform of June 1948. Its main technical results were the contraction of the money supply through the drastic devaluation of the Reichsmark, and the reorganization of the public and private debt structure. Its economic, psychological, and social implications can hardly be exaggerated. Black and grey markets collapsed, literally almost overnight; hoarded caches of raw materials and finished goods found their way back into the market; incentive and confidence in a reliable currency were restored to economic life. Although an inflationary rise occurred soon afterward, tax and banking policies and the restraint of the labor movement in wage demands kept it within manageable proportions; by 1949, rising unemployment, caused in part by the influx of a large number of refugees into the Western zones, further curbed inflationary tendencies.

In addition to initiating the currency reform and channeling counterpart funds into critical sectors of the economy, Allied economic policy made a most important and lasting impact on the West German economy by stressing the need to free markets and liberalize trade. Initially, these policies were conceived of as complementing the Allied program for decartelization and the decentralization of the German economy; they received an added and decisive impetus from the Marshall Plan, which was intended by Washington to bring about European recovery not only through the massive injection of American aid but also through the long-range liberalization of European trade-and-payments policies. Postwar European trade was heavily restricted by bilateral payments agreements, which were the result of hard-currency shortages, and which practically amounted to a sophisticated form of an international bartering economy. The bizonal Joint Export and Import Agency (JEIA), which was under the control of the Anglo-American occupation authorities and in full charge of export-import dealings, was seemingly determined to make Bizonia an example of trade-and-payments liberalization to be emulated by the members of the OEEC—the coordinating administrative organization through which Marshall Plan funds were channeled, and which was to insure a general liberalization of European trade. At first, the stringent policies followed by the Joint Export and Import Agency hurt German exports and forced JEIA to backtrack to a series of bilateral trade-and-payments agreements, but ultimately they contributed substantially to the competitiveness and viability of the German economy after the establishment of the Federal Republic.[9]

The impact of East-West tensions on Germany's economic reconstruction was also reflected in the Western powers' changing attitude on the question of dismantling and reparations.[10] At the Yalta Conference, the Soviet Union had put forth claims for German reparations amounting to the equivalent of ten billion dollars. The United States recognized the legitimacy of Russian reparation demands but refused to be committed to a specific amount at that time and wanted the question postponed until a general settlement of the German question had been effected. The overall total of reparations, including French and British demands, was then to be determined in relation to the industrial capacity that Germany was allowed in order to maintain a self-sufficient economy. Both the United States and Great Britain were wary of permitting reparations to be made from current production, since this might require heavy Anglo-American support of a depleted German economy. The United States therefore agreed that reparations should be made largely by dismantling industrial equipment; this would at the same time help prevent the reconstruction of the German war industry.

In the summer of 1945, the Russians immediately began large-scale dismantling in their zone of occupation, but, as already noted, failed to contribute their share of commodities to the supposedly united economy of the four zones. In the Western zones a number of plants were also dismantled and shipped, and the French occupation authorities were second only to the Russians in extracting the maximum economic benefit from their zone of occupation; but as early as March 1946 the increasing tensions between the Soviet Union and the Western powers led the American military governor, General Lucius D. Clay, to halt shipments to the Soviet Union.

The occupying powers' fundamentally different plans for the political and economic future of Germany were inevitably reflected in their economic policies, and contributed to the economic split of Germany. The Russians and the French were primarily interested in being compensated for the losses and destruction they had suffered from German invasion and occupation. The United States and Great Britain, on the other hand, found it very expensive to administer and feed their zones of occupation, and aimed to create a self-sufficient German economy in order to ease the load on American and British taxpayers and lay the economic foundations for a stable political order. Furthermore, the Russians not only failed to contribute to the economies of the other zones, but proceeded to nationalize the remaining industrial plants in their zone, and carried out drastic agrarian reforms.

After protracted negotiations at the Moscow Conference in the spring of 1947, it was agreed that the Western powers would continue to dismantle plants in their zones and contribute to

Russian reparation demands. However, in the light of the new levels of permissible industrial production that were established for Bizonia in August, the Western powers shelved dismantling plans, and later in the year the dismantling list was further reduced to retain industrial plants that could be of use for Marshall Plan programs. In view of the developing Cold War and the Marshall Plan program, it no longer made sense to deplete West Germany's economic potential through dismantling and at the same time try to sustain the Western zones through infusion of aid. The first success of the newly established Bonn Government was to obtain a further reduction of the dismantling list in November 1949.

REUNIFICATION

The Saar

During World War II, the future status of the Saar territory had been repeatedly discussed among the Allies, and there was general agreement that the industrial complex of the Saar basin was to be separated from Germany.[11] In addition to seeking the separation of the Ruhr and the Rhineland from Germany, the absorption of the Saar into the French economy became a major goal of French policy.

At the end of the war, however, France found little effective encouragement for such separation plans. France was not represented at the Potsdam Conference, and since the Anglo-American powers opposed a definitive settlement of Germany's borders before a final peace conference—in order to avoid legitimizing the de facto annexation of the Oder-Neisse territory and East Prussia by Poland and the Soviet Union—they found it difficult to support a permanent revision of Germany's western borders. France was also disappointed with the provisions of the Potsdam Agreement that envisaged the ultimate establishment of a central German government and the treatment of Germany as an economic unit. In fact, these factors were closely related; France intended to exploit the resources of her zone of occupation as much as possible, and feared that the establishment of some form of central German political structure would tend to freeze and consolidate Germany's western borders and frustrate French plans to pry the important industrial and natural resources of the Saar from international control.

After France failed to gain the support of her wartime Allies at the Foreign Ministers' Conference in London in September 1945, the French resorted to more drastic unilateral steps. In December, the Saar mines were sequestered by France—the Saar being in the French zone of occupation—and in January 1946, Georges Bidault again outlined French plans for the Saar in the French National Assembly:

> The Saar mines, ownership of which was given to France by the Treaty of Versailles, are to become French property once again and, as a corollary to this, the territory is to be included in the French customs and monetary system, the two economies being complementary. French troops will be permanently stationed in the Saar to guarantee the future of such an arrangement. As for the eventual status of the territory, it will be the subject of a decision to be taken with our great Allies at a later date.[12]

In February 1946, the French demands were again presented to the Allies, and by the time of the Foreign Ministers' Conference in Paris in July, the United States and Great Britain were ready to give at least verbal support to French claims on the Saar. The Soviet Union sharply objected, and Molotov, in a sweeping attack on the German policy of the Western powers, called for the political unity of Germany, criticized the provisions of Joint Chiefs of Staff Directive 1067 and the pastoralization of Germany envisaged in the Morgenthau Plan, and condemned French designs on the Saar, Ruhr, and Rhineland.

Being frustrated at the conference table, the French again took matters into their own hands. At the Foreign Ministers' Conference in New York in December 1946, France intimated that "special circumstances" might cause her to make certain "administrative arrangements" in the Saar; and on December 2, French customs officials manned the administrative boundaries between the Saar and Rheinland-Pfalz and began to control the passage of goods, money, and persons. In other words, the Saar was administratively carved out of the French zone of occupation and economically tied to metropolitan France. British reaction was ambivalent, but Moscow objected strongly, and General Clay criticized the measure as a unilateral decision that circumvented the authority of the Allied Control Council.

From here on, French policy on the Saar consistently sought to obtain the Allies' legitimization of the integrative measures already undertaken, in order to consolidate the Franco-Saar economic union politically and contractually. At the Moscow Conference in the spring of 1947, the French Government submitted a note reiterating the French position: the Saar was to be removed from the authority of the Control Council; the Saar population was to obtain separate citizenship status; France was to be in charge of foreign affairs; and a French High Commissioner was to head legislative and administrative bodies chosen in popular and secret elections. No agreement could be reached at the conference, and in May the French established a commission to draft a constitution for the Saar based on the principles of the French memorandum submitted in Moscow. In June 1947, a Saarmark replaced the Reichsmark as a transitional monetary unit, before the French *franc* was introduced. In October general elections were held for a constituent assembly, and resulted in an 87 per cent mandate for economic union with France. In November, France approved the draft of the constitution, and the franc became legal tender. Customs barriers between the Saar and France were abolished and imposed instead between the Saar and Germany.[13]

After the de facto annexation of the Saar, France still had to secure its political and contractual legitimization, especially if a more or less centralized German political structure should come into being. Again, being on record as opposing a permanent unilateral border settlement on the Oder-Neisse question, the United States and Great Britain found it somewhat difficult to lend their official approval to French action in the Saar. Their implicit approval was soon forthcoming, however. During the London Six Power Conference of February 1948, the economic fusion of the Saar with France was in effect given a stamp of approval, with the understanding that the Ruhr was not to be separated from Germany and that no special provisions would be made for the Rhineland. It is no coincidence that the London Conference also produced the so-called London Documents, which set forth the general outlines for a West German constitution that were handed to the German minister-presidents on July 1; there is little doubt that French acquiescence to the formation of a West German government was obtained by Allied legitimization of France's economic annexation of the Saar. In April 1948, after France, the United States, and Britain had reached agreement on adjustments of reparations and coal deliveries, the Saar was officially joined in an economic union with France, and commercial dealings between the Saar and Germany were henceforth treated as foreign trade operations.[14]

West Germany and East Germany

During World War II, the Allies had considered a variety of proposals for the dismemberment of Germany.[15] By the time of the Yalta Conference in February 1945, the issue had become more pressing, since the defeat of Germany was imminent. Stalin urged a specific and binding settlement of the political future of postwar Germany, and wished to have the likelihood of partition inserted in the final communiqué. He also reluctantly agreed to the formation of a French zone of occupation, provided it would be carved out of the areas allotted to the United States and Great Britain. Roosevelt and Churchill, however, favored a "cooling off" period in postwar Europe, and preferred to leave the final decision on the political organization of Germany to a peace conference. Still, the Big Three were generally in accord that a breakup of Germany would be desirable in principle, and instructed their foreign ministers to work out provisions for it that could be incorporated in the German surrender document.

In the months between Yalta and the Potsdam Conference, the Big Three apparently had second thoughts about partition. Throughout the war, the Soviet Union had in effect pursued a two-pronged policy toward Germany. One element stressed the punitive and disintegrative features of the various dismemberment proposals, and the other envisaged in effect a future German-Soviet reconciliation, presumably on the basis of Soviet predominance in central Europe. On the same day that the final German capitulation document was signed in Berlin (a less elaborate surrender document had been signed the day before at Rheims), Stalin declared in a proclamation to the German people that the Soviet Union did not intend to dismember Germany.

The British also had reconsidered the question of partition. In addition to Churchill's general misgivings about Soviet intentions, the British Treasury came forth with an impressive array of economic arguments that made it seem desirable to treat Germany as an economic unit. Since the British zone of occupation was primarily industrial rather than agricultural, and could, moreover, be expected to attract a large number of refugees, there loomed the possibility that Britain would have to support an economically depleted zone, and in effect pay Germany's reparation bills. Similar possibilities were considered in Washington, and were reinforced by the feeling that the United States should not be committed to a lengthy period of occupation. Although President Truman was apparently still oriented by Roosevelt's initial dismemberment plans when he arrived at Potsdam, he did not subsequently press for the division of Germany.[16]

The apparent willingness of the Big Three to shelve dismemberment plans should not obscure the fact that their differing plans for their zones of occupation foreshadowed the partition of Germany. Although provisions were made for the uniform treatment of the German population, and there was agreement that Germany should be treated as an economic unit, deep fissures already existed. The Soviet Union refused to agree that Germany's ability to pay for her imports should have priority over reparation deliveries from current production, and could not be persuaded to negotiate a trade treaty. At least the economic division of Germany seemed already in the offing.

In the meantime, the administrative tasks of occupation needed immediate attention and regulation. On June 5, 1945, the Allies issued a statement providing that "Germany, within her frontiers as they were on 31st December, 1937, will, for the purposes of occupation, be divided into four zones," and that the Four Powers "will hereafter determine the boundaries of Germany or any part thereof and the status of Germany or of any area at present being part of German territory."[17] This divisive zonal arrangement was somewhat qualified by the special provisions made for Berlin and the establishment of an organ pertaining to the whole of Germany, the Allied Control Council.

Fundamental differences about the kind of German society that should ultimately prevail, and lack of agreement on economic policies, especially Soviet reparation demands, soon led to abrasive encounters and acrimonious debates among the representatives on the Allied Control Council. At the two Foreign Ministers' Conferences in 1946, no agreement on the future political organization of Germany could be reached, and the economic fusion of the American and British zones of occupation followed in January 1947. At the fourth session of the Council of Foreign Ministers in Moscow in April 1947—which coincided with the announcement of the Truman Doctrine that the United States would come to the aid of Greece and Turkey—Germany was the main topic on the agenda. The Soviet Union apparently still had hopes that a unified Germany would present opportunities for gaining control of key positions, if not for a complete Soviet take-over; Molotov rejected the "federalization" of Germany and suggested the formation of a provisional German government capable of guaranteeing the political and economic unity of Germany and responsible for German obligations toward the Allies. The Western powers were already deeply suspicious of Soviet motives, and the German question was again complicated by the reparations issue and by American insistence that the status of the Oder-Neisse territories could not be divorced from a general settlement of the political future of Germany. Molotov vehemently rejected this as no longer debatable, and the Russians countered by demanding Soviet participation in a Four Power control arrangement over the Ruhr and ten billion dollars in reparations from current production, to be spread out over a period of up to twenty years.[18]

The year 1948 brought momentous events, which, in effect,

sealed the already existing de facto division of Germany. In February 1948, the Western powers decided at the Six Power Conference in London to fuse their zones of occupation and further consolidate their economic integration in anticipation of the forthcoming European Recovery Program. The Soviet Union called the conference a violation of the previous Four Power agreements on Germany, and indicated that it would reject any decisions taken. On March 20, when the Western representatives on the Control Council in Berlin refused to divulge the agreements on Germany reached at the conference, the Soviet delegation walked out. Meanwhile, the coup d'etat in Czechoslovakia had occurred on February 25 while the London Six Power Conference was in session, and the West had reacted with the Brussels Treaty on mutual defense, signed by Britain, France, Belgium, the Netherlands, and Luxembourg on March 17. At about the same time, the Soviets began to impose the first traffic restrictions on the access routes to Berlin; these were to culminate in the blockade. During the summer, they gradually increased the strictures on traffic between the Western zones and Berlin, and on June 16 the Soviet representatives walked out of the Allied Kommandatura.[19]

The currency reform introduced in the Western zones on June 20 further aggravated these tensions. The Russians now declared that they considered all sectors of Berlin to be part of the Soviet zone with regard to economic matters, and that they would forthwith introduce an Eastmark as legal tender in all of Berlin. The Western powers refused to budge, and announced that beginning June 25 the Westmark would be legal tender in the Western sectors of Berlin. On June 24, the Russians imposed a complete blockade on Berlin, and in July for the first time they claimed that Berlin was an integral part of the Soviet zone because of Western violations of the Four Power agreements. While the airlift was being put into operation, the West began negotiations that resulted in the North Atlantic Treaty of April 1949.[20]

The Berlin blockade and the two currency reforms undoubtedly mark the explicit and rigid division of Germany that had been foreshadowed since 1945. Economically the partition was complete, and not even the inflated Reichsmark remained as a unifying symbol. Militarily, the Soviet threat to Berlin pointed to the relative weakness of the West and led to the creation of a Western alliance directed against the Eastern bloc. The division of Germany had occurred, and needed only to be institutionalized with the establishment of the two German governments in Bonn and Pankow.

The Oder-Neisse Territories

Germany's future eastern borders were a topic of discussion as early as the Stalin-Eden meeting in Moscow in December 1941.[21] At that time, Stalin suggested the Curzon Line as the future Russian-Polish border, and recommended that Poland be compensated with East Prussia. The issue was again discussed at Teheran in November 1943, and although no definitive conclusions were reached, there was an implied, if ambiguous, agreement among the Big Three that Poland was to be compensated in the West for the eastern Polish territories Stalin had claimed.

At Yalta the main disagreements among the Big Three over the Polish question revolved around which Polish government to recognize—the London exiles or the Lublin government sponsored by the Soviet Union—and the Russians' insistence that Polish territory be extended to the western Neisse. The Western powers considered the southern half of East Prussia, Upper Silesia, and the territory to the Oder sufficient compensation for Poland, and the final communiqué left the question open and unresolved. As far as actual possession of the territory was concerned, however, settlement was already under way: while the Yalta Conference was still in progress, Soviet troops had crossed the Oder north of Breslau. Russian occupation of the territory thus presented the Western Allies with a fait accompli by the time the issue came up again at the Potsdam Conference. At Potsdam the United States and Great Britain stressed again that they would be unwilling to commit themselves to a permanent solution until the signing of a final peace treaty with Germany, but nonetheless bargained for a softening of Soviet reparation demands in return for their acquiescence to an established state of affairs.

At the meeting of the Council of Foreign Ministers in Moscow in the spring of 1947, the eastern boundaries of Germany were a major topic. The American position on the Oder-Neisse issue had by then sharpened considerably, and Secretary of State George Marshall presented the Western argument forcefully and specifically. The United States demanded that the Oder-Neisse question be resolved in such a way that future German-Polish relations could develop amicably and that irredentist sentiments would not grow in Germany. In response to Marshall's suggestion that the territory east of the Oder-Neisse Line be made available to the German economy as a whole, Molotov rejected a discussion of the entire question, and declared that although the Potsdam Conference formally had no choice but to postpone a final settlement until a peace conference, the substance of the issue was settled and allowed of no revision. At the London meeting at the end of the year, Marshall again demanded the utilization of Silesia's industrial capacity in a unified German economy, and Great Britain proposed the establishment of a study commission to examine the question of Germany's boundaries. No agreement could be reached, millions of Germans had already been expelled from the Oder-Neisse territories, and Poland had undertaken an extensive program through which the territories were to be effectively incorporated by resettling them with Polish nationals.

2. *The International System and the Pursuit of Goals, 1949–1955*

An international system is a pattern of relations among the major powers in world politics, which is characterized by the nature and scope of their objectives and the capabilities available for their implementation. This pattern emerges from the power relationships among nation-states in the system, the goals they pursue, and the coalitions they form to achieve common purposes. The sum total of these relations, the international system, represents the strictures on and opportunities for realizing national foreign policy goals, and serves as the operational environment in which objectives meet with success or failure.

This chapter gives an account of West Germany's pursuit of its foreign policy goals from 1949 to 1955. The degree of compatibility between the international system and these objectives, and the degree of complementarity among them, will be assessed more explicitly in the next chapter. Although the specific restraints and opportunities that the international system implied for Bonn's foreign policy projects will be of concern throughout the following pages, it is useful to preface the discussion with a brief general statement of the starkest international patterns of power and purpose that prevailed during that period.[1]

In the decade from the end of World War II until West Germany became a member of NATO in 1955, Europe was the major arena of the conflict that came to be known as the Cold War. There were two related reasons for this: Europe, temporarily exhausted, had become an inviting vacuum of power; and Europe, potentially strong, was viewed as the major prize that the two emerging, and soon contending, superpowers meant to deny one another at all costs. The contest over the control of

Europe ended in a deadlock when East and West Germany were fully incorporated into the two Cold War camps, and when the developing nuclear stalemate and its attendant restraints made a drastic revision of the European status quo increasingly unlikely.

By the end of World War II, the power pattern of the international system had been fundamentally transformed. Largely, it was the conduct of the war and the victory of the Allied powers that accounted for the change in the power structure, and shaped the course of international politics in the war's aftermath. Most importantly, the centers of world power had shifted away from Europe and toward the United States and the Soviet Union. The Axis powers' spheres of influence in Europe and Asia had disintegrated. But even the wartime allies of the United States and the Soviet Union had become secondary powers. Those with colonial empires soon found it increasingly difficult and costly to prevent or even delay their dissolution, the Soviet Union had extended its control over part of the Balkans and central Europe, and the United States had emerged as the major power in the affairs of Western Europe and the Far East. The outstanding characteristic of the postwar international system was the emergence of two superpowers, and the great disparity of strength that set them apart from, and above, other nations.

This polarization of power did not as yet extend to nuclear capabilities. From the end of World War II until 1952, the United States enjoyed first a monopoly and later a pronounced superiority in nuclear weapons and the aircraft capable of delivering them. During that phase the Soviet Union's conventional forces far outstripped those of the West and posed a particular threat to Western Europe. Between 1952 and 1955, both superpowers acquired thermonuclear capabilities, and the Soviet Union not only maintained a significant superiority in conventional force levels but also developed nuclear delivery systems capable of threatening Western Europe. The continental United States, however, was still invulnerable to Soviet nuclear weapons, and the Soviet nuclear threat against Western Europe could be credibly countered by American threats to devastate the Soviet Union. Strictly speaking, the capability pattern of the pre-1955 international system was bipolar only in the sense that there were two superpowers and two alliance blocs, and that both Cold War camps perceived a certain compensatory balance between Soviet superiority in land power and American superiority in nuclear air power.

Almost from the beginning of the postwar period, there were disagreements between the two major powers, and after a period of "attempted accommodation" on the part of the United States, the tensions between the superpowers took on increasingly serious proportions. There is no need to spell out step by step the escalation of this conflict, or to speculate on the motivations that inspired the conduct of the Soviet Union and the United States, whether they were geopolitically predestined, ideologically propelled, based on legitimate security concerns, or caused by misunderstanding.[2] In any event, Washington and Moscow became not only the centers of a polarized pattern of power, but also the leaders of contending ideological camps, which disagreed fundamentally on the ultimate purposes and values that should govern the application of this power.

The major patterns of the objectives pursued by the major powers in the international system are less easily summarized. In large part, the postwar tensions between the United States and the Soviet Union, which culminated in a full-scale East-West confrontation, were due to the Soviet subjection of Eastern Europe and Moscow's apparent plan to gain control of all of Germany.[3] Initially, the Soviet Union attempted to extend its power into central Europe as far as it could without risking an open conflict with the Western powers. The 1947 and 1948 Soviet proposals for a withdrawal of all occupation forces from Germany and the establishment of a Four Power German government were apparently part of a master plan for the political conquest of Germany. The failure of this policy, which led to the Berlin blockade, marks the beginning of the Cold War.

At first the Western powers framed a series of ad hoc responses, which did not jell into a consciously articulated policy program until the enunciation of the doctrine of containment. Washington's containment policy, mainly implemented by the mobilization of the military and economic resources of the United

States and Western Europe, became a key element in the increasing polarization of capabilities and spheres of influence in the international system. Containment, to successfully stop Soviet designs in central Europe and elsewhere, seemed to require an unequivocal extension of American "presence" in Europe from the Atlantic seaboard to the East German border. Soviet pressures, and Western measures to contain these pressures, necessarily led to a "tightening" of bipolarity and a corresponding clarification of East-West spheres of influence in central Europe. In Germany, the ultimate success of containment—at the expense of German unification—was reflected by the Soviet Union's final abandonment of serious attempts to unite Germany on Soviet terms. By 1955, the Soviet Union had settled on a policy of "two Germanies," and sought to obtain legal recognition of the de facto division of Germany and Europe. The Cold War balance in Europe had become essentially stable. It was against this background of systemic power relationships and patterns of purpose that the Bonn Government sought to advance its three major foreign policy projects—security, recovery, and reunification.

SECURITY AND REARMAMENT

No regular West German armed forces were established between 1949 and 1955. Hence, the security of the Federal Republic was essentially determined by the capabilities and intentions of the Soviet bloc and by the countervailing power and purpose of the Western alliance. Even so, the Bonn Government's decision to implement the goal of national security by rearming within the framework of the Western alliance affected the power pattern of the international system importantly. Bonn's security policies between 1949 and 1955 laid the groundwork for an increasingly significant German contribution to the Western alliance, in whose security benefits the Federal Republic expected to share. Equally important, the rearmament of West Germany became the linchpin that held together the entire foreign policy of the Bonn Government, with fundamental implications for the entire range of the foreign policy projects the Adenauer Administration was committed to.

By 1949, the lines of political and military demarcation in central Europe had hardened considerably. The creation of Cominform, the Communist coup in Czechoslovakia, and the gradual solidification of Soviet control over the East European satellites had substantially tightened the cohesion of the Eastern bloc, and had effectively excluded Western influence. Similarly in the West, the Marshall Plan and the OEEC, the establishment of NATO, the quelling of the strike movement in France, and the electoral defeat of pro-Soviet elements in Italy had led to a neutralization of Soviet influence. Both Cold War camps had consolidated their positions and established clearly delineated spheres of influence. The establishment of two German states was the climax of this polarization, and both sides soon began to reinforce by military means the political division of Europe and Germany.

The Berlin blockade had already demonstrated to the West the need to be militarily prepared for Cold War encounters in which the Soviet Union was willing to resort to a show of physical strength. The outbreak of the Korean War in June 1950 served as a further warning that Cold War tensions required a large-scale mobilization of Western resources, and that reliance on American air and naval power to deter Soviet aggression with conventional forces would have to be reexamined. In particular, the apparent parallels between the situation in divided Korea and the split of Germany highlighted the possibility that the Soviet Union would resort to more overt hostilities in central Europe. In view of the military buildup in East Germany, widespread apprehensions in the West that the Soviet Union might contemplate aggression in Europe did not lack a basis in fact.*

* The nature of East Germany's paramilitary forces was summarized in a protest note from the United States to the Soviet Union in May 1950: "There has been created in the part of Germany that is subject to Soviet control a police force which has, by reason of its military training and equipment, the character of an army. . . . It amounts to about 50,000 men. It is not an ordinary police force, and it does not have ordinary police duties. It receives basic infantry, artillery, and armored training, and is equipped with military weapons, including machine guns, howitzers, anti-aircraft cannon, mortars and tanks. It must be regarded, therefore, as a military force." Beate Ruhm von Oppen, ed., *Documents on Germany under Occupation, 1945–1954* (London: Oxford University Press, 1955), p. 493.

France began to demand a "forward" strategy in Europe, and the United States embarked on a program of rearmament, imposed a variety of economic controls, and undertook steps to consolidate and extend the Western military alliance. Marshall Plan allocations were gradually rechanneled from predominantly economic sectors to projects contributing more directly to European security.

The rearmament of West Germany, the country situated on the front line of the Western alliance, now came to be considered essential for a viable Western defense posture in Europe. The main problem posed by the realization that the resources of the Federal Republic should be enlisted for the Western cause was how to control a West German military contingent. As early as 1948, European "federalists" had advocated the creation of a supranational European military establishment, in part because such an arrangement would provide an effective method of supervising a rearmed Germany. The possibility of rearming Germany under international auspices had also been raised by Winston Churchill in the spring of 1950, and he repeated this proposal in the Council of Europe on the first day of the Korean War. On the whole, the Truman Administration was in favor of rearming Germany, though Administration spokesmen agreed with Paris and London on the need for close international supervision of German military contingents.[4]

The implications of these developments were not lost on the Adenauer Government. In November 1949, the German Government still declared its "earnest determination to maintain the demilitarization of the federal territory and to endeavour by all means in its power to prevent the re-creation of armed forces of any kind."[5] Nevertheless, at the end of the year Adenauer suggested the creation of West German paramilitary contingents that would serve as part of a general Western anti-Communist military force. In part, this shift was undoubtedly motivated by the buildup of strong paramilitary "police" forces in East Germany, and reflected a concern with the security position of the Federal Republic. More importantly, perhaps, Adenauer was fully aware of the political lever rearmament could provide for the pursuit of West German sovereignty and the attainment of his fundamental goal—equal partnership for West Germany in a Western European union. Bonn now was presented with a range of opportunities to trade German support of the West, especially military support, for Allied concessions in the areas of political and economic recovery. These considerations will be treated below in connection with the goal of West Germany's recovery.

The first clear-cut indications that the Western powers expected the Federal Republic to contribute to the Western defense effort were soon forthcoming. In September 1950, the Western powers announced their decision to end the formal state of war with Germany; and West Germany and West Berlin, although already covered by Article 6 of the North Atlantic Treaty, were again specifically included in the Western defense perimeter. Most likely this emphasis was renewed to avoid ambiguity like that of the American declaration on its defense perimeter in the Far East, which some critics of American policy thought contributed to the North Koreans' expectation that their invasion of South Korea would not trigger an American response.

The Allies agreed to reinforce their troops in West Germany, and encouraged the establishment of German mobile police units, to be organized on a Land basis but available to the Federal Government in emergencies. The creation of a separate, national German army was regarded as undesirable, but plans to incorporate German units at the lower echelons of an integrated European army were being formulated. At the same time, the NATO Council decided to accelerate the defense measures spelled out in the North Atlantic Treaty of April 1949, and instructed the NATO Defense Committee to draw up plans for the efficient and speedy inclusion of West German contingents in a Western defense establishment.

The widely recognized need to seek a West German military contribution raised some serious problems within NATO. The United States proposed that the biggest German unit should be a division, and recommended using ten German divisions in a NATO defense force. France submitted the so-called Pleven

Plan for a unified European army, and insisted on much smaller German units; the French plan called for "the complete fusion of all human and material elements" of the proposed European forces that were to be placed at the disposal of a unified Atlantic community. It was not these integrative features that caused contention between France and the United States, as much as repeated French attempts to curtail Germany's political influence in an international military arrangement and to limit Germany's military functions to an essentially auxiliary role. For example, in connection with the signing of the Schuman Plan for the European Coal and Steel Community, France made a proposal that German troops serve as labor battalions—a proposal that was unsuccessful primarily because the United States strongly supported German objections. From the beginning of the rearmament debate, France was very reluctant to consent unless German units were small and effectively supervised by an international body in which German influence would be minimal.[6]

The French Government was also troubled by its lack of success in enlisting Great Britain in a Western European defense arrangement to counterbalance a rearmed Germany. As negotiations proceeded to establish the European Defense Community, Great Britain stood off under both a Labour government and the Conservative government that replaced it in October 1951. This situation presented France with a real dilemma. Already deeply suspicious of the special Anglo-American "understanding" that had been cemented during the occupation of Germany, France nevertheless felt obliged to commit both the United States and the United Kingdom to involvement in Europe to make up for French weakness. This appeared especially necessary because French resources were already severely strained by costly commitments in Africa and Asia. At the same time, France wished to forestall the formation of another special understanding—between the United States and West Germany —apparently in the offing owing to fundamental strategic calculations that made the equal partnership of the Federal Republic in the Western Cold War alliance seem desirable. The French position became even more problematic in the following years because of the Eisenhower Administration's impatience with the vagaries of the Fourth Republic's domestic politics, and because Eisenhower, Dulles, and Adenauer concurred on methods of dealing with the Soviet Union.

To repeat, however, the most important factor in the shifting power relationships within the Western alliance was the growing importance of West Germany for the defense posture of the West. The gradually widening role that NATO planners assigned to West German military contingents provided Bonn with a bargaining lever of increasing effectiveness although there was not yet a single West German soldier under arms. For these considerations we must turn to the changing strategic context that evolved in the early 1950's as a result of the shifting power relationships between East and West.

The NATO Conference at Lisbon in February 1952 marked an important juncture in the reformulation of Western military strategy, and had an important effect on the security position of the Federal Republic. The decisions reached at Lisbon reflect the first "formal" recognition that the value of the American nuclear deterrent could be expected to decline and that the capability patterns of the international system were shifting in favor of the Soviet Union.

NATO planners had from the beginning distinguished among three defense plans; in addition to two stopgap emergency plans, they had formulated a so-called long-term requirements plan, which was based on the contingency of a main Soviet thrust across the North German plain, and which spelled out the force levels required to meet that threat and defend Europe in a major war. In that respect, the force goals agreed upon at Lisbon, which came close to the requirements of the long-term plan, were no drastic innovation. But there was a feeling of increased urgency. The Soviet Union had already exploded nuclear devices, and it was to be expected that the differential advantage still being provided by American strategic nuclear capabilities would be gradually diminishing. At Lisbon, the North Atlantic Council agreed on a force goal of 96 divisions, of which 35 to 40 were to be battle-ready on the line, the remainder to be capable of mobilization within a month after D-Day.[7] In light of these requirements, it was not surprising that the Council members "reaffirmed the urgency, for the defense of Western Europe, of establishing at the earliest possible date a militarily effective European Defense Force, including a German contribution."[8]

There was no intention, however, of matching Soviet conventional forces in Europe. The decision to equip NATO with a conventional army powerful enough to sustain a prolonged engagement with Soviet ground troops was intended to compensate for the diminishing advantage of the American nuclear deterrent rather than to provide a conventional alternative. The primary purpose of a large NATO army was to prevent the Soviet Union from effecting a fait accompli with a conventional attack while threatening a nuclear strike against Western Europe. Since the Soviet Union was not yet capable of threatening the United States with nuclear destruction, a Soviet threat to attack Western Europe could be credibly countered by an American threat to devastate the Soviet Union with a nuclear counterstrike.[9]

The implications of the Lisbon strategy aroused some misgivings in Bonn that foreshadowed the much more serious concerns voiced in later years. The Lisbon Plan apparently accepted the possibility of a more or less "prolonged engagement" with Soviet troops, and, implicitly, of fighting a "limited war" in Europe during which the Federal Republic, due to its forward position, would necessarily suffer the most. The Soviet action to be prevented would presumably involve hostilities on West German territory under any circumstances. As it was, the conventional force goals envisaged at the Lisbon meeting proved unrealistically ambitious. They met with a good deal of domestic opposition in many NATO countries, and there are good reasons to suspect that many member countries viewed the fixing of the Lisbon force goals as largely an academic exercise.[10] Implementation would have proven costly and politically controversial, and many Europeans regarded conventional forces primarily as a trip-wire that would trigger an immediate American nuclear response if they were attacked. For this function, it seemed, a much smaller contingent would suffice. The Atlantic alliance continued to rely primarily on the American nuclear deterrent, and when the Eisenhower Administration enunciated its doctrine of "massive and instant retaliation" by means and at places of Washington's choosing, it merely added an official stamp of approval to the existing and accepted deterrence posture.

Understandably enough, the "automaticity" of an American nuclear response to a conventional provocation, which was reemphasized in the doctrine of massive retaliation, appeared attractive to Bonn; it seemed to reinforce the credibility of deterrence and reduce the likelihood that West Germany would become a battlefield in a conventional war. But Washington's "new look" strategy of massive retaliation, which was coupled with the announcement that American standing forces would be reduced by 18 per cent over the next four years, was rapidly being called into question by the shifting power relationship between the United States and the Soviet Union. Massive retaliation depended heavily on the B-47 bomber bases overseas, which were beginning to become vulnerable to Soviet attack; in August 1953 the Soviet Union set off its first H-bomb, and during 1954 Moscow began to display a considerable number of long-range bombers. Although NATO's Lisbon force goals were far from implementation, Soviet conventional forces had been consistently modernized since the end of World War II.

To be sure, this increase in power was in part balanced by the advances made by NATO. By 1954 NATO had approximately fifteen divisions under arms, and considerable progress had been made in planning and constructing an elaborate infrastructure of communications networks, fuel pipelines, port facilities, supply lines, and headquarters installations. The teamwork developed in joint maneuvers and joint planning, coupled with the physical apparatus of a coordinated infrastructure, had transformed NATO from a traditional military alliance into an integrated coalition army. Nonetheless, the absolute and relative increase of Soviet power, particularly on the nuclear level, required a searching reappraisal of American strategy. Throughout 1954 the Pentagon was engaged in reformulating the American deterrence posture in order to arrive at a credible nuclear strategy to complement the doctrine of massive retaliation. This culminated in the decision to reinforce the Western forward line of defense with tactical nuclear weapons.

Both increasing Soviet strength and the successful establishment of an integrated Western alliance led to the announcement at the NATO Council meeting of December 1954 that the Lisbon force goal would be revised: thirty standing divisions were to be deployed in the central defense sector, and these divisions would be supplied with "modern"—that is to say, atomic—weapons. During 1953 the United States had developed tactical "battlefield" atomic weapons that were expected to be operational and ready for deployment soon thereafter. Reliance on tactical nuclear weapons to offset the conventional force superiority of the Soviet bloc seemed highly attractive, since it promised fiscal and manpower savings in addition to making up for the diminishing credibility of American strategic nuclear retaliation. Deployment of tactical nuclear weapons in Europe was also intended to compensate for the failure to establish the conventional force goals accepted at Lisbon in 1952. NATO planning was now officially based on the principle that tactical nuclear weapons would be used to counter almost any type of aggression, and the NATO Council authorized SACEUR to formulate contingency planning on that basis.[11]

For West German security, the implications of the shift in NATO planning were ambiguous, if not contradictory. General Norstad explained that the primary function of the thirty divisions that were to be deployed in the central sector was to implement NATO's commitment to a "forward strategy" in the case of an all-out war. This kind of calculation apparently stemmed from the expectation that an all-out nuclear war would be of short duration, and thus would not provide time for the mobilization and redeployment of reserve contingents. Coupled with this assumption was the hope that a forward strategy with tactical nuclear weapons would allow the defenders to destroy the massed forces of the attacker before the attack could begin. But tactical atomic weapons can also be employed effectively by the attacker if the defender's strategy is based on holding an inflexible forward line. Since the Soviet Union also had developed tactical nuclear weapons, the differential advantage that NATO planners hoped to gain was already being called into question. Consequently, NATO planners assigned a second, related function to the thirty-division force goal, namely, to deal with minor aggression and to prevent the Soviet Union from confronting the West with a fait accompli through a rapid and limited surprise attack. To accomplish this mission, NATO's new forward nuclear strategy was supplemented with a doctrine of flexible defense, which called for highly mobile units to retreat and advance as battlefield conditions required, and to roll with the punch of the major Soviet thrust.[12]

This dual purpose of NATO planning, which prepared for the contingency of defense and simultaneously tried to sustain the credibility of nuclear deterrence, met with cautious official response in Bonn. The concept of mobile strategy and elastic defense had already stirred up a lively debate in the German press and among German military experts because it seemed to accept the possibility that an attacker would penetrate deeply into West German territory; this would subject West Germany to being first overrun and then "liberated." But whatever misgivings Government circles may have entertained in private, the political and contractual commitments that had already been made, and the attendant reward of sovereignty, hardly allowed a reversal or even a public reappraisal of the Government's rearmament policy. American generals were called upon to make reassuring speeches in Germany, stressing the effectiveness of tactical nuclear weapons and their value for deterrence, but conspicuously omitting references to NATO's strategy of mobile defense. In March 1955, Adenauer flatly argued that only membership in NATO could obviate the possibility that the Federal Republic would become a battlefield in a hot war between the Soviet Union and the United States.[13]

The Adenauer Government could hardly neglect to exploit the political leverage provided by the decision to fortify NATO with battlefield nuclear weapons. Under the new strategy, West

German conventional forces were even more indispensable than before. The twelve divisions that West Germany had agreed to provide under the Paris Agreements were now assigned two functions: one was to carry the major burden in defending the central sector (especially since the other NATO members had not met their share of the Lisbon force goals); the other was to provide the strong forward position of ground troops, which was required by the new strategy to force the enemy to attack in concentration so as to make tactical nuclear counterstrikes efficacious. In addition to being part and parcel of the Western ground forces, the German contingents had become an integral element in Washington's attempt to reinforce the American strategic nuclear position. The importance of these functions had increased enormously since the early plans for Germany's rearmament after the outbreak of the Korean War. Without having proceeded beyond the planning stage, "by the beginning of 1954, German rearmament—which had at the time of Lisbon been seen only as one component of a balanced force designed to complement the nuclear superiority of the United States—had become, in SACEUR's view, the sine qua non of a new nuclear strategy for Europe."[14]

This shifting military-strategic scene, which reflected far-reaching transformations of the capability pattern of the international system, was the background for the Western powers' deliberations on the European Defense Community. Throughout 1952 and 1953, the French National Assembly was deeply divided over the question of German rearmament.[15] Aside from widespread misgivings about the resurgence of German military and political power, matters were complicated by the fact that both Bonn and Paris tied the issue to the unresolved Saar question. At a time when the success of French policy hinged on firm and continuous leadership, the Fourth Republic went through recurring political crises that were skillfully exploited by Adenauer, who pressed insistently for a satisfactory settlement of the Saar question, for full and equal membership in the Western alliance, and for the speedy restoration of German sovereignty. During January and February 1952, these demands, presented with a supporting vote of the Bundestag, led to the "high-water mark of sixteen months of trading by the Bonn Government on the basis of a contribution of nonexistent German troops to a nonexistent European Army."[16] The United States was constantly prodding the French Government not to stand in the way of Germany's rearmament, and Robert Schuman already thought it necessary to caution the French Assembly that it would be wise to accept a compromise version of the Pleven Plan, which would meet at least some of the German demands for equal status, since the United States would undoubtedly support the creation of a German *national* army if an integrated European army were to fall by the wayside through French intransigence.

The strategic planning of the NATO Lisbon Conference already reflected the changing power relationship between West Germany and France. Although technically denied membership in NATO, the Federal Republic was accorded de facto membership under an arrangement whereby EDC became a part of NATO and the North Atlantic Treaty was extended to cover the territory of the European Defense Community. West Germany was promised the restoration of sovereignty, and the only major concession to French demands was the provision that German contingents would be integrated at the corps level, thus preventing German generals from commanding German national corps.

On May 27, 1952, the EDC treaty was signed by the Federal Republic, France, Italy, and the Benelux countries. The connection between West German rearmament and West German sovereignty was now specifically acknowledged in contractual provisions.* On the previous day, the occupying powers and the West German Government had signed the so-called Bonn Conventions. They provided for the end of the occupation regime by abolishing the Occupation Statute and the Allied High Commission, and anticipated, with certain reservations, the restora-

* The EDC was also politically and legally linked to European integration. Its executive body was to be a Commissariat whose resignation could be forced by the ECSC Assembly, to be enlarged for this contingency by three additional members each from France, Germany, and Italy.

tion of German sovereignty in both external and internal affairs. The Western Allies reserved the right to station troops in Germany and to decide questions involving the whole of Germany—including reunification, a final peace treaty, and Berlin. These Conventions were to go into effect at the same time as the EDC treaty.

With the defeat of the EDC in the French National Assembly in August 1954, the treaty structure that was to rearm the Federal Republic and restore German sovereignty collapsed. The entire Western defense system seemed threatened, and the United States implied the possibility of American disengagement in Europe because of French obstructionism. The situation appeared especially serious, since plans to deploy tactical nuclear weapons on NATO's forward line in Germany were already being formulated, and because the new strategy assigned new and crucial functions to the proposed German contingents. It was in the wake of these disquieting developments that Anthony Eden went on his celebrated mission to Italy and the Benelux countries, with the purpose of arranging for Germany to join NATO and providing for Germany's and Italy's membership in an expanded and revived Brussels Treaty Organization. The outcome for the Federal Republic was a full success. Although the political restrictions of the Bonn Conventions were essentially retained, Germany was to be granted full equality as a member of NATO, with the proviso that Bonn was to renounce the manufacture of atomic, biological, and chemical weapons and certain other types of arms, such as guided missiles and rockets, submarines, and other types of vessels. These provisions did not preclude the possession or use of nuclear weapons; Germany did not renounce a nuclear strategy but rather the independent production of nuclear weapons on German territory. The Federal Republic agreed to provide NATO with a national contingent of twelve divisions, and the members of NATO pledged in turn to support the reunification of Germany with all diplomatic means, and to regard the West German Government as the only legitimate spokesman for all of Germany. Great Britain promised to keep at least four divisions and an air-force contingent on the Continent. In addition, an effective international control over German forces was to be provided through the Council of the Western European Union. In October, Germany was officially invited to join NATO and the enlarged Brussels Treaty Organization.

France had failed to prevent West Germany from setting up a national military contingent. But the French were now somewhat mollified by the presence of Great Britain in the Western European Union and by Adenauer's agreement to support the autonomy of the Saar in a plebiscite to be preceded by a free election campaign. In October, the French National Assembly passed a new defense bill, and on October 23, the Federal Republic joined the Brussels Treaty Organization. On the same day, the occupying powers and West Germany signed a slightly altered version of the 1952 Bonn Conventions, which had been adjusted to take account of the new European defense structure. These so-called Paris Agreements were ratified by Germany in February 1955, and went into effect on May 5. On the same day, the Occupation Statute was revoked, and the Allied High Commissioners became ambassadors. On May 9, West Germany became a member of NATO, and in July a group of German officers took up their duties at SHAPE.

RECOVERY

Political Recovery

The new German state, which had been established by the three Western occupation powers in 1949 under the Occupation Statute, was endowed with only a limited measure of sovereignty. The Allied High Commission, which succeeded the military governors of the occupation regime, in effect controlled the Federal Republic's political and economic relations with other countries, and was invested with broad powers to regulate, or at least supervise, domestic political and economic developments. In particular, the High Commissioners were charged with preventing the recartelization of German industrial complexes, and ensuring that the political development of the new state would proceed along democratic lines.

In Chapter 4, I shall deal in some detail with the motives and attitudes of various political groups in the Federal Republic concerning major foreign policy goals. Here, however, a discussion of the specific meaning that Adenauer attached to political recovery is desirable, since it had an immediate bearing on how this goal was pursued in the international system.

For Adenauer and his supporters, the goal of political recovery meant, in its widest implications, the right to have a foreign policy and the return of a democratic Germany to the society of free nations. More specifically, he aimed to include Germany as an equal and respected partner in a Western European union, which would irrevocably tie the Federal Republic to the cultural and political traditions of Western Europe and forestall the recurrence of a Nazi, or any other, dictatorial regime. The content and direction of Germany's sociopolitical order was to be shaped by a close and permanent attachment to the cultural values of the Western democracies. This aim necessarily required a fundamental and lasting rapprochement with France and the United States, and the restoration of legal independence, so that Germany could participate in a European integrative venture on the basis of equality and with freely given consent. The sovereignty that Adenauer sought to have restored to the West German state was thus of a rather special kind: he was willing to subsume some of its elements, once they were gained, to contractual agreements that would bind Germany to the West in integrative international structures. As a consequence, he could advance his demands in the name of European integration and the Western alliance, rather than in terms of a discredited German nationalism.

Considering the growing importance of the planned German military contribution, it is not surprising that Bonn's political leverage increased enormously. The successful pursuit of political recovery at crucial points ran parallel to the developments that led to the rearmament of Germany. The new relationship that began to form between West Germany and the Western powers because of Cold War tensions, and especially because of the implications of the Korean War, was explicitly acknowledged in September 1950 in the protocol of the Western Foreign Ministers' Conference:

The United States recognizes the right of Germany to participate in her own and the common defense within an integrated European defense system under conditions of equality. . . .

We believe it must be obvious to the German people that the nature and efficacy and extent to which Germany can be protected depend in a large measure on German participation in its own defense. Neutrality has never been an effective bar to aggression against an unprotected country.[17]

In September 1950, the Western powers ended the formal state of war with Germany; and in March 1951, the Occupation Statute was revised, and Allied control over Bonn's diplomatic relations was relaxed. A more liberal agreement on industrial controls was negotiated soon afterward, and later in the year ceilings on German coal production were lifted. Also, plans to replace Allied control over the Ruhr coal and steel industries with the ECSC, in which Germany would participate as an equal member, had been considered since the spring of 1950. In the fall of 1951, the Western powers agreed that in return for Germany's rearmament the Occupation Statute would be replaced by a treaty restoring sovereignty, and that West Germany would be admitted to the ECSC on the basis of equality. Since these so-called Bonn Conventions were to take effect at the same time as the treaty for the EDC, they had to lie legally dormant until the EDC was replaced by the WEU and German membership in NATO. In fact, however, the Allied High Commission anticipated the provisions of the Conventions, and already acted in accordance with them as much as possible in its dealings with the German Government. From the beginning, the tie-up between German rearmament and the restoration of sovereignty was so immediate and so clearly acknowledged in treaty provisions that it was obvious the Federal Republic "was to pay for its sovereignty by being irrevocably bound to the western military alliance through the European Defense Community on which the validity of the whole arrangement rested."[18]

In this relationship, West Germany's bargaining position vis-à-vis the Anglo-American powers was relatively uncomplicated and effective. Owing to the shifting strategic balance between the United States and the Soviet Union, Washington was determined to enlist Germany's power potential, and Adenauer could always point to the Socialist opposition in Bonn, which strongly pressed him to deliver on the sovereignty issue, and generally raised fundamental objections to rearmament because of its implications for reunification. With respect to France, the situation was much more complex and precarious. As early as April 1950, shortly before the launching of the Schuman Plan for the ECSC, France had proposed the formation of an Atlantic Supreme Council, which seemed designed to enhance French and European influence in the Atlantic alliance and which perhaps anticipated a Franco-German entente to strengthen the French position in Europe and to allow closer supervision of the new West German state. The Pleven Plan for the European Defense Community thus had antecedents in European economic integration, the Saar question, and the overall power position of France and Western Europe in the Atlantic alliance.

I have already noted the French dilemma—the need for a strong Anglo-American military commitment on the Continent to compensate for French weakness, and a simultaneous desire to curtail Anglo-American and German influence in Western Europe. The military dilemma had economic and political parallels. French fears that West Germany's political and economic recovery would proceed along national lines with a minimum of international supervision made international control arrangements seem imperative. At least they would help supervise German resurgence, and at best they might help enlist for French purposes Germany's political and economic potential, thus buttressing the French position vis-à-vis the Anglo-American powers. At the same time, France consistently sought to curtail West German influence in these international arrangements, and demanded tight international control before consenting to German rearmament.

On the whole, these crosscurrents of interest among the

Western powers posed no insuperable obstacle to Bonn's political and economic recovery policy, since the United States constantly pushed for a solution that would bring West Germany into the Western alliance at the earliest possible time. But the goal of *political* recovery was subjected to conflicting pressures that resulted not only from the disagreements between the United States and France but from the dual nature of the goal itself. Political recovery had two distinct aspects: the essentially legal aspect entailed in the restoration of sovereignty, and the more substantive political aspect, which, for Adenauer, meant the inclusion of Germany in a Western European union. These two aspects take on a special meaning in the post-1955 period, when the legal element had essentially been accomplished, although the political element was still a point of contention on both the international and the domestic political scenes. But even before 1955, the tensions between the legal and political dimensions of recovery posed serious problems for Bonn. The Western powers had enough interest in European integrative measures to allow the Federal Republic to pursue its recovery policy—in a European context—forcefully and effectively. In fact, the considerable congruence of French, Italian, Dutch, Belgian, and West German concepts of European integration was of crucial importance throughout the period under discussion, and immeasurably aided Bonn's pursuit of a viable Europe policy. But as a consequence of the persistent French attempts to curtail Germany's influence and relegate the Federal Republic to a secondary place in the alliance, the legal aspects of recovery—in terms of equality and the restoration of full sovereignty—generally had to be pursued with the support of the United States, in the face of French reluctance if not outright opposition. At the same time, the long-range political content that Adenauer attached to the goal of political recovery—a European union and a fundamental reconciliation with France—required not merely France's acquiescence but its sympathetic cooperation. This situation, even though at times awkward for Bonn, was still manageable, as long as the Western alliance was fairly cohesive and Bonn could advance its claim in the name of an integrated

Western alliance. But the pre-1955 tensions between the legal and political dimensions of recovery foreshadowed the much more serious dilemma that German leaders had to face after 1955, when they saw that taking sides with either the United States or France tended to widen the developing fissures in the Atlantic alliance.

Both the legal-political and the economic dimensions of the goal of recovery were advanced by Germany's participation in a number of international organizations. In the Petersberg Protocol of 1949 the Allies had agreed to promote German membership in international organizations, and West Germany subsequently became a member of the Council of Europe, the European Payments Union, the World Health Organization, the International Labor Organization, the Food and Agriculture Organization, UNESCO, GATT, and the World Bank. In addition to practical benefits, this aspect of political restoration was welcomed by the Bonn Government as a symbol that West Germany was on the way to being readmitted to the society of nations as an equal member.

With the demise of the EDC, Germany's progress toward political recovery seemed to come to an abrupt halt. But NATO and the enlarged Brussels Treaty Organization quickly supplied an alternative contractual framework with which to restore German sovereignty. The Paris Agreements of October 1954 incorporated essentially the same provisions as the Bonn Conventions of 1952. Aside from the restrictions on armaments already mentioned, the three Western powers retained their rights regarding German reunification, a final German peace treaty, and Berlin. The political connections that had consistently linked a number of foreign policy issues were most poignantly reflected in the legal interlocking of the components of the Paris Agreements. The following were signed in conjunction on October 23, 1954: the protocol for terminating the occupation regime, the declaration that officially invited Germany to join NATO and the Brussels Pact, the Saar Agreement, and the Status of Forces Convention retaining certain rights for the Western Allies. On the day the Paris Agreements took effect, May 5, 1955, the Federal Republic became a sovereign state.

Economic Recovery

Before examining the impact of the international system and the Bonn Government's foreign policy on the course of West Germany's economic recovery, it is helpful to briefly review the general economic conditions the Adenauer Government inherited in the fall of 1949.[19]

The convalescent West German economy of the late 1940's posed four major problems for economic reconstruction: first, a large quantity of industrial equipment had either been destroyed or dismantled, and production in key industries was curtailed by Allied controls; second, a severe balance-of-payments deficit hampered foreign trade; third, insufficient investment slowed down economic growth; and last, unemployment had risen to 10 per cent of the labor force.

Even though the economic philosophy and the corresponding economic program espoused by the Government—the "social market economy"—assigned in theory and practice a considerable role to government, it also relied heavily on the free play of market forces and individual incentive. Both elements would have been undercut severely if confidence in the new currency had been shaken by inflation. The monetary system had just recently sustained a most drastic cure through the currency reform, and inflationary trends would have had disastrous psychological and economic effects. Furthermore, inflation would have made it difficult for the Government to realize its commitment to liberalizing internal and external trade, and exports would have suffered so that the balance-of-payments problem could not have been remedied.

This situation seemed to call for a tight monetary and fiscal policy, and whenever possible a balanced budget. In view of the high level of unemployment, such a conservative policy was at times painful to follow and hard to defend politically. But it had a very beneficial effect on German exports, which became highly competitive as a result of the uninflated price levels and the domestic underconsumption caused by unemployment. The producer was forced to concentrate on export markets; satisfactory exports in turn allowed a general, if gradual, liberalization of import restrictions. Liberalization of external trade complemented what the Government was trying to achieve by relaxing controls on domestic markets. "By freeing other European countries' exports to Germany [liberalization] encouraged reciprocal concessions and became a stimulus to exports. By exposing the German domestic market to foreign competition, it stimulated competition at home. Although the freeing of her foreign trade created some tense situations and one or two minor upsets, it became the keynote of Germany's policy."[20]

In the spring of 1950, the West German economy still suffered from stagnation, and unemployment had risen to 12 per cent of the labor force. The Government was now hard pressed to stimulate the economy through development spending. But Ludwig Erhard, the Minister of Economics, stuck to what he considered to be of the highest priority: the stability of the currency in an economy that had experienced two disastrous inflations in one generation. The Government persisted in seeking to improve the balance of payments through a tight monetary policy, which was intended to create a buyers' market domestically and force the producer to turn to export markets. An additional reason for the reluctance to accelerate the economy through government spending was Erhard's diagnosis of the unemployment malaise as not readily amenable to governmental remedies: the labor force had grown substantially, largely because of the influx of refugees; and industry was not working at full capacity because of coal, steel, and power shortages, which, in turn, were largely the result of Allied controls over production.

The Cold War polarization of tensions in the international system had a profound, though at times somewhat general and indirect, impact on the course of Germany's economic revival. In the first place, as already noted, the economic reconstruction program advanced by the American and British occupation authorities prior to 1949 guided the West German economy in a direction that, although not irreversible, would have proven costly and disruptive if redirected fundamentally. To the extent that the establishment of Bizonia was an outgrowth of the tensions between the Soviet Union and the Western powers, the

Cold War had left an imprint on the West German economy even prior to the establishment of the Federal Republic. After 1949, East-West tensions continued to promote a readiness on the part of the Western powers, and especially the United States, to assist West Germany in the quest for economic recovery—if only to lay the economic and social foundations for the political and military integration of West Germany in the Western alliance. In addition to creating this generally favorable political climate, the Cold War conflict produced specifically economic repercussions as well: the political and economic impact of the Korean War and the establishment of the European Coal and Steel Community—both results of East-West tensions—had a considerable effect on the course of West Germany's economic revival.

Furthermore, in the early 1950's the West German economy could gain maximum benefits from the political developments in the international system. During that period, the major characteristic of the economy was its actual and potential excess capacity. In part because of Allied controls over production in key industries, and in part because of the conservative economic policies pursued by the Bonn Government, the production facilities and the labor force of West Germany were only partially used. Rearmament spending, which stimulated the economies of a number of Western countries, had a special effect on the West German economy, because excess capacity and the tight monetary policies previously pursued by the Government allowed this boost to take place without an excessive rise in the price level. Excess capacity checked inflationary trends and greatly aided in the competitive marketing of German exports. This generally favorable economic situation caused some problems as well. Although the economy was now beginning to pick up substantially, once again balance-of-payments deficits became a serious, if short-range, concern. Following the outbreak of the Korean War, West Germany created large balance-of-payments deficits by rapid, nervous purchases of raw materials at rising prices, on credit obtained from the European Payments Union. The rate of investment was unsatisfactory, in part because of a substantial drop in the rate of savings, which resulted from domestic consumers' hoarding commodities; recent deprivation was still so fresh in the minds of German consumers that they could not react to international crises with equanimity. By the end of 1950, Germany's deficit to members of the European Payments Union had become so serious that the Government was forced to revert to import restrictions. This measure, undertaken reluctantly, eased the balance-of-payments deficit, and the credit extended by the EPU was repaid by May 1951. The balance-of-payments problem was further alleviated when the export of finished goods began to catch up with the excessive purchases of raw materials.

An additional effect of the Korean War was the lifting of Allied controls over production in key industries. In September 1950, the Western foreign ministers agreed that Allied controls over production in prohibited and limited industries should be reviewed "in the light of the developing relationship with the Federal Republic," and that West Germany would henceforth be allowed to produce steel "outside the present limitation where this will facilitate the defense effort of the West."[21] In the following years, almost all aspects of West Germany's economic recovery came to be regarded as "facilitating the defense effort of the West"; limitations on shipping and on the production of aluminum and important chemicals were also gradually abolished, and the 1955 Agreement on Industrial Controls, which became an adjunct to the treaty structure restoring West German sovereignty, officially removed the remaining economic controls.

The gradual lifting of Allied controls on key industries largely brought about the reconstruction of German industry and the upswing of the economy because it removed bottlenecks that had hampered economic recovery since the late 1940's. A year after the outbreak of the Korean War, West Germany had doubled its exports without serious inflation, and restrictions on imports from EPU countries could be reduced again in January 1952. Still, economic growth had slowed down, there was considerable unemployment, and the Government was again urged to follow a more aggressive program to stimulate the economy. But it stood pat and merely resorted to the relatively mild device of easing credit by lowering bank reserve requirements and the discount rate. Apparently Erhard and his advisers anticipated that EDC armaments contracts would provide another boom, and they sought to prepare and cushion the economy by retaining excess capacity. For the time being, this expectation remained unfulfilled. However, by the end of 1952, inventory adjustments—necessary because of the excessive purchases of raw materials at the beginning of the Korean War—shifted the economy's attention to consumer goods, and as exports improved further, the economy as a whole picked up again. Between 1952 and 1954, exports and the gross national product continued to rise steadily, and by the end of 1954 the gold and foreign-exchange reserves of the Federal Republic amounted to over $2.5 billion. Unemployment had dropped below 5 per cent of the labor force, but was high enough to keep the wage-price level relatively stable. The wage-price level was further buttressed by the restraint shown by the trade unions. By the end of 1954, American offshore procurement contracts, promised in April 1953, provided an added stimulus.

Such integrative economic structures as the European Coal and Steel Community (and later, the European Economic Community) had a considerable impact on West Germany's economic reconstruction.[22] Nonetheless, Adenauer evaluated German participation in the Schuman Plan largely on political grounds. Again, it was largely the Cold War that accounted for the establishment of the first integrative European structure.

In May 1950, the French foreign minister proposed a coal and steel common market that would include France, West Germany, the Benelux countries, and Italy. This proposal can be attributed to two aspects of the Cold War pattern of the international system. In the first place, the rearmament of West Germany seemed inevitable, and France was determined to create at least a rudimentary international body for supervising it before agreeing to German rearmament; international arrangements for regulating the production and marketing of coal and steel looked like an effective check on the war potential of Germany. Secondly, France was acutely conscious that German influence within the Western alliance was increasing, because the Western defense system needed the Federal Republic. The industrial complex of the Ruhr was as yet under the control of the International Ruhr Authority, which had been created by the occupation powers. But French policymakers were afraid that unless international supervision over the Ruhr continued in one form or another, the growing influence of Germany might sooner or later lead to the scrapping of Allied restraints, and allow Germany unfettered control over the industry of the Ruhr basin. Furthermore, France hoped that the ECSC would ease Franco-German tensions over the Saar question.[23]

For Robert Schuman, necessity was combined with virtue in any event. The ECSC promised to become the first step toward the political and economic integration of Western Europe, which he personally favored, and which could be expected to meet with the warm response of Adenauer and Italian Prime Minister de Gasperi, both of whom were tied to Schuman by strong political, cultural, and religious bonds, and a fundamental commitment to Western European union. For West Germany, the establishment of the ECSC meant the abolition of the International Ruhr Authority, and represented a significant advance toward the restoration of German sovereignty: the Schuman Plan replaced an Allied instrument of control with an international organization in which the Federal Republic would participate as an equal member. The ECSC promised gains both for the legal aspect of political recovery and for Adenauer's larger aspiration —a fundamental reconciliation with France in the context of a Western European community. The establishment of the ECSC exemplifies the kind of mixed legal-political advances the Bonn Government made through its policy of reconciliation and cooperation with the West. The payoff for Bonn was not primarily in terms of the more traditional values of sovereignty—such as unfettered freedom of action and political mobility—but rather in gaining an equal legal status in an integrative international structure to which the Federal Republic was bound both contractually and politically.

West Germany gained economic benefits as well. The Schuman Plan removed the steel-production bottlenecks that had hampered economic reconstruction, and its provisions held out the promise that coordinated management of coal and steel, which had been outlawed by the Allies and from which the German industrialists expected great benefits, would be reinstated. Although German business and industrial circles were not unanimous in their assessment of the economic benefits of the Schuman Plan, as will be seen in Chapter 4, the lifting of Allied coal and steel controls was crucial because it freed basic raw materials at a time when their shortage seriously retarded economic reconstruction.

There is no need to exaggerate the direct impact of the Cold War on the course of West Germany's reconstruction. No doubt purely indigenous factors were of crucial importance. Nonetheless, the Cold War tensions of the international system provided a general political climate that was highly conducive to the successful pursuit of economic recovery. In such specific instances as the lifting of Allied controls over production, the economic stimulus provided by the Korean War, and the establishment of the ECSC, the impact of external circumstances was directly beneficial to economic reconstruction. Most important, perhaps, *economic* recovery rested on the *political* basis that was laid by Adenauer's policy of accommodation with the Western powers. This fundamental political relationship in turn stemmed from the need to enlist the power potential of West Germany for the Western alliance; that is, it emerged from the polarization of power and purpose in the international system.

REUNIFICATION

The Saar

The unresolved status of the Saar territory, aside from its aspects as a unification project, posed a major obstacle to the Franco-German rapprochement that was the cornerstone of Adenauer's Europe policy. Friction over the Saar question generally poisoned relations between Bonn and Paris, and constantly intruded in the negotiations on the Schuman Plan and the European Defense Community. Disagreement over the Saar threatened the entire treaty structure that was to rearm the Federal Republic and restore German sovereignty.[24]

Soon after the establishment of the Federal Republic, the French Government renewed its efforts to obtain a contractual agreement that would legalize the de facto union of the French and Saar economies. Early in 1950, the French and Saar governments negotiated the so-called Franco-Saar Conventions, which further solidified French control over the Saar economy, especially in the mining and steel industry. The reaction in Bonn was extremely sharp. The Adenauer Government issued a lengthy memorandum asserting that the Saar was part of Germany as defined by the Allied declaration of June 1945, and that consequently there could be no legitimate alterations of the 1937 German frontiers prior to a peace treaty. The statement criticized the lack of freedom of expression in the Saar Landtag elections of 1947, and refused to interpret the election results as indicating the Saar population's desire for economic union with France and political separation from Germany. It also castigated the Conventions as a thinly disguised attempt to annex the Saar, effecting a fait accompli that would be difficult to reverse, and suggested as an alternative an international Saar authority and special customs arrangements, which would not entail the political separation of the Saar from Germany.

Both France and Germany were very much aware that the Saar dispute was strongly affected by larger developments in the international system. Timing became a crucial consideration. Germany, confident of improving her bargaining power within the Western alliance because of her commitments to Western defense, sought to keep the Saar situation in a state of flux. France, for the same reason, attempted to secure as speedily as possible treaty arrangements that would be difficult to renegotiate and would permanently settle the question in her favor.

Bonn emphatically rejected French attempts to give the Saar political autonomy and economic links with France. Adenauer declared that such a solution would be unacceptable not only because the Saar was rightfully German territory, but also because it made no sense to create new "midget" states at a stage of European political development when boundaries were supposed to be eliminated.[25] As with other issues, Adenauer's commitment to the European cause allowed him to pursue foreign policy objectives in the name of Western European unity rather than in terms of German nationalism.

The Schuman Plan at first failed to contribute to a meeting of minds on the Saar. On the contrary, the blueprint for the international administration of coal and steel in the ECSC seemed to foreshadow international control of the Saar basin. This was strongly resisted in Paris. France had no interest in subjecting the Saar economy to international surveillance, since the Saar economy was already effectively fused with the French economy. Again, timing was of the essence. France now sought to have the Saar admitted to the ECSC as an autonomous political entity; and since Bonn adamantly refused to sanction this proposal, France announced early in 1952 that the French High Commissioner in the Saar would become an ambassador and that French diplomatic delegations would henceforth include a representative of the Saar. This meant, of course, that the political separation of the Saar from Germany would be made even more specific and visible, if only symbolically, and that France was preparing the way for having the Saar represented "autonomously" in the ECSC. The acrimonious nature of the dispute became particularly evident when Bonn retaliated with a letter to the Council of Europe threatening to present the question of the curtailment of democratic freedoms in the Saar to the Committee of Ministers.

Off and on throughout 1952 the Saar issue was quietly negotiated. Although the United States and Great Britain had initially supported French claims on the Saar, by the fall of 1952 Anthony Eden was willing to perform as mediator in the discussion between France and Germany, and during 1953 the

French found it increasingly difficult to obtain support for their Saar policy within the Western alliance. The communiqué issued after Adenauer and Schuman conferred in Paris in March 1953 stated rather vaguely that the Saar question was to be negotiated by France and Germany before the conclusion of an all-German peace treaty; but aside from this ambivalent German concession, no agreement on specifics could be reached. In October Adenauer again rejected a final settlement before a peace treaty, and suggested that in the meantime the Saar should be placed under the supervision of a European organization such as the ECSC Council of Ministers. It became increasingly obvious that the Federal Republic's influence within the Western alliance was growing substantially in the wake of the NATO Lisbon Conference, and that support for French policy within the Western alliance was diminishing at the same time.

The temporary Cold War détente following Stalin's death in 1953 brought about a general relaxation of efforts to integrate Europe. But Germany's rapid economic and political recovery increased the Bonn Government's confidence that its Saar policy could be brought to a successful conclusion. In July the Bundestag passed a unanimous resolution asserting that the Saar was part of Germany, and giving the Government a parliamentary mandate to demand democratic freedoms in the Saar, and its return to Germany. Encouraged by the fall elections, which could be interpreted as a vote of confidence for his foreign policies, Adenauer approached Georges Bidault in September, even before the new German Government had been formed, and suggested that discussions on the Saar be reopened. In April and May 1954, negotiations were resumed and Bonn again insisted that the Europeanization of the Saar must be economic as well as political, and that Germany's economic relations with the Saar must be essentially the same as France's. The United States applied considerable pressure to bring the issue to a conclusion, and German demands were largely satisfied. In May 1954 a Franco-German agreement was signed when the Committee of Ministers of the Council of Europe met in Strasbourg. The Saar issue seemed to be moving toward an amicable solution.

But the head of the French delegation could not get his Government to accept the agreement; and three months later, with the defeat of the EDC in the French National Assembly, Mèndes-France thought he had the lever he needed to improve the French bargaining position. It seemed that France now could deny the Federal Republic access not only to the Atlantic alliance but also to sovereignty. But the swift Eden mission that paved the way for German membership in NATO and the WEU pointed out the French miscalculation of the Franco-German power relationship within the Western alliance. While the French Assembly sought to delay West German rearmament by refusing to ratify the EDC, the Pentagon was already considering plans to deploy tactical nuclear weapons in West Germany, and had assigned increasingly important functions to West German contingents. As part of the Paris Agreements of October 1954, France and Germany finally reached a compromise settlement, which provided: (1) that the Saar would be placed under a European statute within the framework of the Western European Union and that this statute, after approval by a referendum, would not be called into question until the conclusion of a peace treaty; (2) that a European Commissioner would represent the Saar in foreign affairs and matters of defense; and (3) that France would retain close economic ties with the Saar, with Germany acceding to similar relations over a period of time. The referendum was to be preceded by free campaigning for or against the statute; and in May 1955 the WEU Council set forth the guidelines that were to govern the referendum, and established an International Commission to handle supervision and certification.[26]

This outcome was a moderate success for Bonn. There was, of course, the strong implication that the Saar was the price for French acquiescence to German membership in NATO. Nevertheless, Adenauer denied that the agreement meant a permanent separation of the Saar from Germany, and events were soon to prove him right. When the Europeanization statute was submitted to the Saar voters in October 1955, it was rejected by 67 per cent of them, 367,000 votes going to pro-German parties,

162,300 to pro-European parties.[27] Both the French and German Governments showed concern over the possible effect of the referendum on Franco-German relations. Adenauer immediately declared that good relations between France and Germany should not be endangered by this development, and the French Government replied in a similar vein.

For the time being, the results of the referendum merely continued the status quo, but in effect they were interpreted by both France and Germany as a vote for reunion with Germany. In December, the incumbent pro-French government of the Saar was decisively defeated at the polls. A pro-German majority was elected, and forthwith declared its intention to end the separation of the Saar from Germany. Negotiations between Paris and Bonn produced an agreement in October 1956 providing for the restoration of German political sovereignty over the Saar on January 1, 1957. France was given 25 years to phase out her mining efforts in the lucrative Warndt coal deposits, which would yield her an estimated 66 million tons of coal in that period; and Germany agreed to deliver 1.2 million tons of coal annually beginning in 1962, plus a third of the total output of the Saar mines. French demands for a Moselle canal were also accepted in principle, with the understanding that the German Government would make a large financial contribution and agree to important concessions on toll rights. Economic reunification with Germany was to be accomplished by 1960, but subsequent cooperation between France and Germany made it possible to advance that date to July 1959, when the Saar was included in the German currency and customs system as an integral part of the Federal Republic.[28] Although the economic price paid by Germany was heavy, as an issue of reunification the Saar question had been resolved successfully.

West Germany and East Germany

The most fundamental obstacle to the goal of reunifying East and West Germany was the need for the consent of both Cold War camps. In contrast to other foreign policy projects, the unification of Germany required at least the acquiescence, if not the direct support, of both the United States and the Soviet Union. Realization of this led the Bonn Government to pursue a single-minded unification policy, which, even though its more active elements were addressed primarily to the Western alliance, was in fact aimed at both centers of power.

Because of Germany's relative weakness, the most immediate aim of the Government's unification policy was to enlist the active support of the Western powers, especially the United States, and to ensure that the West would not treat the "German question" as a secondary issue that could conceivably be traded off in an overall American-Soviet settlement of the Cold War. This objective was based on the not unjustified assumption that the Western powers would view the prospect of a unified Germany with some apprehension; it was to be implemented by increasing German political leverage within the Western alliance in order to ensure on the political plane the Western powers' legal and moral commitment to unification and to regard the Bonn Government as the only legitimate spokesman for all of Germany. This power calculation was supplemented by continuously reassuring the West that the Federal Republic would faithfully fulfill her treaty obligations, forswear the use of force to achieve unification, and lead a united Germany to develop along peaceful and democratic lines.

The Bonn unification policy's second dimension, which was aimed at the Soviet bloc, was more vague and passive, precisely because it was merely an extension of the first dimension. The "Eastern corollary" to Bonn's Western-oriented alliance policy was based on the assumption that the pressures a united West could bring to bear on the Soviet Union would sooner or later induce Moscow to settle the German question on terms acceptable to Bonn. Negotiations with the Soviet Union on the basis of Western strength thus presupposed a future East-West power relationship that would be largely unfavorable to the Soviet Union.

The Eastern dimension of Adenauer's unification policy, in particular, presupposed shifts of international power and purpose that Bonn could influence only marginally. More than in any other foreign policy project, in pursuing unification the Bonn Government's role was essentially indirect and passive, and was circumscribed by the interest calculations of the two superpowers. While both Cold War camps considered it politic to give at least verbal support to German aspirations for reunification, neither side could be expected to support the creation of a unified Germany that would be genuinely free to conduct its external affairs. The first choice of either side—to draw a united Germany into its orbit under effective supervision—could be successfully vetoed by the other side, given the power pattern prevailing in the international system. On the other hand, securing the allegiance and power potential of the part of Germany that each Cold War camp already occupied promised a substantial increase of strength for either side. The existing state of affairs was tolerable and contained a modicum of stability. East Germany served the Soviet Union by keeping its satellites in check; loss of control over East Germany would have resulted in a serious loss of prestige, not to speak of the possible "domino" effect among the East-bloc countries. For the Western strategy of containment, West Germany became the indispensable forward bastion in central Europe, whose loss would have decisively settled the European Cold War balance in Moscow's favor.

Both Cold War camps were on record as favoring a united Germany; but the realities of power allowed neither side to go beyond repeating its interpretation of what constituted an equitable solution to the German problem. The Western powers insisted on free elections in both parts of Germany, and on freedom for a united Germany to join alliances; the Soviet Union demanded the withdrawal of Western military forces, and the establishment of a German State Council with equal representation for the two existing governments in Bonn and Pankow. The very existence of these two governments limited both sides' room to maneuver. The West had solemnly pledged to recognize Bonn as the only legitimate government for all of Germany, and the Soviet Union was similarly committed to the Pankow regime, promising to preserve its "social achievements." Both East and

West Germany were being integrated in the power structures of the Cold War alliance and were expected to contribute substantially to their viability.

By 1952 the unification question had become inextricably tied to West German rearmament. Following the outbreak of the Korean War and the resulting plans for rearming the Federal Republic, the East-bloc foreign ministers met in Prague in the fall of 1950 and spelled out a number of preconditions for negotiating with the West on German reunification: no rearmament of West Germany, no reconstruction of West Germany's military-industrial potential, the conclusion of a peace treaty and the withdrawal of occupation forces, and an all-German government established on the basis of equal representation for both East and West Germany.[29] The East German Government made similar overtures directly to Bonn, but the Western powers and the Adenauer Government insisted adamantly that free elections precede the establishment of an all-German government. Toward this purpose, in the fall of 1951 the Western powers and the Bonn Government, supported with a Bundestag resolution, requested the United Nations to set up a neutral committee to supervise free elections in both parts of Germany. A United Nations commission was in fact established, consisting of members from Brazil, Iceland, the Netherlands, Pakistan, and Poland; but the East German Government did not recognize the UN decision. Poland withdrew its representative, and the commission was denied entry into East Germany in the following year.

All subsequent diplomatic moves by the Soviet Union attempted to forestall the rearmament of West Germany and prevent the integration of West German military contingents in a Western defense system. The subsequently famous Soviet note of March 10, 1952, deserves special attention, since the proposals presented in it followed in the wake of the NATO Lisbon Conference of February 1952, and came a few months prior to the signing of the EDC treaty.

In the spring of 1952, the Soviet Union launched a major

propaganda campaign to disrupt the Western alliance by stirring up popular opposition to German rearmament in France and Britain, while simultaneously offering Germany, if united and neutralized, a national military establishment that would have been considerably more independent than the one planned for West German forces under the EDC. In the note of March 10, the Soviet Union called for the neutralization of Germany and the withdrawal of occupation forces, including those of the Soviet Union, and dropped its previous demand that the American overseas bases be scrapped as a Western concession. Crucial paragraphs provided that "the existence of organizations inimical to democracy and to the maintenance of peace must not be permitted on the territory of Germany," and that Germany would be obliged "not to enter into any kind of coalition or military alliance directed against any power which took part, with its armed forces, in the war against Germany."[30] In a subsequent note, the Soviet Union threatened that there would be "new difficulties" for reunification if West Germany joined the European Defense Community.

On March 25 the Western powers replied to the Soviet Union that the all-German government the Soviets had suggested as the basis for negotiating a peace treaty would have to be established through free elections in East and West Germany. The Western note, which closely reflected Adenauer's own thinking, rejected detailed discussions on a peace treaty until conditions had been created for free elections, and until a freely elected all-German government had been established. It also questioned the Soviet note's reference to the German frontiers determined by the Potsdam agreement, and stressed that no definitive German frontiers were as yet established. As to the limitations on a German government's freedom to join alliances, the West argued that "the all-German government should be free both before and after the conclusion of a peace treaty to enter into associations compatible with the principles and purposes of the United Nations."[31]

The Western proposals can only be viewed as unrealistic. By insisting on free elections and subsequent freedom to join alliances, the West presented the Soviet Union with the prospect that not only West Germany but a unified Germany would become a member of the Western alliance. On the other hand, the Soviet Union expected the West to accept, or help create, a power vacuum in the heart of Europe, with many opportunities for Soviet manipulations and interference, at a time when clearly delineated spheres of influence held the most promise for effective containment. For Adenauer, acceptance of the Soviet proposal would have meant the end of his most fundamental political aim—including Germany in a Western European union. The West, and Adenauer, had to weigh the uncertain and risky prospect of a neutralized Germany against the certainty of a Western increment of power at a crucial stage in the Cold War.

In the eyes of many of Adenauer's critics, the rejection of the Soviet proposals signified a careless or even cynical failure to explore a last opportunity for unification. But to the Western powers and the Bonn Government, Moscow's plan appeared to be at best a stratagem to disrupt the Western alliance, and at worst a design to extend Soviet control over all of Germany. The Soviet proposals were fraught with risks and uncertainties and could have ushered in an important shift in the power balance of the Cold War. The treaty establishing the EDC and restoring West German sovereignty was about to be signed, and perhaps most importantly, the NATO strategy and the conventional force goals formulated at the Lisbon Conference made a German contribution to the Western defense effort appear indispensable. Furthermore, at this time Washington's policy of containment was expected to benefit most from a "forward strategy" and a clear-cut political and military line with which to unequivocally confront the Eastern bloc. The Western powers' misgivings were reinforced by the Soviet disarmament plans submitted to the United Nations on March 19, calling for a ban on nuclear weapons and for the reduction of conventional force levels by one-third: the Soviet proposals for Germany appeared to be part of a master plan to disrupt the Western defense structure.[32]

Adenauer's calculated decision to secure the West German position within the Western alliance before negotiating with the

Soviet Union on reunification led Bonn to pursue an increasingly static and unimaginative Eastern policy. In large part, this "non-policy" was the result of the apparent lack of alternatives in the face of the East-West power balance, the risky nature of the Soviet proposals, and Adenauer's preoccupation with integrating Germany in a Western European union. In addition, the Western powers most likely would have viewed German overtures to the Soviet Union with apprehension, and a more active Eastern policy could have jeopardized the entire treaty structure that was to restore sovereignty to the Federal Republic. This would have undermined the power base from which Adenauer expected to deal with the Soviet Union at some future date. In combination, these factors almost inevitably made Bonn's Eastern policy appear flaccid and colorless—especially in contrast to the political acumen and tenacity displayed by Adenauer in his dealings with the Western powers.

The static nature of Bonn's Eastern policy was clearly exemplified by its implacable position on the Oder-Neisse issue. After the East German Government and all the other East-bloc states recognized the Polish claim on the Oder-Neisse territories and East Prussia, the Adenauer Government adamantly refused to regard the existing state of affairs as anything but provisional and subject to revision. This legal claim, which rested on the Potsdam provision that no permanent revision of Germany's borders could take place before a final all-German peace treaty, was buttressed by the consistent, if rather perfunctory, support of the Western powers until De Gaulle recognized the Oder-Neisse line as permanent in 1959. Aside from the legal merits of the question, the Adenauer Government probably intended to preserve its concession as a trump card to be played at a time when the larger question of Germany's unification would be on the agenda. But the legalistic rigidity of Bonn's position precluded a more dynamic Eastern policy—which might have aimed at the political isolation of East Germany within the Eastern bloc—and gave Moscow the opportunity to strengthen its hold over the satellites, especially Poland, by posing as the protector of the status quo against the "revisionist" and "revanchist" designs of the Federal Republic. In later years, critics of Bonn's foreign policy raised similar objections to the so-called Hallstein doctrine, which provides that the Federal Republic shall withhold or withdraw diplomatic recognition from governments (except the Soviet Union) that recognize the East German regime.

The death of Stalin in 1953 ushered in a new phase in Soviet policy on German unification. In the first place, it can be argued that Soviet interest in a united Germany was essentially a Stalinist phenomenon,[33] and that after Stalin's death the new rulers in the Kremlin began to regard the status quo in central Europe as an acceptable outcome—and under the circumstances the best possible outcome—of Soviet policy. Soviet diplomacy now shifted its line of attack and began probing the internal cohesion of NATO more insistently. This, in October 1953, prompted the Western powers to reaffirm their interest in solving the German question and to propose a Four Power conference on Germany. But the new administration in Washington was not inclined to be more flexible on the German question than its predecessor, especially in light of the shifting strategic circumstances; and the dialogue between East and West on the problem of unification became increasingly doctrinaire and unrealistic. The Soviet Union continued to call for the neutralization of Germany, and the West kept insisting on free elections at a time when the East German uprising of 1953 must have forcefully reminded the Soviet Union that its hold on East Germany depended on the presence of Russian tanks, and that it could expect no gains from elections.

When the four foreign ministers met in Berlin in February 1954, Anthony Eden presented the first version of his "Eden Plan for German Reunification in Freedom," which called for free elections as the prerequisite for reunification, but which also proposed a European collective-security system designed to allay Soviet fears of a united, non-neutralized Germany. The Soviet Union again insisted that elections would have to be arranged through negotiations between East and West Germany and countered the Eden Plan by proposing the almost complete withdrawal of occupation troops from a neutralized Germany whose safety would be guaranteed by a European security pact. The Soviet Union was willing to concede that NATO need not be dissolved as a prerequisite for such an arrangement, although the United States was specifically excluded from the proposed European security treaty.[34]

The crucial difference between the two proposals was, of course, whether a united Germany would be free to join the Western alliance. While this prospect was obviously unacceptable to the Soviet Union, the Western powers openly implied for the first time that it might be the only outcome acceptable to the West. The changing East-West power relationship—namely, the explosion of a thermonuclear device in the Soviet Union and the development of a long-range Soviet bomber as a delivery instrument—finally left "no hope whatever that Western forces could be withdrawn from West Germany, for then the only deterrent to a lightning occupation of the whole country by the still overwhelmingly superior Russian forces would be an American threat of all-out war, whose credibility, always somewhat ambiguous for moral and political reasons, was now beginning to be further undermined by Soviet technical advances."[35]

The strategic and political calculations that made West Germany seem indispensable to a viable Western defense posture were reinforced by the decision to strengthen the Western defense perimeter with tactical nuclear weapons. After the Federal Republic had been invited to join NATO, the Soviet Union renewed its attempts to keep West Germany from joining the Western alliance and again proposed a Four Power conference on Germany. At the conference, however, the specific proposals and the Western reply did not go beyond well-worn statements of familiar positions.

During this reassessment of NATO strategy, the Soviet Union again probed Western intentions on the German question. By the end of 1954, the planned West German military contribution had become an essential element in the overall nuclear deterrence posture of the Western alliance. In January 1955, shortly after the NATO decision to deploy tactical nuclear weapons and a few months before Germany formally joined NATO, the Soviet Union intimated that international supervision of free elections might be feasible after all if the two German governments could reach an agreement. Adenauer, who had disclosed that the Western powers' pledge to actively support reunification depended on German ratification of the Paris Agreements,[36] argued that this new Soviet proposal was merely a tactical diversion and that the Soviet Union could readily sabotage free elections, since they required the agreement of both Germanies and the Four Powers. Furthermore, the Soviet plan would mean neutralizing a unified Germany that would be deprived of effective Western protection, while allowing Soviet intervention in internal German affairs whenever the Soviets chose to interpret German policies as not proceeding along "peace-loving and democratic" lines. Bonn was convinced that the Soviet Union was not offering unification in exchange for the scrapping of the Paris Agreements, but a series of preliminaries that could be withdrawn at any time. Adenauer explained that he was not actually following a "policy of strength," which would be ridiculous with only twelve German divisions, but rather was seeking the integration of Western Europe because only then could effective negotiations on reunification take place.[37]

In February 1955, in a final attempt to dissuade Bonn from joining NATO, the Soviet Union repeated that the Paris Agreements would become the chief obstacle to a settlement of the German question and would make German reunification "impossible for a long time to come." Rejection of the Agreements, on the other hand, would make it "possible to hold free, all-German elections this year with the aim of reestablishing Germany's unity on a peaceful and democratic basis."[38] A week after Germany joined NATO, the East-bloc countries signed the Warsaw Security Pact and incorporated East Germany in the East European military alliance.

The Big Four Summit Conference in July 1955 marked the end of a five-year period of East-West maneuvering during which the line of demarcation running through Germany had become increasingly sharp. Moscow had failed to deny the Western alliance the increase in power expected from a West German military contribution. But the Western powers had also failed to achieve the superiority of power that was the central assumption and prerequisite of Adenauer's Eastern policy. On the contrary, the absolute and relative strength of the Soviet Union had increased substantially, and the Cold War balance of power was moving toward a deadlock, of which the central European state of affairs was one manifestation.

By 1955 not even the Western-oriented dimension of Bonn's reunification policy had succeeded entirely. To be sure, the growing weight of German influence in Western councils was acknowledged both legally and politically, and with the ratification of the Paris Agreements, the Western powers had reaffirmed their pledge to use all diplomatic means to support the unification of Germany. But the development of Soviet nuclear capabilities also led to a serious Western reappraisal of the potential dangers in central Europe and to a corresponding inclination to "de-fuse" the Cold War in general and the German question in particular. In Bonn, the implications of this raised serious misgivings that were not entirely unfounded, although they were perhaps somewhat exaggerated. For example, after Soviet policy had failed to prevent the ratification of the Paris Agreements, Moscow began to renew its proposals for disarmament negotiations. In some Western quarters these overtures were received with a good deal of interest. But Moscow did not fail to suggest that since the German status quo had now in effect been solidified, the division of Germany might serve as the basis for an agreement between the superpowers on some measure of arms control—implying that the Soviet Union would discuss arms control in return for an indirect Western recognition of the political status quo in Germany. In fact, this general theme became the keynote of Moscow's Germany policy after 1955.

The Geneva Summit produced no agreement either on the German question, arms control, or any other Cold War issue.

The Western powers, and especially Great Britain, apparently assumed that Western strength was now at its peak, particularly on the level of nuclear capabilities, and could be expected to decline relatively. In the second version of the Eden Plan, presented at Geneva, Great Britain proposed to solve the German issue by offering a demilitarized zone in central Europe, an agreement to curtail armaments, and a European mutual-security pact. Since the Soviet Union apparently had already settled on a policy of two Germanies, the coupling of the German question with arms-control measures caused dismay and apprehension in Bonn because "for the first time these . . . areas of negotiations, sharply separated until then, were brought in contact with each other. For the first time also it was officially indicated by British and French statesmen that the demarcation line between the zones of Four Power occupation in Germany could serve at least temporarily as a basis for arms-control arrangements between the Four Powers."[39]

No agreement could be reached at Geneva, and the failure of Bonn's unification policy became manifest in the fall, when the Federal Republic felt it necessary to establish diplomatic relations with the Soviet Union. With this step, Adenauer in effect admitted the cogency of the Kremlin's two-Germanies policy, and underlined the division of Germany by lending it a certain de jure recognition. Moreover, Bonn's Western-oriented unification policy was not completely successful either; Adenauer was haunted by the fear that a Cold War détente or overall settlement could conceivably take place on the basis of a tacit, or even explicit, recognition of the German status quo. Both the Eastern and the Western dimensions of Bonn's unification policy were being undermined by the shifting East-West power relationship, which stiffened the Soviet attitude and further diminished the West's willingness to take undue risks for the cause of German unity.

3. *Goal Compatibilities and the International System, 1949–1955*

Having examined the goals of security, recovery, and reunification separately, it is now possible to assess more explicitly their respective degrees of compatibility with the conditions of the international system and their mutual complementarity. Compared with the post-1955 period, the degrees of compatibility between West German foreign policy projects and systemic circumstances from 1949 to 1955 are relatively clear-cut, direct, and easily discernible—primarily because the major patterns of power and purpose in the international system were simplified by their polarization in the Cold War struggle. Clearly, the bipolar structure of the international system was highly conducive to the goal of recovery, and quite detrimental to the unification of East and West Germany on terms acceptable to Bonn and the Western powers.

The sharp contrasts among these degrees of compatibility were created by an essentially bipolar systemic backdrop. At the same time, these bipolar patterns contained the political impulses that were to lead to a much more intricately patterned international system after the middle 1950's. As a consequence, the degrees of compatibility among German foreign policy goals became much more complex and ambiguous after 1955. It is essential at this point to stress a most important attribute of the international system from the end of World War II to the middle 1950's. This system is often summarily described as "bipolar"; however, though the major patterns of alignment and tension in the Cold War may be usefully categorized as "bipolar," it was a previously nonexistent but gradually developing bipolarity on the nuclear level that had the most pronounced impact on the international system of the early 1950's. It was precisely the gradual transition from an American monopoly of strategic nuclear capabilities to a Russo-American duopoly that caused a major shift of power in the international system and led to reappraisals of NATO strategy. It was the polarization of alignment and tension, combined with the evolving nuclear polarization, that provided the most salient systemic effects on West German foreign policy goals.

Security, Rearmament, Recovery, and the Saar

In retrospect we can say that West Germany's goal of security was compatible with the strictures and challenges of the international system because the territorial integrity of the Federal Republic was in fact maintained successfully. But even with the benefit of hindsight, it is difficult to assess the specific nature of the threat posed to West German security. In the absence of Cold War tensions, West Germany's security from external dangers presumably would have posed no foreign policy problem for the Federal Republic. Bonn's security concerns developed against the background of the capabilities and intentions of the major Cold War antagonists. It is of course difficult to speculate about the ambitions of the decision makers in the Kremlin, and the extent to which they may have contemplated the use of force to obtain their objectives; in any event, after the outbreak of the Korean War Bonn and the Western powers seemed genuinely concerned that the Soviet Union might resort to armed aggression in central Europe. As the Korean conflict clearly proved, the Communist camp was not deterred from risking conventional war in places and circumstances where Western interests and commitments seemed ambiguous. On the other hand, each Cold War camp probably viewed the situation in central Europe quite differently. The stakes were high, spheres of influence were already beginning to be clearly drawn, Western interests were forcefully and unambiguously articulated, and the armies of the two superpowers directly confronted each other across the Cold War boundary dividing Germany. Western determination had been tested by Soviet probing actions, and a major Soviet transgression could be expected to trigger a swift and probably escalated Western response.

West German security was thus essentially a function of the East-West power relationship. As the military power of the Soviet bloc increased both absolutely and relatively, by the middle 1950's the security position of the Federal Republic may have become more problematic. On the other hand, the increase in Soviet strength was at least in part balanced by the mobilization of Western resources and by their coordination in NATO; and West Germany had been specifically included in the Western alliance, which itself was covered by the protective umbrella of the still credible American strategic nuclear deterrent. Furthermore, by 1955 the Soviet Union had settled on a two-Germanies policy, which seemed to reflect a readiness to forswear the use of force for changing the status quo in Europe, especially since Moscow apparently regarded the existing state of affairs as acceptable, and subsequently sought to solidify it politically. With the integration of East and West Germany in the Cold War camps, the European front of the Cold War had been clarified considerably; both sides had consolidated their positions and established thresholds of provocation that the opponent could ignore only at the risk of general war.

Against this background, from 1949 to 1955 the connection between the larger goal of security and the policy of implementing it with rearmament was somewhat tenuous. West Germany's borders were already formally guaranteed by the Western powers, and the West had made it a point to specifically include West Germany and West Berlin in its defense perimeter. No doubt a German military contingent was expected to strengthen the Western position considerably, but this was a moot consideration because no German army had as yet been established. The major change was in the political and legal status of West Germany in the Western defense structure. By committing itself to contribute to the Western defense effort, West Germany elevated its status from that of a military protectorate to that of an essentially equal and sovereign ally. This may have enhanced the credibility of Western promises to come to the aid of the Federal Republic, and by extending NATO's "presence" unequivocally to the East German border, the American nuclear deterrent may have covered the Federal Republic more convincingly. But the major effect of West German rearmament at that stage was political and psychological rather than military.

The political consequences of German rearmament can hardly be exaggerated. Clearly, it was the link that held together the complex treaty structure and the underlying bargaining relationship between the Bonn Government and the Western powers. The Government's chances of achieving its goals of security, recovery, and reunification were directly affected by the decision to join the Western defense system. Equally important, rearmament connected the conditions of the international system with the entire aggregate of West German foreign policy goals. Without the Cold War bipolarization of tensions and interests, there would have been little reason for the Western powers to press for a reconstruction of Germany's military potential a few years after the disintegration of the Nazi regime and the Wehrmacht. Without the need to rearm Germany, there would have been less incentive to accommodate the Bonn Government on issues of recovery and reunification. Rearmament was the bridge between the Cold War attributes of the international system and the successes and failures of Bonn's foreign policy; the strictures and opportunities of the international system, which impinged upon all German foreign policy projects, were largely channeled through the issue of German rearmament.

The Western powers' interest in West Germany was not limited to its military potential. A German military contingent could perhaps have been established by conscripting West Germans under the command of Allied occupation authorities. But this would not have provided a lasting integration of West Germany in the Western alliance. To merely "deputize" a German army under Western command—which France had implicitly suggested in the beginning of the rearmament debate—would have placed a West German military contribution in a sociopolitical and economic void. Moreover, the apparent designs of the Soviet Union went beyond military challenges; the Soviets continuously probed the resiliency of the sociopolitical order prevailing in the Western states. In such circumstances, it would have been insufficient to commit a potential ally only on the military plane. Obtaining a West German military contribution was an immediate and important goal of the Western powers. But beyond that, the Federal Republic was to be integrated in the Western alliance through more fundamental and penetrating elements of support: commitment to a Western system of values, interdependence of economies, political consultation and perhaps supervision, domestic consensus and political stability, and so forth. This point cannot be stressed too strongly because these larger considerations gave Bonn a much wider and more effective range of bargaining power than that provided by the question of rearmament alone.

Thus, the connection between rearmament and political recovery was bound to be very close. The sequence of events speaks for itself: in the Bonn Conventions and the Paris Agreements, Bonn traded rearmament and the allegiance of the Federal Republic to the Western cause for the restoration of sovereignty and for the Western commitment to recognize the Bonn Government as the only legitimate spokesman for all of Germany. As the Federal Republic turned more and more toward the West, the restoration of sovereignty became less of a concession for the West, especially since many sovereignty values that were being restored were immediately "frozen" in the international organizations Germany joined. When this happened —as in the cases of the OEEC, the European Payments Union, NATO, the Western European Union, the Schuman Plan, etc.— the primary payoff for Bonn was in terms of equality rather than independence, strictly speaking.

From Adenauer's perspective, "diluting" gains of sovereignty by joining integrative organizations was intrinsically unobjectionable. The content that Adenauer and other "Europeans" attached to the goal of political recovery—namely the integration of West Germany in a tightly knit Western European community—made it easier for the Bonn Government to consent to the curtailing of Germany's freedom of action, so long as it brought gains of equality. Just as important, it would have been much more difficult for Bonn to extract concessions from the Western powers if the restored elements of sovereignty had not been subject to international surveillance. The creation of international and supranational organizations had a positive and perhaps decisive influence on the speedy political recovery of West Germany. They provided mechanisms for controlling German sovereignty as soon as it was granted, and they made the restoration of sovereignty less risky and less painful for the Western powers, especially France. In turn, the mounting pressures to grant West Germany important political and economic concessions provided a powerful impetus for establishing integrative structures that could supervise the Federal Republic. In this two-way interaction, Adenauer's Europe-oriented policy was an essential precondition for successful political and economic recovery. It eased the way for political recovery because its integrative features, tirelessly stressed by Adenauer, demonstrated Germany's willingness to tie herself to the West and resist the temptation to pursue a "seesaw-balancing" policy with the East and West.

The pursuit of the goal of security—implemented as it was by close alignment with the West and the decision to rearm—thus not only was compatible with the goal of political recovery but was its prerequisite. The quest for security and the aim of political recovery, with the meaning attached to recovery by Adenauer, were mutually reinforcing under the bipolar Cold War patterns prevailing in the international system.

Similarly complementary connections existed between systemic conditions and economic recovery, and between economic recovery and political recovery. A depleted or unstable West German economy would have posed a serious liability for the Western alliance. A shaky economic order would have undermined political stability and opened up opportunities for Soviet maneuvers. Because of the integrative features of the Western alliance, the faltering or inefficient economy of one alliance partner would have weakened the economic structure of the entire bloc, not to speak of its adverse consequences on military preparedness. The tensions of the Cold War created an atmosphere in the West that was generally sympathetic with German aspirations to restore a viable economy. A more direct and specific manifestation of the effect of the Cold War on the German economy was the lifting of Allied controls over industrial production, and the stimulus provided by the Korean War and by subsequent rearmament contracts. Although these were important factors, one need not suggest for that reason that the German economy could not have reached a recovery takeoff point without Cold War tensions. The economic policies pursued by the Bonn Government, and the material and human resources of Germany probably were the primary reasons for the speedy recovery of the German economy. Nonetheless, reconstruction proceeded in the context of an international political situation that was highly conducive to economic revival.

The achievement of economic recovery was skillfully complemented and underpinned by the Bonn Government's policy on political recovery, and by extension, its policy on security and rearmament. Especially in such mixed political-economic ventures as the Schuman Plan, political and economic gains went hand in hand, and were achieved through a calculated, coordinated strategy that encompassed both dimensions and advanced German demands in the name of European and Atlantic unity. The Government's determination to liberalize domestic and international trade was in the long run advantageous politically as well as economically, since it underlined Bonn's commitment to political "internationalism." By forgoing traditional protectionism, Bonn rejected the economic corollary to political nationalism. Both inclinations could count on a sympathetic and appreciative response in Western capitals, especially in Washington. Again, it should be stressed that these compatibilities rested on the particular content that the Government read into both the political and economic aspects of recovery, in addition to the permissive and encouraging circumstances of the international system.

The pursuit of economic and political recovery also had an important bearing on the successful conclusion of the Saar issue. It is not often fully appreciated that the Saar issue was an issue of reunification. But recognizing the Saar as specifically a unification problem underlines the fact that unification of East and West Germany was doomed primarily because of the polarization of power and purpose in the Cold War struggle. The Cold War had the opposite effect on the Saar question; without East-West tensions, the Saar probably would not have been returned to Germany for some time.

After the war, France had hoped to steer a middle course between the Anglo-American powers and the Soviet Union, and to maximize, in the role of balancer, her severely limited political and physical resources. At first France expected the Soviet Union to be generally sympathetic to her claims on Germany, but Moscow, after initial ambivalence, soon began to oppose French designs on the Ruhr, the Rhineland, and the Saar. As tensions mounted between the Soviet Union and the Western powers, the USSR became less and less interested in supporting French policy on Germany, and France felt obliged to lean closer to the Anglo-American side to avoid becoming isolated politically. At the same time, the United States and Great Britain could ill afford to alienate French policy makers or risk the development of French "neutralism," particularly since the French Communist Party already was powerful in the Fourth Republic's domestic politics.

In these circumstances, the United States and Great Britain initially did not find it difficult to support French claims on the Saar. No overriding principles or interests stood in the way, and although both the United Kingdom and the United States had been annoyed by French delays and intransigence on some occupation policies, they supported French policy on the Saar consistently. In May 1951, when Adenauer complained to the Allied High Commission about French attempts to separate the Saar from Germany, the Western powers replied unequivocally that they did not find French policy on the Saar in any way contradictory to the Allies' June 1945 announcement that no permanent German border revisions were to take place prior to a final peace treaty. With the growing importance of the Federal Republic for the Western alliance, and with the realization that the Saar issue might delay an effective European defense system, American and British attitudes gradually changed. More and more, the Anglo-American powers began to act as mediators in the dispute between France and Germany, rather than as advocates of French aspirations. While they did not directly and openly renounce their commitment to support French claims, they let it be known that they favored an amicable settlement in the interests of a united Europe and Atlantic security.

The rejection of the EDC in the French Assembly in August 1954 strengthened Prime Minister Mèndes-France's hand in the immediate give-and-take of Franco-German negotiations on the Saar, because now it seemed as if France could deny West Germany access to the Western alliance and, ipso facto, to the restoration of sovereignty. But French procrastination proved a serious long-run handicap within the Western alliance, as the members became increasingly impatient with what they viewed as French chauvinism and obstructionism. Although French policy on the Saar displayed continuity of aims, it was seriously weakened by the disruptive politics of the Fourth Republic, which invited unfavorable comparison with the stable and increasingly self-confident Government of the Federal Republic. Adenauer advanced German demands in the name of Europe and the democratic right of self-determination; he appealed to the very values that the international community of Western Europe was to be built on. The United States and Great Britain pushed for the speedy establishment of a viable European defense organization, and began to look upon the time-consuming and erratic political processes of the Fourth Republic with increasing disfavor. No doubt there was a close connection between German rearmament and the Franco-German understanding that was finally reached on the Saar question. French acquiescence in the Paris Agreements, which paved the way for West German membership in NATO and the restoration of sovereignty, was obtained by German concessions on the Saar question. Most important, however, Bonn's increasing leverage derived from Cold War tensions and from the growing importance of West Germany for a viable Western defense posture.

Neither the shift in alliances nor the changes that had come about in the international climate would have sufficed to create a change in the balance of moral force between France and Germany had there not been a parallel change in the balance of material force. . . . Economic and political recovery served not only to give Germany back her power of attraction over the Saar. It also conferred upon her demands in the international field a weight impossible for a state of more modest resources. The means at her disposal, her ever-increasing power, and the dynamism of her economy, forced those with whom she dealt to give her a hearing and to take her desires into consideration. Those managing the affairs of the Federal Republic moreover found renewed confidence in a consideration of her power and a conviction that the change in the balance of strength would lead inevitably to a solution of the Saar problem favorable to Germany.[1]

Two distinct but closely related patterns of the international system thus combined to create the propitious setting that allowed the Federal Republic to pursue its Saar policy successfully. First, East-West tensions created the incentive for the Western powers to seek a German contribution to the Western alliance in return for the restoration of sovereignty, and they provided a climate conducive to economic recovery. These developments significantly enhanced Germany's bargaining position within the Western bloc, and were skillfully complemented by Adenauer's Europe policy and his insistence that the Saar question be resolved equitably for the sake of Western unity. Second, Germany's opponent on the Saar issue, France, was severely restricted in her freedom of action by the bipolarization of power and alignments in the international system, which required her to lean on the Anglo-American powers so as not to become isolated politically. The only major tension, if not direct incompatibility, between pursuing the Saar project and pursuing other West German foreign policy goals pertained to the goal of political recovery and especially its aim to accomplish a fundamental rapprochement between France and Germany. From the beginning, the Saar contest stood in the way of a Franco-German reconciliation, and the acrimonious nature of the dispute was hardly conducive to bringing about the collaboration and understanding that Adenauer sought to further so insistently.

On the whole, there was a striking degree of compatibility between the conditions of the international system and West Germany's foreign policy goals of security-rearmament, political and economic recovery, and the Saar question. These goals had an equally pronounced mutual complementarity, which was clearly reflected in the interlocking provisions of the Paris Agreements. The complementarities were not absolute, and required some adjustment and compromise on the part of the Bonn Government; but the respective degrees of compatibility between these individual goals and the international system were so pronounced that their mutual complementarity is hardly surprising, especially since the issue of rearmament provided a constant and crucial link between the major patterns of the international system on one hand, and the goals of political and economic recovery and the Saar question on the other.

The Reunification of East and West Germany

The goal of unifying East and West Germany was of an entirely different order because it could be achieved only with the consent of both Cold War camps. The polarization of major systemic patterns precluded the unification of Germany because the line of partition between the Cold War spheres of influence coincided with the division of Germany. Each side had to weigh the risk that a Germany united on its opponent's terms would decisively upset the balance of power in Europe. The Western powers, reasonably certain that a Germany united on the basis of democratic processes would side with the West, insisted on free elections prior to the formation of an all-German government and called for restoring freedom of action to that government. The Soviet Union advocated the neutralization of a united Germany and the formation of a government in which

East and West Germany would be represented equally. The risks for the Soviet Union were high, especially because Soviet control over Eastern Europe might have been jeopardized by a "domino" effect caused by the loss of East Germany. The West also had ample cause to be suspicious of Soviet proposals, which apparently aimed at Germany's neutralization but most likely were designed to create political conditions that could be exploited for infiltration and the ultimate domination of all of Germany. At a minimum, the Soviet proposals would have deprived the West of the power potential of West Germany—which was becoming more and more indispensable for Western strategy—and would have led to the de facto recognition of the East German regime. Because of the increasingly symmetrical power pattern in Europe, both camps were faced with a double-or-nothing situation where each side had good reason to expect that acceptance of the opponent's proposal would have a negative outcome. For each side the unification of Germany—on the opponent's terms—was fraught with risks and uncertainties. The stakes were high, and involved not only the two Germanies but the cohesion and viability of the two alliance blocs. The very importance of the issue thus prevented the two camps from making, at another front of the Cold War struggle, a "global deal" that would bring a solution to the German question, even though this possibility was frequently alluded to in German political circles.

In addition, the territorial dividing line that ran through Germany was clear-cut and manned on both sides by the armed forces of the major Cold War antagonists. The "trip-wire" setting, and the opportunities it seemed to offer for effective containment with a "forward strategy," was precisely what the United States sought to establish on all Cold War fronts. It is difficult to imagine why the United States should have been anxious to replace this relatively tolerable and apparently stable status quo with the uncertainties that would have followed from accepting Soviet proposals.[2]

With all these contingencies prevailing, the military, economic, and political alignment of either half of Germany with one of the Cold War camps could not possibly have helped make unification acceptable to both superpowers. The inclusion of West Germany in the Western alliance tended to "tighten" bipolarity and consequently exacerbated the conditions that made unification difficult in the first place. This is not to say that unification, on terms acceptable to Bonn and the West, could necessarily have been achieved if West Germany had not aligned herself with the West, or if the Federal Republic had not contributed to the Western defense effort by joining NATO; the Soviet Union could have sabotaged unification at any juncture in the sequence of steps that it proposed for bringing unification about. It is to say, however, that unless circumstances changed, Bonn could not have hoped to improve the chances for reunification by pursuing a policy of integration with the West.

The policy makers of the Federal Republic, and especially Konrad Adenauer, were fully aware of this. In fact, their long-range calculations anticipated a point where circumstances would not be the same; and Bonn's unification policies were designed to bring about these more propitious circumstances as quickly as possible. Probably the single most important development that threw grave doubts on these expectations was the Soviet Union's acquisition of nuclear capabilities. Since this had such far-reaching effects on the general attributes of the international system, it will be considered more fully and explicitly in a later chapter. There is no doubt that the actual and potential military strength of the Soviet Union had increased in kind as well as in degree. A Western policy of "roll back" and liberation now became inconceivable in light of the retaliatory power the Soviet Union was developing, as events in Hungary were soon to demonstrate.

Even the possibility of exerting strong diplomatic pressures on the Soviet Union to bring about a satisfactory solution of the German problem became increasingly unlikely. To be sure, the Soviet Union, while increasing her military power, had been facing serious internal political problems. The death of Stalin in March 1953, the resulting struggle for succession, and the June uprising in East Germany showed up serious weaknesses in the East bloc's power structure. According to Nikita Khrushchev, certain persons in the Kremlin, notably Beria, were apparently willing to trade what they considered a serious liability in East Germany for an East-West détente that might have included a German settlement. It is doubtful, however, that the Soviet Union was ever willing to sacrifice her hold over East Germany; and Adenauer in any case did not seem anxious to fully explore the possibilities that may have existed in the summer of 1953. Moreover, at a time when the Kremlin's rulers were jockeying for position in the race for power, a settlement of the German question acceptable to the West would have carried serious risks not only for its possible proponents in the Kremlin but for the cohesion of the entire Soviet bloc.

The political consolidation of the Eastern bloc and of Khrushchev's position in the Kremlin, coupled with the Soviet Union's improved military position, was soon reflected in Moscow's German policy. The opposite of Adenauer's premise for a policy of strength toward the Soviet Union in fact occurred: instead of becoming more conciliatory on the German question with the passage of time, the Russians' attitudes on unification stiffened in exactly the way they themselves had predicted. With the realization that it had not succeeded in preventing German membership in NATO, the Soviet Union shifted to a two-Germanies policy that found its most specific expression in establishing diplomatic relations with Bonn. In July 1955, Khrushchev stated that the unification of such differently developing countries as East and West Germany could not possibly take place at the expense of East Germany, and later that year, during Adenauer's visit to Moscow, Khrushchev declared himself to be no longer even interested in bringing up the question of a possible West German withdrawal from NATO. The Soviet Union was apparently convinced that the status quo in central Europe was tolerable for the time being, and that time was working for the Kremlin; this was reflected in Khrushchev's remark to Adenauer that "the wind is not blowing in our face."[3]

Clearly, Adenauer's hope of dealing successfully with the Soviet Union from a "position of strength" had not materialized by the end of 1955. Equally serious for unification prospects was the fact that by 1955 Adenauer himself seemed to detect a weakening of the Western resolve to confront the Soviet Union unequivocally and forcefully on the German question. Both the Eastern and Western dimensions of Bonn's unification policy were being called into question, in large part because the shifting power relationship between the Cold War camps strengthened Moscow's hand and patently increased the risks faced by the Western powers should a military conflagration occur.

One must conclude that the Cold War polarization of power and purpose, which had caused the split of Germany and subsequently diminished Germany's chances for unification, was further accentuated by Bonn's policy of close alignment with the West, especially on the military level. Since the policy of integration and rearmament was highly conducive to furthering the solution of the Saar issue and the goals of political and economic recovery—as conceived and advanced by Adenauer—all of these projects were more or less incompatible with the aim of unification under the prevailing systemic circumstances. It is worth noting again that during the period under discussion a developing East-West polarization of nuclear capabilities was gradually being superimposed on the already existing polarization of tensions, perceived interests, and Cold War alignments. This "tightening" of bipolarity—both on the level of capabilities and with respect to the cohesion and integration of the Cold War alliances—was transitory. In fact, it can be argued that it was precisely the polarization on the nuclear level that led to a loosening of the Western alliance on the political level after 1955. This large transformation of the international system, and its implications for West German foreign policy projects, will be treated in Part 2.

4. *Patterns of Consensus and the Domestic Political System, 1949–1955*

This chapter does not aim to give a detailed account of the domestic political struggle over the content and direction of West German foreign policy.[1] Instead, it aims to point out that the external patterns of compatibility or incompatibility between foreign policy goals and the international system were reflected to a striking degree on the domestic political scene in patterns of consensus or dissent.

The polarization of power and purpose in the international system gave rise to a similarly polarized conflict on the domestic political scene—not because the Government and the opposition were divided along pro-Western or pro-Soviet lines, but because incompatibilities between major foreign policy goals raised the issue of which foreign policy projects should be given priority. In the preceding two chapters I have noted that the fairly clear-cut patterns of the pre-1955 international system provided stark contrasts among the compatibilities of foreign policy goals in their external dimensions—especially between the goal of reunifying East and West Germany and the goals of political and economic recovery. This pattern was the backdrop for similarly sharp cleavages in the domestic political system. So long as the opposition saw the conditions of the international system as allowing acceptable alternatives to the Government's foreign policies—perhaps with a reversed order of priority—consensus was impossible.

The reflection of external patterns of compatibility on internal patterns of consensus or dissent is particularly significant because all political parties and relevant interest groups in the Federal Republic assumed that external circumstances would have far-reaching effects on the future course and content of the domestic political order. The contest over foreign policy was regarded as setting the framework for domestic policy and the social content of the German body politic. In their abstract formulation, the major projects of security, recovery, and reunification were not subject to contention; no significant political group in West Germany questioned their intrinsic merit. It was on the level of implementation that the conflict was sharp and sustained. All disagreements over the Government's foreign policy arose from the questions of what content should be placed in the abstract formulation of foreign policy goals and what priorities should be established for their pursuit.

The issue of priorities inevitably developed from the recognition that international conditions would not allow the Bonn Government to pursue all major foreign policy goals with equal success. Not even the Government claimed that unification could be actively pursued at the same time as security and recovery: Adenauer contended that the pursuit of security and recovery within the framework of the Western alliance would lay the groundwork for a *subsequent* resolution of the unification issue. Disagreement over the validity of this assumption, and the sociopolitical implications of the security and recovery policies that the Government followed in the interim, caused key divisions between the major political groups in the Federal Republic.

SECURITY AND REARMAMENT

Domestic political responses to the proposed rearmament of Germany ranged from complete acceptance to complete rejection. The underlying reasons for these attitudes were primarily the anticipated repercussions of rearmament on the political programs advocated by the contending parties; rearmament was viewed as a crucial instrumentality that would either enhance or impede the various groups' political aspirations for the sociopolitical, cultural, and economic development of German society. Since the outcome of foreign policy projects was widely recognized as having a fundamental effect on long-range domestic political developments, and since rearmament was clearly the link that held together the Government's entire foreign policy program, rearmament became the key issue of the domestic contest over foreign policy. For the very reason that rearmament was the central connection between the international system and Bonn's foreign policy projects, rearmament and its perceived implications became the focal point of the domestic struggle over foreign policy questions.

From the beginning of the Federal Republic in 1949, Konrad Adenauer stood out as the key architect of its foreign policy. The substantial constitutional powers provided for the Chancellor's office in the Basic Law were fully complemented by his forceful personality and political acumen. Adenauer was head of both the Government and the strongest political party, and he devoted the greater part of his time and energy to the conduct of foreign affairs. In fact, he initially held the post of Foreign Minister concurrently with the chancellorship. With the passage of time, Adenauer not only reshaped the CDU in his own image but also established the reputation, both at home and abroad, of having led West Germany to political stability and having laid the political foundations for Germany's rapid economic recovery. All this meant that Adenauer would, for better or worse, emerge as the strongest single influence on the formation of West German foreign policy.[2]

For Adenauer, all West German foreign policy goals, including that of security, derived their fundamental meaning and purpose from the vision of a European political and economic community. His overriding aim was to integrate Germany in this community and to irrevocably tie the structure and direction of German society to the cultural and political forces of Western Europe. This was to be achieved by making Germany an equal and respected partner of the Western powers and by forging a fundamental and lasting reconciliation with France. In the larger context of world politics, and especially for the purpose of meeting the Communist challenge, a purposefully united Western Europe was to be anchored to the power of the United States in the framework of an Atlantic alliance.[3]

The "policy of strength" that Adenauer advocated for dealing with the Communist world presupposed not only a determined Western diplomatic and moral posture, but necessarily required a respectable Western military establishment to which a number of German divisions would make a noteworthy contribution. Although the Bonn Government rejected the use of force for achieving foreign policy aims, Adenauer on many occasions expressed his belief that the Soviet Union was run by "realists" who understood the language of power rather than that of equity or moral persuasion. In addition to seeing its contribution to West German security, Adenauer viewed rearmament as a token of Germany's determination to align herself wholeheartedly with the West, and as an indispensable bargaining lever in expediting the restoration of German sovereignty and laying the groundwork for the recovery of German influence in world affairs.[4]

Adenauer never allowed the connection between rearmament and sovereignty to go unnoticed. Before and after the signing of the EDC treaties, he repeatedly stressed this tie, and argued that one could not expect the Western allies to relinquish the rights stemming from the unconditional Nazi surrender unless the Federal Republic compensated them by agreeing to rearmament. At the time when the Bonn Conventions were signed, Adenauer went to great lengths to trace the story of Germany's postwar recovery, and assigned the EDC treaties the major place in the progress toward sovereignty and security.[5]

Although they were firmly guided by the chancellor, the Christian Democrats in the Bundestag and the Cabinet did not always line up unanimously or enthusiastically behind his rearmament policies. For example, Dr. Gustav Heinemann, the CDU Minister of the Interior, resigned over the issue of rearmament and helped organize protest meetings throughout West Germany. But on the whole, the CDU/CSU parliamentarians supported Adenauer's pro-Western policy and were willing to follow through with its specific implications, including that of rearmament.[6] Conviction and party discipline were generally reinforcing; it was only in later years that Adenauer began to meet with serious opposition within his own party. Nonetheless, the variations in the amount of enthusiasm for Adenauer's Europe policy within the CDU/CSU are worth noting, if only because they are an element in the overall spectrum of political attitudes that ranged from outright rejection to support with an almost ideological fervor.

The Christian Democratic Union was founded after the war by lay leaders of the Roman Catholic and Protestant churches, with the support of businessmen and trade-union leaders. From the beginning, the CDU and its Bavarian branch, the CSU, aimed to attract a wide and heterogeneous group of supporters, and eschewed any specific ideological orientation except an adherence to general "Christian principles." Although there was a pronounced socialistic strain up to and including the party's Ahlen Program of 1947, by 1949 the CDU/CSU had become economically more conservative, in that it grew distinctly oriented toward small business, agriculture, and industry. At the same time, the party was still committed to labor-management codetermination and other policies favored by its trade-union wing. By espousing this moderate social and economic program, the CDU/CSU sought to tap the apparently large reservoir of political moderates who rejected the Communists and Socialists on the left and the neo-nationalists on the right. The party's success at the polls seemed to prove the validity of this strategy.[7] Nonetheless, the coalition between Catholic and Protestant elements in the CDU/CSU was at times an uneasy one, and had to be shielded from disruptive influences. This was particularly true regarding some aspects of Adenauer's policy for an integrated Europe. No major figure in the Christian Democratic Union was opposed to European integration or to rapprochement with France. But the Catholic overtones of the gradually emerging Europe of the Six—the neo-Carolingian realm, as the Socialists derisively called it—could not be expected to meet with the enthusiastic support of the Protestant elements in the CDU/CSU. The tension within the major party, which was also notable on domestic issues, did not prevent the CDU/CSU from uniting behind the Government on such major issues as German rearmament; but the central motivation of Adenauer's foreign policy program, the integration of Germany in a Western European union, was not shared equally by all elements of the CDU/CSU because it carried the implication that Catholic political and cultural elements might predominate in an "international coalition."

Similar but more pronounced tensions existed between the CDU/CSU and its coalition partners. Adenauer had no difficulty in enlisting the support of the Free Democratic Party (FDP) and the German Party (DP) for his policy of rearmament. But his underlying motivation—tying Germany's political and cultural destiny to the cause of Western Europe—could not count on the unqualified support of the FDP and DP. These parties had joined the CDU/CSU in the coalition governments established after the 1949 and 1953 elections; although the Free Democrats suffered from internal tensions that arose in part from their regional political efforts and the heterogeneous nature of their political support, they maintained the balance of power between the CDU/CSU and the Socialists. The FDP brought together republican Liberals who cherished the tenuous political traditions of 1848, business interests that preferred a more pronounced laissez-faire economic liberalism than that advocated by the CDU, and anticlerical middle-class voters who resented the Catholic tinge of the CDU/CSU.

In both international and domestic politics, the Free Democrats toyed with the idea of a "third force." Some of them would have liked Germany to play a more independent role in European politics than Adenauer's integrative, pro-Western program would allow; they tended to stress national self-interest in the pursuit of foreign policy aims, and on the whole were less willing to make an attempt to conciliate the Western powers, an attempt that was basic to the CDU's foreign policy program. The Free Democrats were not nearly as committed to Adenauer's "little Europe" policy as were the Christian Democrats, and they generally opted for a wider framework of European cooperation, which would include at least Great Britain. On the domestic political plane, the FDP also consistently tried to enlarge its role as a possible "third force" between the CDU/CSU and the Socialists, by presenting a foreign policy program that stressed reunification and the national interest without the economic and social policies advocated by the Socialists. But the FDP's emphasis on national self-interest and mobility in international affairs, coupled with the nationalistic sentiments of some groups in the party, presented no obstacles to pursuing a "policy of strength" and to exploiting the opportunities inherent in Adenauer's rearmament-sovereignty barter with the Western powers. While the substitution of the Western European Union for the European Defense Community disappointed many of the ardent integrationists in the CDU/CSU, the FDP was satisfied with the course of events that led to the establishment of a more traditional German military establishment not integrated at the lowest echelons.[8]

The German Party (DP) was even less enthusiastic about European integration than the FDP, but found it equally easy to support the rearmament of the Federal Republic. This party's flirtation with a German *Grossraum* policy in Europe made it generally hostile to a full accommodation of the Western powers. The role of a predominant balancer, which the DP envisaged for Germany, required independent strength and political mobility unencumbered by international integrative measures. The pronouncements of the German Party were liberally sprinkled with terms like "foreign domination," and they detailed the dangers that would come from a German "spirit of self-sacrifice" and "self-abnegation." The DP's apparently enthusiastic appeal for the support of former Nazis, and the strongly nationalistic statements of many of its spokesmen, placed the party as a whole on the right wing of the governing coalition.[9]

From 1949 to 1955, while the coalition partners, for their own reasons, consistently supported West German rearmament, the Socialists were its most determined and vociferous opponents. The priorities that the Social Democrats assigned to West German foreign policy projects were, just like those of Adenauer and of the supporters of a Western European community, determined by fundamental preferences for a certain kind of German society. Both the Government and the opposition consciously attempted to manipulate the international system to create external circumstances propitious for achieving far-reaching domestic goals.

The Social Democratic Party is the oldest extant German party. Its Marxist-reformist program drew considerable support during the Weimar era, especially in Northern and Eastern Germany. Hence the division between East and West Germany considerably weakened the party by cutting if off from many of its traditional bases of political strength. In addition, a large number of SPD leaders originally came from East of the Elbe and had a particularly keen concern for the fate of their compatriots there.[10]

These factors no doubt partially explain why the Socialists consistently stressed the urgency of reunification and implacably opposed rearmament as being fundamentally incompatible with its achievement. But there were more basic reasons for the SPD's preoccupation with unification. In the first place, although the Socialists echoed the Government's call for a European community and a rapprochement with France, they were also deeply disturbed about the prospect of a European union with strong Catholic and conservative tendencies. The Socialists' blueprint for a new social and political order in Germany was Marxist-reformist, at least initially, and had pronounced antibourgeois and anticlerical overtones. They had little hope that the economic and political values of socialism would prevail in the Western European union advocated by the Christian Democrats. On the contrary, the SPD feared that Adenauer was fully justified in expecting to strengthen his conservative political and economic program by forming an "international coalition" among the conservative elements of Western Europe. The SPD felt a much closer affinity with the sociopolitical and cultural attributes of Great Britain and the Scandinavian countries, whose political and socioeconomic life had been significantly shaped by their Socialist parties. The European community the Socialists envisaged, as well as Germany's place in it, was determined by their image of what social order should prevail in the Federal Republic and in a united Germany. Just as Adenauer anticipated support for his Western European vision from the considerable congruence of foreign policy concepts among French, Italian, Dutch, and Belgian leaders, so the Socialists expected that their aspirations for German society would be advanced internationally by a larger European community, which would include Scandinavia and Great Britain. Furthermore, the SPD version of European integration was far looser than the supranational aspirations of the "Europeans" in the governing coalition, and hence led the Socialists to reject most specific steps in this direction taken by the Adenauer Administration.[11]

The Socialists' reluctance to participate in the formation of a Catholic, ultramontanist Europe was strengthened by the fear that they would once again be accused by the extreme right of being too "internationalist," as had happened in Weimer Germany. To forestall this attack, after the war the SPD adopted a "sort of preventive nationalism" that led to a highly critical attitude toward the occupying powers and the conciliatory integrationist program of Konrad Adenauer. With its long tradition of rejecting nationalism in favor of international solidarity and the common interests of the working classes, the SPD found itself in the paradoxical position of appearing more nationalistic than its political opponents on the moderate right.[12]

The Socialists' wary attitude toward Western European integration and the incompatibility they perceived between rearmament and reunification made the SPD the major voice of organized opposition to the entire range of interlocked foreign policies pursued by the Government. From 1949 through the middle 1950's, the Socialists' outlook remained essentially unchanged: they fought Germany's membership in the EDC, in the Coal and Steel Community, in the WEU and NATO. The SPD's four major objections to rearmament can be summarized as follows: it would render unification more difficult, if not impossible, by attaching West Germany too closely to one of the Cold War camps; it would increase world tensions and antagonize the Soviet Union without substantially improving the Western defense posture; it was dangerous for the fledgling German democracy because it would bring to the fore militarist elements and other objectionable remnants of the old order; and finally, it paved the way to Germany's integration in a Western European group that threatened to split free Europe and showed conservative-clerical tendencies.

In view of this overall outlook, it is not surprising that the Socialists engaged the governing coalition in heated battles over rearmament. For both Adenauer and the opposition, rearmament was the crux of the entire foreign policy program, having fundamental implications for domestic policy and the future course of German society. The Cold War attributes of the international system, which led the Western powers to insist on a German contribution to Western defense in return for German sovereignty, thus imposed the framework for the domestic contest over foreign policy alternatives. This inevitably led the Socialists to criticize the Western powers' policy on Germany, and in fact SPD spokesmen tended to imply that the Western powers not only showed little interest in German unification but were ready to impede it by drawing the Federal Republic into the Western defense system. Generally, the Socialists felt that by virtue of occupation the Western powers had undertaken the responsibility for Germany's defense; the rights of occupation implied obligations of defense, and as long as West Germany had not regained full sovereignty the Socialists were unwilling to concede that Germany should contribute to the Western defense effort.[13]

The Socialists' insistent demands for sovereignty and equal status in any planned European venture implied, however, that once these conditions had been met they would scrap their opposition to rearmament. But though the SPD consistently harassed the Government and questioned the constitutionality of rearmament, it was neither completely united nor entirely consistent in its opposition. A number of SPD spokesmen admitted that they were not fundamentally opposed to rearmament nor necessarily adverse to German membership in NATO, if the Federal Republic were invited. In attacking the provisions of the EDC, the SPD frequently pointed to the restrictive control arrangements of the EDC treaty, and argued that it would be intolerable to have German contingents reduced to the status of "foreign legionnaires." There was thus the implication that at least some Socialists could be induced to support German rearmament if control arrangements were less restrictive. This interpretation was strongly opposed by certain members of the party. There was also disagreement over the ethical propriety of "neutralism" in the Cold War struggle, and at times the party split into a radical, anti-American, neutralist faction and a more moderate, pro-Western, less doctrinaire faction.[14]

The ambivalence of the SPD's opposition was highlighted after the defeat of the EDC in the French Assembly. The Socialists took this opportunity to castigate the Government for having failed in its Europe policy, but they also had to admit that many of the EDC features that they had found unacceptable were subsequently omitted in the provisions made for German membership in NATO and the WEU. They now shifted to arguing that German membership in NATO would be unnecessary because international tensions had abated considerably since the Government first launched its rearmament campaign. As was to be expected, the Socialists welcomed the inclusion of Great Britain in the proposed European military alliance, but they kept objecting that rearmament and unification would be incompatible, and that Germany should abstain from rearming at a time when an East-West détente appeared feasible. By now the Socialists were careful to reject the label of "neutralism" for their position, and insisted that their fundamental political and moral commitment was on the side of Western values, if not always on the side of Western policies. Still, they stated that it would be unreasonable to expect the Soviet Union to give up its hold over East Germany by allowing free elections if a united Germany could subsequently join a Western military alliance. This argument was capped with the proposal to establish a central European collective-security system, which would guarantee the security of a united Germany and take into consideration the legitimate interests of both Cold War camps.[15]

Clearly, there were some embarrassing inconsistencies and

ambiguities in the SPD's position. By constantly reiterating their objections to second-class status for Germany in a European defense arrangement, the Socialists intimated that they were willing to consent to rearmament if only German sovereignty and equality were restored in the process. This merely echoed the Government's long-standing policy and strengthened Adenauer's hand in both domestic and international politics. Secondly, while the Socialists showed a keen appreciation of power when it came to pointing out that the Soviet Union could not be expected to consent to German unification on Western terms, they constantly denied the importance of a West German military contribution to the Western defense effort. This argument was not very convincing at a time when the Western powers adamantly insisted on West German rearmament, and when it was clear that Adenauer could extract major concessions from the West in the goal areas of political and economic recovery. In opposing rearmament, the Socialists tirelessly stressed its damaging effect on the chances for unification. But their own proposals for reunification, which focused on the neutralization of Germany and the creation of a central European collective-security system, assumed the Soviet Union's genuine willingness to permit the unification of Germany on the basis of democratic principles. The Socialists seemed oblivious to military-strategic calculations, and throughout the debate on rearmament, their criticism had a somewhat shrill, unreal quality. They cast the Government as a willing dupe of the Western powers, and posed rather simplistically as the only champions of unification. In December 1954, after NATO had assigned crucial new functions to the planned German contingents, and when the entire treaty structure that was to restore German sovereignty was about to come into effect, SPD spokesmen still held forth with the platitudinous argument that twelve German divisions were relatively unimportant in terms of the overall East-West balance of power.

By 1955, the apparent incompatibility of rearmament and unification on the international scene had polarized the domestic contest on foreign policy to such an extent that it was possible to say "Germany is now presented with two clear foreign policy alternatives—for the first time since the war. The first—Adenauer's—sees a strong two-thirds of the country wholly allied with the free world in the hope that a 'policy of strength' will sooner or later force the Russians to pull the Iron Curtain back at least as far as the Oder. The Socialist alternative seeks to achieve immediate unification by offering to trade the scheduled twelve German divisions against [the] twenty million civilians of the East Zone."[16]

The Socialists' efforts to gain support for their opposition to rearmament met with uneven success. Unquestionably, most West Germans viewed rearmament without enthusiasm. In addition to the sobering experiences of World War II, German public opinion was influenced by previous Allied policies, and by the reeducation campaign that had sought to eradicate any physical and psychological remnants of militarism. The rather sudden shift of attitudes and values that accompanied the Western powers' decision to seek a military partnership with West Germany was thus greeted with a good deal of cynicism. A spirit of "without me" was prevalent, and it was widely felt that Germany could only lose in a military encounter between East and West, since Germany would necessarily bear the brunt of the fighting. Overcoming the psychological and moral disarmament of postwar Germany was a major difficulty for the Government, as was shown by the bitter struggle over amending the Basic Law to make conscription legal.[17]

On the surface, this climate of opinion seemed to provide the Socialists with rich political opportunities. German membership in the EDC and NATO lacked popular support, and almost 80 per cent of respondents in a survey agreed with the SPD that the decision to rearm should have been subject to a plebiscite.[18] But in the 1953 elections, for which the Socialists had chosen rearmament as a key issue, they barely managed to hang on to the 29 per cent of the votes they had obtained in 1949, while the CDU/CSU gained 14 per cent over the 31 per cent it had received in 1949. Of course inability to exploit the rearmament issue was not the Socialists' only problem. They suffered from several political handicaps that made it difficult for them to increase their support at the polls; in particular, they were still hurt by the doctrinaire image the party had created under the leadership of Kurt Schumacher, and by the apparent lack of relevance of a Marxist political dogma for a society whose class structure seemed to be gradually shifting without ideological prodding. Economic reconstruction was proceeding apace, and many West Germans apparently clearly understood that rearmament was the prerequisite for political and economic recovery—a connection constantly stressed by Adenauer—and appeared unwilling to jeopardize recovery by holding out on rearmament.

Rearmament was a price most Germans would have preferred not to pay. But the objections to rearmament, although widespread, were constantly counteracted by practical considerations, and furthermore lacked effective political representation at the seat of power in Bonn. The opposition to rearmament had a dispersed constituency—in the trade unions, churches, and among university students—and it had a difficult time coordinating its demands forcefully. With the exception of the Socialists, whose rigidity prevented them from exerting any great influence on the political process, the elements opposing rearmament were not effectively channeled and were subjected to divisive cross-pressures. The practical and immediate requirements of economic reconstruction, the desire for an adequate standard of living after years of deprivation, the gains promised in return for collaborating with the Western powers—in short, the recognition that the Government's policy showed a way to stability, recovery, and international "respectability"—made opposition to rearmament an essentially emotional issue that had to face a daily test against expediency and the hope for "normalcy."[19]

The attitude of organized labor is a case in point.[20] Although the Socialists and the trade-union movement collaborated closely on many domestic issues, on a number of foreign policy questions the unions either had no clearly enunciated position or sided with the Government. Taking an official stand on the rearmament issue posed a special problem for the labor movement because of internal disagreements. From the beginning, many of the rank and file and many minor officials opposed rearmament. The top leaders were more ambivalent; they were more fully aware of the intricate relationship between rearmament and the Government's entire range of recovery goals, and they recognized that the union movement had an important stake in recovery. But when the leaders of the German Trade Union Federation (DGB) reluctantly endorsed the Government's rearmament policy, a number of them were purged at the DGB convention in 1952. Subsequently, the DGB tried to avoid taking an official stand on rearmament, and issued noncommittal statements to the effect that it considered the question "political" and therefore primarily the responsibility of the political parties. The refusal to express an official viewpoint, however, did not satisfy rearmament's more determined opponents in union circles, who regarded the DGB's "neutrality" as an implicit endorsement of Government policy. At the 1954 DGB convention, the initial resolution on rearmament was equivocal and did not directly oppose it. This statement failed to pass, and was replaced by a much stronger one, which argued that participation in the EDC would endanger the prospect of unification and would increase world tensions. In the spring of 1955, the DGB, along with SPD leaders and the chairmen of all industrial unions, officially participated in drafting and supporting the so-called Pauls-Kirche Manifesto, which strongly condemned rearmament, and called for renewed attempts to negotiate unification before West Germany became militarily entangled with one of the Cold War camps.[21]

Thus, although the opponents of rearmament finally succeeded in obtaining from the labor movement a public declaration that amounted to a repudiation of Government policy, the trade unions had in effect remained on the sidelines of the rearmament struggle. In union circles views on foreign policy generally varied widely, making it difficult for the labor movement to speak with one voice and exert its general political influence on foreign policy issues. This prevented the union movement from applying consistent pressure either on the Government or on the opposition, and allowed the rank-and-file members to shape their attitudes more by the general public discussion than by a specific trade-union position. The general aversion to rearmament, although freely expressed, was denied the channel of a consistent trade-union position and had to turn directly to the Social Democrats for political representation.

Neither was there effective opposition to rearmament among businessmen. Although not homogeneous in their attitudes, business and industrial spokesmen were on the whole more pro-Government than the trade-union leaders. Interviews conducted during the summer of 1954 brought to light a notable diversity of viewpoints among businessmen, but showed that they generally tended to support rearmament as an integral part of the Government's overall foreign policy program.[22] Some businessmen, although not opposed to rearmament as such, criticized the provisions of the EDC because they would restrict Germany's freedom of action; others said that for the sake of European unity and because of French misgivings, European economic integration and political coordination should precede German rearmament. A large number of businessmen believed that rearmament was the key to success for projects of political and economic recovery, even though they expressed doubts about the military efficacy of the EDC and a German military contribution. Opinions were also somewhat divided on possible alternatives to the EDC, after its demise in August 1954. Businessmen who appeared more internationally minded preferred the NATO solution, and suggested that French apprehensions and delaying tactics be met with patience and understanding; others, who had a more nationalistic perspective, either were skeptical of the NATO solution and supported it only because it was the best that Germany could get under the circumstances, or opposed NATO because they believed Germany could be rearmed on more independent terms that would allow greater political mobility. Among the large majority of businessmen who favored either the EDC or NATO, many seemed concerned, nonetheless, that a military alliance with the West could jeopardize reunification. The "internationalists" appeared willing to assign a higher priority to European integration and a recovery of German influence in Western councils than to reunification, at least for the time being. This viewpoint, of course, reflected Adenauer's position and that of a large majority of the CDU/CSU. The "nationalists," in advocating a flexibility that would allow German interests to be advanced more forcefully, came very close to the line taken by the Free Democrats. The attitudes of a large number of businessmen on rearmament were thus effectively and rather accurately represented by the two major coalition partners in the Government, who also enjoyed the confidence of the business community on the issues of economic and political recovery.

Because of the military's direct professional interest and expertise, it is appropriate to conclude the discussion of the consensus pattern on rearmament with a brief statement of the military's position.[23] The Blank Office, the predecessor of the Defense Ministry, had taken great pains to disrupt all threads of continuity between the old Wehrmacht and the proposed new Bundeswehr by carefully screening applicants for the new military establishment. Although many of the former Wehrmacht generals were thoroughly discredited, and in any event spoke as private individuals, their contribution to the rearmament dialogue is of some significance if only because the contest between the Government and the opposition lacked any sustained discussion of military-strategic matters. In defending their plans for arming the Federal Republic, Government spokesmen frequently were rather high-handed and tried to sell German membership in NATO as the cure-all for West Germany's security needs. The Socialists were equally simplistic, and refused to let a serious discussion of military-strategic issues interfere with their wholesale rejection of rearmament.

Some ex-generals, for instance Rudel and Ramcke, who had been closely identified with the Nazis, were strongly opposed to German rearmament in the context of the Western alliance, and were openly neutralist if not pro-Soviet. Other former military leaders favored rearming Germany, but were extremely skeptical of the military efficacy of the integrative features of the EDC, and apparently thought it would be better to postpone rearmament until political circumstances and the climate of opinion at home and abroad allowed the establishment of a national military contingent.[24]

Although the tough-minded determination conveyed by the Eisenhower Administration's doctrine of massive retaliation was generally well received in German military circles—in the Blank Office as well as among many of the purged ex-generals—the implications of the 1954 NATO decision to deploy tactical nuclear weapons was received with some misgivings. The cause célèbre of Colonel Bonin is an instructive example.[25] Bonin, who had been Chief of Operations on the German General Staff during World War II, had been appointed Chief of Planning in the Blank Office in June 1952. He soon began to criticize the adequacy of NATO planning for the defense of West Germany, and in particular argued for the forward deployment of German contingents near the East German border. Bonin's planning in effect called for a national German defense strategy, and the political implications made it seem desirable to relieve Bonin of his planning functions in 1953. He was sent abroad on "study trips," and after he returned in the summer of 1954, he proposed the deployment of a German force of about 150,000 volunteers along the zonal borders in defensive "blocking units" at a depth of about fifty kilometers. This was to be an all-German force, operating separately from NATO contingents, which would have been pulled back behind the Rhine. Bonin's plan, based primarily on the contingency of a Soviet attack with tanks, was officially rejected by the Blank Office both because it contravened NATO planning and because it was considered militarily inadequate; furthermore, it seemed to emphasize the division of Germany by drawing a clear-cut military boundary between East and West Germany.

After the collapse of the EDC in August 1954, and after the December NATO decision to deploy tactical nuclear weapons, Bonin took his case to the public and began to cap his military proposals with political arguments. He vehemently attacked the NATO concept of mobile strategy and flexible defense, on the grounds that it would carry a war deep into German territory and that this kind of planning would make it difficult for young Germans to identify with Western defense objectives. The crux of Bonin's argument was that a strong forward defense with a small German national army would facilitate unification by allowing the withdrawal of Western and Soviet forces from Germany. Although Bonin's proposals failed to rally the support of strategic planners in the Blank Office, who criticized them largely on military grounds, the neutralist political implications of his views produced interesting reactions in Bonn. This was at a time when the Soviet Union was making last-minute efforts to prevent West Germany's accession to NATO with announcements designed to portend unification; while Adenauer and the Blank Office were adamant in rejecting Bonin's line of thinking, the Ministry of All-German Affairs, which had previously supplied Bonin with travel funds to publicize his cause, showed considerable interest. Erich Mende, later chief of the FDP and already influential in party circles, came out for Bonin, and other FDP and DP spokesmen called for a serious consideration of the neutralist possibilities implicit in Bonin's proposals. The Socialists were divided. Bonin's views came close to the SPD position, but Bonin's past in the Wehrmacht, and the militarist reputation he had gained from his opposition to the reformists in the Blank Office, made it difficult for the SPD to embrace his argument in public and without reservations. Nonetheless, the SPD freely used Bonin's arguments for supporting their opposition to NATO and for attacking Adenauer and the Blank Office.[26]

In the present context, the Bonin case is significant because it brought the strategic-political implications of NATO strategy to a public discussion, which the political parties previously had been either unwilling or unable to engage in. In so doing, the Bonin affair pointed up the fact that although the coalition partners in the Government could agree on rearmament as such, their different underlying motivations led them to interpret the implications of NATO strategy in significantly different terms. As soon as important elements in the FDP and DP perceived a strategic alternative to the one implicit in Adenauer's pro-NATO policy—an alternative that promised more political flexibility for the Federal Republic, appeared less damaging to the prospects for unification, and did not entail strong integrative features within a Western military alliance—the CDU's coalition partners were seriously interested in pursuing this possibility even if it meant undercutting NATO strategy. The consensus on rearming Germany within the governing coalition was broadly based, but was subject to divisive cross-pressures as soon as strategic-political alternatives that were more congenial to the FDP's and DP's overall programmatic preferences seemed to present themselves.

RECOVERY

Political Recovery

No political group of any consequence was opposed to the restoration of German sovereignty as such. As an abstract value, sovereignty and political recovery posed no domestic political issue. But the specific content of the Government's recovery policies, and their anticipated consequences for other foreign policy issues and for the future course and content of West German society, were contested consistently. Especially the implications of linking German political recovery to a Western European union were subject to intense political debate because of possible repercussions on the chances for reunification. While rearmament became a key issue because it provided the Government with the political lever needed to advance Adenauer's overall foreign policy preferences in the international system, political recovery was a major substantive issue because it represented the specific values that the contending parties wished to instill in the German body politic. The choice of a route to political recovery was the choice of a direction for German society; the pursuit of political recovery in the international system was regarded as having a long-range effect on the future domestic order.

The specific meaning that Adenauer and a majority of the CDU/CSU parliamentarians attached to German sovereignty has already been noted: first, for Adenauer it symbolized the return of Germany to the society of free nations; second, in order to create the lasting European union that was Adenauer's most cherished foreign policy goal, it was essential that Germany join as an equal partner with freely given consent; third, it would enhance the stability of German democracy by forestalling extremist appeals and by instilling a feeling of self-confidence and responsibility in the newly established body politic; fourth, it would add to the attractions of the Federal Republic, and invite favorable comparisons with East Germany, thus enhancing the prospects for unification; fifth, it would increase the political and diplomatic leverage of the Federal Republic within the Western alliance; finally, sovereignty was expected to bring gains for the CDU/CSU on the domestic political scene.[27]

The Free Democrats were not particularly impressed with, or committed to, the kind of Western European international coalition that Adenauer and the European "federalists" in the CDU sought to create. Consequently, the FDP's advocacy of West German sovereignty was tinged with more nationalistic appeals, and they were much less ready to "freeze" gains of sovereignty in integrative and supervisory European structures. The right wing of the party in particular was much less patient and conciliatory toward French delaying tactics and more inclined to advance German demands in terms of national self-interest, freedom from external restraints, diplomatic flexibility, and a generally more traditional, perhaps chauvinistic, view of national sovereignty. Furthermore, the FDP right wing's efforts to attract frankly nationalistic elements in Northern Germany led the party as a whole to champion national independence and sovereignty much more stridently and inflexibly than the CDU/CSU. On the other hand, the business and industrial circles that were attracted by the FDP's laissez-faire economic program had a substantial stake in the Government's pro-Western policy and acted as an important check on the right wing. A further restraint was provided by the party's Liberal element, whose major spokesman, Theodor Heuss, enjoyed general respect because of the urbanity and sensitivity with which he performed his duties as President of the Republic.[28]

The German Party and the spokesmen for refugee interests were not encumbered by such restraints. The DP's wish to see a united Germany as a European balancer of East and West, and the party's strongly nationalistic program, called for freedom of action and a tough posture vis-à-vis both East and West. To them the restoration of sovereignty meant the opportunity to engage in power politics, and freedom to play East against West unencumbered by contractual restraints that would bind the Federal Republic to the Western alliance.[29]

The Socialists' overall political program and their overriding preoccupation with reunification, which provided the cue to most of their foreign policy attitudes, inevitably shaped their position on sovereignty and political recovery. Their hostility toward German membership in a Western European community that they saw as having a conservative bias, its potential repercussions on unification, and the fear that the Socialists could once again be accused of self-abnegating "internationalism," made the SPD the most outspoken advocate of German self-interest. This had been foreshadowed in the SPD's cautious response to the establishment of the Federal Republic. During the negotiations preceding the adoption of the Basic Law in 1949, the Socialists repeatedly voiced the fear that an unqualified acceptance of the Basic Law would leave the SPD open to the charge that it shared responsibility for the split of Germany. Hence the Socialists accused the CDU of having accommodated the occupation powers too willingly, and SPD spokesmen frequently pointed to the similarity between the CDU's viewpoint and the Western powers' viewpoint on certain constitutional features, especially federalism. Although the Socialists ended up voting for the final version of the Basic Law, they stressed its provisional nature more than the Christian Democrats, and implied that the restraining circumstances of the occupation had not allowed a more satisfactory result.[30]

It is important to return to the distinction—made previously in discussing political recovery in its international setting—between the legal aspects of the restoration of *sovereignty* and the politically more substantive nature of *political recovery.* Adenauer's determination to make West Germany an equal partner in a Western European union (as a goal of political recovery) allowed him to view international integrative ventures with equanimity, even though they curtailed Bonn's freedom of action by tying West Germany contractually and politically to the Western powers. But for the Socialists the two-pronged legal-political aspect of political recovery posed a vexing problem. Although they consistently pushed for full equality and legal sovereignty, they could not really accept the restoration of sovereignty without qualification, because of its possible effect on unification—an implication that they themselves had raised since the drafting of the Basic Law. Putting undue stress on West Germany's legal sovereignty—even the kind of stress the SPD envisaged, that is, unencumbered by entanglement with the Western Cold War alliance—appeared politically and psychologically unwise because it emphasized the division of Germany and tended to shift the responsibility for reunification from the Allied powers to the two German governments.[31]

The crux of the matter was always the question of what was to be done with the legal aspects of sovereignty that were being restored to the Federal Republic. Because sovereignty, rearmament, and integrative Western European structures were always tied up legally and politically on the international scene, the gains in sovereignty achieved by the Bonn Government were never "disposable" for purposes other than the ones earmarked in the contractual provisions. The interests of the Western powers obviously complemented Adenauer's plans for integrating Germany in a Western European union; they were necessarily adverse to the SPD's call for mobility of action that might lead to reunification, and detrimental to the SPD's long-range plans for Germany's domestic order as well. For Adenauer, necessity was combined with virtue; for the Socialists, the international barter that restored sovereignty in exchange for rearmament was objectionable on most grounds. This was no compromise as far as the Socialists were concerned: many of the restored legal aspects of sovereignty immediately tied the Federal Republic to a budding Western European union that the SPD opposed on intrinsic grounds, and Germany's participation in a military alliance directed against the Soviet Union would jeopardize unification and make Germany a potential battlefield of an East-West war.

Economic Recovery

The one major domestic issue of the Government's international economic policy was the creation of the European Coal and Steel Community.* While the Socialists objected strenuously, the Government anticipated from West Germany's par-

* Although it is difficult to separate the international from the domestic elements of economic policy, some major economic issues that divided West German political parties would properly be regarded as "domestic" or internal, and are thus not directly relevant to our inquiry. The initial economic program of the CDU, formulated in 1947, envisaged the "planning and guidance of the economy to a considerable extent for a long time to come," although the CDU rejected a planned economy as an intrinsic value. By the early 1950's, however, the CDU's economic policy had become quite conservative, in part because the party had attracted the support of a variety of interest groups whose economic outlook was generally conservative. The first coalition government formed in 1949 was "a government with distinctly pro-business leanings. While this term falls far short of describing the many currents and cross-currents that are always present in a great coalition, it does denote the government's outstanding characteristic in the economic field. This aspect was intensified by the necessity for the Christian Democrats to satisfy the demands of the Free Democrats, their main coalition partner, a party containing strong big-business elements. The chief points on which the government differed from the Social Democrats were its tight monetary and fiscal management, implying a rejection of full employment policies; the free market policy; the tax privileges and reductions favoring the upper incomes; and the relatively smaller emphasis given to social conditions." (H. C. Wallich, *Mainsprings of the German Revival* (New Haven: Yale, 1955, pp. 315-16.)

The Free Democrats, strongly identified with business interests and the spokesmen for individualism versus mass society, had from the beginning of the Federal Republic not only supported Erhard's neo-liberal "social market" economy, but at times took credit for being its only consistent and determined supporters. The FDP placed great stress on the inviolability of private property, attacked collectivism, and viewed nationally oriented monopoly capitalism as the betrayal of genuine liberalism. The German Party deviated from the economic and social policies of the CDU/CSU only rarely and insignificantly. It agreed with the principles of neo-liberalism and stressed the need to protect the middle class against the forces of big industrial interests and monopolies.

The Socialists called for the socialization of basic industries, and advocated a unified federal administration of public finances and the removal of the individual fiscal administrations in the Länder since this would have allowed a nationwide program of economic planning. National planning, and far-reaching fiscal reforms to benefit the working class, were the major programmatic items on the SPD's economic-political agenda.[32]

ticipation a number of desirable consequences, among which the economic benefits were not necessarily the most important. The Schuman Plan seemed to show a way to ease tensions over the Saar question, and it might allay French fears that international control of the Ruhr basin would gradually evaporate; furthermore, for the Federal Republic, the ECSC represented a significant gain in sovereignty, since it replaced an Allied instrument of control with an international organization in which West Germany would participate as an equal.[33]

The coalition partners of the CDU/CSU were never fully committed to Adenauer's overall European policy, and found it more difficult to support the Schuman Plan. The Free Democrats initially showed great caution in their attitude on the ECSC. In part, the reluctance of the FDP stemmed from the influence of the coalitions the party had formed with the Socialists in various Länder cabinets, which also colored the FDP's attitude on the EDC. Further, FDP spokesmen expressed concern that the Schuman Plan would have adverse effects on the Saar question and would strengthen the influence of clericalism in West Germany; and some FDP leaders and the industrial interests close to them objected to the stringent anti-cartel orientation of the ECSC. At the same time, the Free Democrats and German business circles were interested in abolishing the Ruhr Statute, the regulatory restrictions imposed on the coal-steel *Verbundwirtschaft*, and the Allied controls over production levels. In the end, the 51 votes of the Free Democrats helped the Government carry the ECSC treaty by a vote of 232 to 143.[34]

The CDU/CSU's smaller coalition partners—the German Party and the GB/BHE Refugee Party—also fell pretty much in line with the CDU/CSU majority. The German Party viewed the ECSC as an enticing instrument with which to attract East Germany to a European power base, and echoed CDU statements on the need for European unity in opposing Soviet pressures. Refugee spokesmen also ended up supporting the ECSC, but wished to be assured that it would not lead to a de jure separation of the Saar from Germany, since they feared that a border settlement in the West prior to an all-German peace treaty would prejudice German claims on the Oder-Neisse territories in the East.[35]

The somewhat ambivalent attitude that prevailed among the CDU's coalition partners—largely because they lacked Adenauer's unequivocal commitment to the Western European cause—was echoed in business circles. Initially, German industrial interests responded very favorably. The president of the Federation of German Industry (BDI) pledged the Federation's support and explicitly placed a higher priority on political recovery than on immediate economic considerations. A prominent trade journal endorsed the Schuman Plan as an important step toward a Franco-German rapprochement, but stressed the need for complete equality among all "industrial partners."[36] Other businessmen soon voiced reservations, however, because they feared that French surplus steel would flood the German market and that the sacrifices demanded of the weakened German economy would be unduly severe. There was additional concern that the ECSC might become too "dirigistic" in outlook, and engage in economic planning; and German coal interests were unhappy about the anti-cartel provisions, which restricted coal sales organizations, since they were convinced that price fixing was essential for profitable coal mining. However, the prospect that reconcentration of coal and steel management would be permitted was warmly welcomed by German industrialists, and on the whole German coal and steel interests saw more advantages than disadvantages in the treaty. Also, as long as the dirigistic implications of the Schuman Plan could be kept in check, free enterprise seemed to win out over state planning, and this neatly fit the economic doctrines embraced by the CDU/CSU and the FDP. The international and domestic political advantages the Government expected to gain from the ECSC were coupled with important economic payoffs:

> If the political advantage of full equality was a potent reason for CDU support of ECSC, economic doctrine and industrial advantage were by no means absent. . . . German industrial interests—identified with the CDU by means of deputies designated by trade associations—

rallied to the plan because its rationale dovetailed with their desire to achieve more "economic" production units, or to reconcentrate the plants just separated by the Allies and especially regain steel control over coal—the famous *Verbundwirtschaft* held out as "inevitable" and "natural" by industry spokesmen. Europeanism was curiously mingled with the political desire for equality and the economic aim of undoing parts of the occupation policy. The convergence of these factors goes a long way in explaining CDU enthusiasm for ECSC.[37]

The Socialists became increasingly isolated in their bitter and at times rather shrill opposition to the Schuman Plan. The public at large seemed apathetic,[38] and despite the close programmatic and personal relationships between the SPD and the labor movement, the Socialists could not even enlist the trade unions in their struggle to prevent German membership in the ECSC. Labor leaders strongly welcomed the removal of allied controls, and they were very sensitive to the need to use labor pressures to check the influence of producer organizations within the ECSC. A large number of union spokesmen felt that the interests of labor should not lack representation in the ECSC by default, and the coal and steel workers' unions in particular perceived an opportunity to extend to the international level the domestic "codetermination" through which they had gained a voice in the management of their industries. The unions found support for their wage and hours demands in the comparative statistical studies undertaken by the ECSC, and although union circles raised objections to the free movement of coal and steel labor among the Six, they wished to take advantage of the Schuman Plan's proposals for a forty-hour week, uniform overtime, and extended vacations. The metal workers, for example, although at times strongly leaning to the left, supported the ECSC because it might strengthen the union's hand in wage negotiations with producers. A more intangible but important element of the unions' support for the Schuman Plan stemmed from the social aspirations of the workers. The political doctrine of supranationalism seemed to enhance the labor movement's chances for social equality and respectability—which business circles were less willing to grant the unions domestically.[39]

This generally favorable reaction of the labor movement was not unanimous, and a minority in union circles supported SPD objections. But the DGB officially endorsed ratification of the ECSC treaty with the proviso that Allied controls would be discontinued at once, and that the sale of industrial holdings to non-German interests would be restricted.

The Socialists' attacks on the Schuman Plan were never directed against integration or Europeanization as such. Nevertheless, their objections were sweeping and led to some of the most abrasive political encounters in the Bundestag. The core of the SPD's criticism was that the ECSC treaty represented a regional alliance organized by reactionary elements who sought to perpetuate capitalism and lay the groundwork for the economic and political control of Western Europe. Socialist spokesmen argued that the Schuman Plan was in effect an attempt to continue occupation policies and that it was designed to decisively shape the development and ultimate characteristics of Germany's economic and social order. By 1953, SPD opposition had become extremely bitter. The Socialists attacked French attempts to seek admission of the Saar as an autonomous entity, and depicted the Schuman Plan as an international conspiracy to impede German unification and to handicap German industry's ability to compete with France on world markets.[40] The Socialists were now in the paradoxical position of uninvited spokesmen for German industrial interests. They contended that the German coal industry was to be made less efficient by punitive contribution schemes and discriminatory taxation, while France would be allowed to keep her stabilizing syndicates. Of course the SPD emphasized the repercussions that would affect the working classes rather than the entrepreneurs:

In our opinion, the plan is unacceptable because it contravenes the elementary interests of the German people. It ties down the German people—to the advantage of one treaty partner. . . . It robs us of the freedom to reconstruct our coal and steel industry on a modern basis and prevents the reform of our economic life. It provides no guarantee for sufficiently free disposition of coal and steel for export so that the necessary imports of foodstuffs and raw materials can be secured. It endangers the establishment of a wider European union. The undemocratic nature of its constitution is at odds with the basic ideas for the reconstruction of Europe according to the principles of democracy and freedom.[41]

In 1954, the SPD position changed significantly. The party program of that year no longer objected to the transfer of economic authority to international agencies, but stressed instead the democratic-parliamentary methods with which the transfer ought to be accomplished. SPD spokesmen now called for extended economic planning, for supranationally coordinated economic analyses, and for counter-cyclical measures and investments. By 1955, the Socialists advocated an internationally coordinated investment policy and business-cycle control, and began criticizing the ECSC for not having gone far enough in this direction.

In part, the SPD's about-face can be explained by the Saar issue, which had figured prominently in SPD objections to the Schuman Plan, and was now largely settled after the pro-German plebiscite. Also, the SPD apparently feared that an entirely negative attitude would give control of the ECSC to industrial interests, and freeze out Socialist influence by default. Moreover, after the demise of the EDC, "the party was no longer compelled, on grounds of consistency, to oppose all supranationalism because it led to militarism and alliances. Hence, its all-German policy could remain intact and pure while economic integration could be supported as well."[42] Internal political isolation and external changes in the international system had led to a significant reversal of the SPD position on a major foreign policy issue.

REUNIFICATION

The Saar

All major political groups in West Germany agreed that the Saar rightfully belonged to Germany.[43] So long as the Government's Saar policy was not tied to the issues of membership in the ECSC and rearmament, no significant disagreements developed between the Government and the opposition. Even so, the Socialists stressed the analogy between the Saar question and the status of the Eastern territories, and cautioned the Government that a compromise on Germany's western borders could weaken the force of German claims in the East.[44]

When the Bonn Government issued its stern memorandum on the Saar question in March 1950, all political parties supported Adenauer's argument that Germany considered the Franco-Saar Conventions unacceptable. The Socialists, however, took exception to the memorandum's proposal that the Saar should be placed under the supervision of an international authority, and suggested that the Government oppose the admission of the Saar to the Council of Europe, since its admission would tend to emphasize the separation of the Saar from Germany.

On the surface, these divergent lines of strategy differed only in degree, but they foreshadowed serious subsequent disagreements between Adenauer and the opposition. For the SPD, the primary issue in the Saar question was one of reunification; the contribution that a solution could make to expediting a Western European union was of secondary importance.[45] In fact, the possibility of such a development was intrinsically objectionable because of the Socialists' aversion to a "little Europe" construct. For Adenauer, these priorities were reversed. The Saar problem was a constant point of friction between France and Germany, and had to be resolved as soon as possible so that Bonn could work at establishing a European union on the basis of a Franco-German reconciliation.

There were also important related issues. The Socialists feared that loss of the Saar mines would strengthen the forces of Western European capitalism, and they hoped to take full advantage of what promised to be an important election issue.[46] The SPD never tired of pointing out that Adenauer's conciliatory Europe policy had failed to resolve the Saar issue, and that France's efforts at "'Europeanization" were nothing less than disguised attempts to annex the Saar herself and permanently deprive Germany of its important raw materials.

During the discussions of Germany's admission to the Council of Europe, held in the summer of 1950, the Government's and the SPD's differing views on the Saar question were also influenced by more general and fundamental considerations. The Government hoped to be able to exert pressure within the Council for a favorable outcome, and seemed temporarily satisfied to leave things unresolved by limiting the Saar to associate membership; in any case, the Saar conflict seemed to be moving toward a compromise solution in the context of the Schuman Plan, and it looked as if at least some of the economic aspects would be resolved through the ECSC provisions about the Saar mines and blast furnaces. Again, this possibility held little attraction for the Socialists, since they strongly opposed the ECSC on its own merits. During debates on the ratification of the ECSC, Government spokesmen again expressed their belief that the Schuman Plan would go a long way toward alleviating the Saar problem because of the integrative measures envisaged for the coal and steel industries of the Six. This argument was strongly supported by the German Party, because it promised a successful solution of the Saar issue and because it would provide an opportunity to represent German interests forcefully and effectively.[47]

By 1952 it became apparent that the Saar question was destined to become a logjam issue: now it was being linked to German participation in the European Defense Community. Again, this tie-up was especially distasteful to the Socialists because of their intrinsic objections to West German participation in a Cold War military alliance. They now attacked Adenauer's arrangement to trade German acquiescence to the de facto separation of the Saar for French consent to German membership in the EDC. The Saar question caused fissures even within the governing coalition. The Free Democrats began to withdraw their support of Adenauer's Saar policy, and FDP spokesmen specifically rejected the isolated Europeanization of the Saar.[48] Not even the CDU/CSU was immune to divisive tensions. The Saarbund, a vociferously militant organization established to lobby for a speedy and complete reunification of the Saar with Germany, had considerable influence within the CDU/CSU and claimed a number of CDU parliamentarians as enrolled supporters. Although the 1953 elections strengthened Adenauer's hand considerably, the so-called "prerequisite policy," which required the Federal Republic to come to terms on the Saar issue before it could be admitted to the EDC, came under increasing attack within the governing coalition.[49]

The opposition to Adenauer's Saar policy was climaxed by the debates over the ratification of the 1954 Paris Agreements. In December, Adenauer had once again summarized his views on the Saar question with the argument that the Agreements constituted a necessary compromise, and that

> since the establishment of the Federal Republic, the Saar question has strained the relations between France and Germany. . . . In Paris [in October] the attempt was made to solve this difficult problem in a way that would prove satisfactory to Germany as well as France. The result of these attempts necessarily constitutes a compromise, which entails advantages and disadvantages for both sides. . . . Because of the connection with the WEU and especially because of the . . . guarantees of the agreement, the [Saar] statute rests on a European basis. The agreement does not create . . . a European territory. . . . France as well as a united Germany would have a free hand . . . during a peace conference to decide what kind of proposition to present to the Saar population for their approval. The Saar agreement constitutes an agreement about the status of the Saar until the peace treaty. Consequently, the agreement does not contravene the belief of the Bundestag and the Federal Government that the Saar, conditional upon the final determination of the borders by a peace treaty, belongs to Germany since it is within the 1937 borders.[50]

Although the Government attempted to convey the impression that the Saar Agreement was provisional, the opposition viewed it as a settlement that would be difficult to dislodge by the time a peace treaty was negotiated, especially since Adenauer's intransigent attitude toward Moscow seemed to postpone an all-German peace conference indefinitely. For the Socialists, any compromise on the Saar was necessarily undesirable; the provisions Adenauer viewed as French concessions—such as agreement to German membership in the WEU and NATO—the Socialists rejected on intrinsic grounds. Matters were further aggravated by the fact that the French Government, in attempting to obtain ratification of the Paris Agreements in the French Assembly, was forced to play up those features of the Saar statute that were most palatable to French public opinion. Naturally, this supplied the opposition in Bonn with cogent arguments why the Federal Republic should not become a party to the Saar Agreement. The proponents of the statute—a majority of the CDU and DP deputies—defended the Agreement by pointing out that it afforded Germany the opportunity to counterbalance French influence in the Saar, and that after all a later settlement on more favorable terms was not precluded; furthermore, the settlement would lead to a Franco-German rapprochement and thus to German sovereignty.[51]

No West German political party found it possible to divorce the Saar issue from the overall context of other foreign policy aims. The domestic political fracas over the Saar quite accurately reflected the intricate connections between the Saar, German rearmament, and German political and economic recovery on the international scene. In addition to the differences of opinion that rested on fundamental programmatic grounds, the diverging attitudes of the Government and the opposition can also be partially explained by the pragmatic demands made upon the party in power. The Government, faced with the daily need to guide German political and economic interests through complex international pressures and counterpressures, was necessarily more amenable to compromise, especially since the overall development of affairs moved toward a European union and toward recovery of German influence, which Adenauer ardently desired. The opposition, deeply distrustful of the general policy trend it saw pursued in Bonn, having an opposite ordering of priorities, and unencumbered by the day-to-day necessity of governing, found it much easier to press its point of view, without mitigating its implacable opposition to Adenauer's overall foreign policy program.[52]

East Germany and West Germany

On innumerable occasions, Konrad Adenauer and other Government spokesmen asserted that they regarded the unification of Germany, by peaceful means and on the basis of freedom, as their most pressing foreign policy objective. According to Adenauer, there were no long-range incompatibilities between unification on the one hand, and rearmament and Western European integration on the other. For Adenauer it was a question of putting first things first. Unification could be achieved only by pressing the Soviet Union to release its hold over East Germany. Since this required strength, which the Federal Republic did not possess, alignment with the Western powers looked like the only possible road to unification. Adenauer regarded rearmament as part and parcel of an effort to increase the leverage of the Federal Republic, leverage that would, in the long run, create the conditions that would make reunification possible.[53]

It was, of course, somewhat paradoxical for Adenauer to reject the SPD's contention that rearmament would increase international tensions, and to suggest at the same time that the Paris Agreements would discomfit and soften the Soviet Union on the German question and ultimately lead to its favorable resolution.[54] Adenauer was most derisive when criticizing the opposition's suggestions on how to achieve unification. He viewed the Socialists' proposals for an armed but neutral Germany as the naive dream of irresponsible amateurs in foreign affairs. A neutralized Germany would be neither a viable entity nor contribute to a relaxation of international tensions. For Adenauer, the neutralization of Germany as a precondition for reunification implied permanent international control and a power vacuum in the heart of Europe; it would destroy the plans to integrate Germany in a Western European community, weaken the Atlantic alliance decisively, and leave a powerless Germany to the designs of the Soviet Union. It would lead neither to unification on the basis of democracy nor to the return of Germany to the society of free nations.

I mentioned the way the CDU's coalition partners viewed unification when I discussed their outlook on rearmament. The Free Democrats generally pressed more vigorously for unification than the CDU/CSU did; but this difference of emphasis was not pronounced enough to make the FDP withdraw its parliamentary support on important foreign policy questions during the period under discussion. The German Party was even more committed to German unification because of its vision of a German mission in central Europe: a divided Germany would not be strong enough to play the predominant role the DP envisaged. Other programmatic DP ideals, such as its almost mystical stress on *Heimat* soil, its militant nationalism, and its organismic view of society tended to reinforce its strong concern with unification. The same held true for the vociferous Refugee Party, whose strident and emotional demands for the return of the Eastern territories* almost automatically entailed a militant

* All major West German political parties consistently refused to accept the Oder-Neisse line as the definitive settlement of Germany's eastern frontiers. The Oder-Neisse issue was overshadowed, however, by the larger problem of the East-West German division; and the refusal of the Eastern-bloc countries to even regard the issue as still negotiable lent a certain lack of immediacy and reality to its discussion. The West German position was, and is, essentially based on the argument that the Potsdam Agreement states specifically that the final determination of Germany's borders should take place at a peace conference, and that the Federal Republic consequently cannot and will not consent to the de facto annexation of the territories by the Soviet Union and Poland.

Naturally enough, refugee groups, and especially the GB/BHE Refugee Party, were among the most vociferous advocates of a determined stand on the Eastern frontiers. Spokesmen for refugee interests stressed that the successful economic and social absorption of refugees in West Germany, while in itself desirable, could not be considered an acceptable substitute for their return to the territories they previously inhabited. The very fact that the refugees were being successfully integrated, however, and the forbidding circumstances on the international scene, rendered the Oder-Neisse issue sterile politically as well as diplomatically. While all political parties were unanimous in supporting the Government's legalistic position, refugee spokesmen had to be content with pressing the Government to make such symbolic gestures as rendering NATO maps "correctly" by indicating the German borders of 1937. The Government also issued administrative directives to its various ministries ordering them to refrain from using the term "Ostzone" for the Soviet-occupied part of Germany, replacing it with "Mitteldeutschland," so as to avoid giving the impression that the Federal Republic considered this part of Germany as its easternmost expanse. See *Vertriebenenproblem, Recht auf die Heimat und Selbstbestimmung im Deutschen Parlament* (Bonn: Bundesministerium für Vertriebene, Flüchtlinge und Kriegsgeschädigte, 1960), pp. 5, 30–31, 41, 47–49, 74–77, 83–85; see also Zoltan M. Szaz, *Germany's Eastern Frontiers* (Chicago: Regnery, 1960), esp. Chapter 8.

preoccupation with reunification. The right wing of the coalition, less fascinated by the prospect of a Western European union, and inclined to favor an independent Germany unencumbered by alignments with either Cold War bloc, was less ready to postpone unification and make sacrifices in the name of a European union.

The Socialists' place in the political spectrum of attitudes on reunification was somewhat paradoxical, because they favored priorities that were also shared by the right wing of the governing coalition—with whom the SPD disagreed on almost every other conceivable issue. There were, of course, significant differences. The nationalists of the right, with their deep-seated hostility to bolshevism and socialism, advocated an extremely tough line in dealing with the Soviet Union. Their call for a "policy of strength" implied at times that force need not necessarily be proscribed to obtain unification. The Socialists, on the other hand, were much more willing than the right wing of the coalition, or for that matter than the CDU, to test Soviet proposals and to assume that the Russians were acting at least partially in good faith. Hence they frequently accused the Government of dragging its feet on unification, of letting opportunities for profitable negotiations pass by, and of lacking initiative, flexibility, and intelligence.[55]

The Socialists agreed with the CDU that unification should be achieved only through peaceful means and that the only acceptable political order in a united Germany would be a genuine democracy. But because of their fundamental commitment to unification and to the kind of German society for which it seemed a precondition, some SPD spokesmen were ready to accommodate the Soviet Union to an extent that would have imposed severe political limitations on a united Germany.[56] In response to the Government's contention that a neutralized Germany would be unable to defend itself against Soviet designs, the Socialists proposed a central European collective-security system that would foster a relaxation of tensions by lifting Germany from the grasp of both Cold War camps:

The present policies of East and West on the [German] problem are irreconcilable. Each is trying to achieve a dominant position in the part of Germany which is on the other side. Since this cannot be done without war, both sides must revise their positions. The only part of Germany which has a freely elected government should take the initiative in developing proposals which might be acceptable to all concerned. After all, the Germans are the most interested element. If they ever get the impression that their own government is laggard in this respect, democracy as such will lose ground.

The common denominator obviously cannot be an invitation that one part of Germany be handed over unconditionally from one military bloc to the other. . . . The desires of all concerned for security must be observed, and this means not what one side conceives to be security for the other but what each side feels would constitute security for itself. . . .

For these reasons the claim that a reunited Germany should be a member of NATO is as much of an obstacle to reunification as would be a Communist demand that reunited Germany must be bolshevized. The suggestion that a reunited Germany should have the right to decide freely about joining military alliances would have the same effect, for if Germany were reunited and could exercise this right she would join the Atlantic Pact. We know that, and so do the Russians. . . .

With these ideas in mind the German Social Democrats for a number of years have been proposing a collective security system for Europe.[57]

In a very real sense, from 1949 to the middle 1950's the Socialists ran a single-issue campaign against their political opponents. The determined quest for unification and the corresponding implacable opposition to rearmament were the major themes with which the Socialists appealed for the voters' support. The single-mindedness of the SPD's commitment provided the cue to all of their responses to foreign policy questions, and the Socialists in effect staked the political future of their party on the outcome of the domestic debate on unification and rearmament.

The results of the 1953 elections may be regarded as a general if not overwhelming vote of confidence in the Government's overall foreign policy program; but they do not for that reason lend themselves to the interpretation that unification lacked widespread support. Most likely, the Socialists were not the most effective champions of unification. Their position on domestic issues was consistently undercut by the Government's extensive economic and social programs, and the noticeable improvement in the standard of living took most of the wind out of the SPD's sails. The Adenauer regime already symbolized political stability; prosperity seemed around the corner; and the CDU strategists apparently had been correct in counting on the moderately conservative temper of the electorate. Furthermore, their preoccupation with unification forced the Socialists to take a negative attitude on all other foreign policy questions. This made it difficult for them to share credit for Adenauer's successes and made it easy for Adenauer to stick them with the labels of doctrinaire rigidity and naive obstructionism. The SPD was deprived of political leverage in Bonn, and found it impossible to gain more than a third of the votes in the single-issue campaign it waged on the national level.

Perhaps the major problem the Socialists faced in converting the general desire for unification into votes was the lack of practicality and immediacy that characterized the German question. This is not saying that the Germans did not want unification. There is evidence that in the early 1950's West Germans began to regard unification as the single most important problem confronting their foreign policy.[58] But in contrast to the immediate economic and political benefits of the Government's pro-Western policy, the question of unification took on increasingly abstract dimensions. West Germany was preoccupied with reconstruction, and aside from the strident advocacy of refugee groups and the consistent support of the SPD, the issue of unification had no effective political representation. The Socialists were essentially excluded from the political process in Bonn; and no powerful interests, whose demands could not be ignored without paying heavy political penalties, "lobbied" for unification. To be sure, most political and economic groups unfailingly professed their commitment to unification, and there is no reason to doubt the sincerity of their sentiments. But German interest groups and the electorate at large apparently were aware that in the international system unification was highly incompatible with political and economic recovery. West Germans were constantly asked to choose between unification and the possible loss of democratic freedoms, or on a less exalted plane, between unification and political and economic "normalcy." Even if a large number of West Germans had been willing to choose a determined pursuit of unification, the daily realities of political and economic life worked against it. In addition to suffering because of the forbidding circumstances of the international system, the cause of unification was undergoing a constant process of attrition on the domestic political scene.[59]

Of all organized interest groups, the trade-union movement was perhaps the only one that sought to lend its political strength to the cause of reunification, and by extension, to the Socialist Party. There was a widely expressed desire to see the East Germans liberated from the Communist yoke, and activist union circles saw unification as a way to revitalize the union movement. A number of labor functionaries attributed the rather flabby state of the movement not only to political apathy and the promise of economic recovery and prosperity but to the shift in political power that resulted from the division of Germany. These circles were convinced that the political predominance of the CDU/CSU stemmed at least in part from the exclusion of the Protestant and traditional working-class strongholds in East Germany from the political processes of the Federal Republic. But the pressures put on the rank-and-file members because of their economic and social interests, and the divided leadership of an already devitalized union movement, could not provide an effective interest lobby for unification. Union leaders and the rank and file had too much at stake in the Government's political and economic recovery program to attempt to sabotage Adenauer's pro-Western policy.[60]

Business circles also found it difficult to exert their influence on behalf of a foreign policy program that would have assigned top priority to unification.[61] To businessmen and industrialists, the ramifications of a determined unification policy appeared far-reaching, and were made no more palatable by their unpredictable nature. In addition to the political and economic repercussions foreseeable from a more flexible Eastern policy prior to unification—for example, the possible disintegration of the carefully nurtured alliance with the Western powers—post-unification tasks would require sweeping sacrifices from the West German economy, and could be expected to result in profound and unpredictable social transformations. In the early 1950's, the so-called Königsteiner Kreis, a group of intellectuals concerned primarily with the economic dimensions of unification, spelled out some of the problems that would probably follow from the combination of the two German economies.[62] Only a few years after the currency reforms were carried out in East and West Germany, the purchasing power of the Western Deutsche Mark had far outstripped that of the Eastern mark. Yet the spokesmen of the Königsteiner Kreis considered it necessary to recommend a 1:1 adjustment between the two currencies in the event of unification in order to avoid the disruptive social consequences of a more realistic ratio of adjustment. On the other hand, East German public funds could hardly be converted on a similar scale because of the great volume of currency involved and the resulting ill effects on the Western mark in international markets.

In addition to monetary and fiscal problems, including the problem of adjusting tax structures, the entire economic systems of East and West Germany had evolved in different directions. Cost correlations were "adjusted" in the planned economy of East Germany, and the lack of consumer goods could be expected to create a "vacuum" market in East Germany on the day of unification. This would almost certainly require the imposition of price ceilings by the Government, and lead to high taxation for West German business, since most East German firms would not be competitive and would have to be subsidized for sociopolitical reasons. On top of these largely economic aspects, there was the likelihood of social and political transformations with unpredictable directions but significant consequences. Thus, the uncertainties and risks of unification appeared high to West German entrepreneurs. A respected commercial daily summarized the problem in rather guarded terms:

In case of a reunification, the West German economy will once again be confronted with entirely new circumstances, which will tax its innate dynamic forces to the utmost. Already one may surmise that the magnitude of the tasks will require international assistance if the painful adjustment process is not to weaken the West German economy in a lasting way. Furthermore, there will be an urgent need to examine all possiblities so as not to be confronted with insoluble tasks . . . that could endanger our own existence.[63]

No doubt the difficulties of pursuing reunification in the international system contributed to the gradual, if perhaps temporary, attrition of the "German question" as a practical, day-to-day concern on the domestic scene. The problems Adenauer faced in furthering the cause of German unity on the international scene were poignantly reflected in the domestic political process. The Western-oriented dimension of Adenauer's unification policies—strengthening the Western alliance and obtaining political leverage for the Federal Republic in Western councils through rearmament—gained the political support of powerful interest groups and a large proportion of the electorate, because these policies also produced important and immediate benefits in the goal areas of political and economic recovery. The Eastern-oriented dimension of Adenauer's unification policy, which anticipated a favorable shift of power in the international system, became increasingly unrealistic in view of international developments that stiffened rather than softened Soviet attitudes on the German question. The SPD's strategy for reunification—an accommodation with the Soviet Union that meant neutralizing a united Germany, and presumably would not disturb the East-West balance of power—could not gain the support of the Western powers, and therefore probably could not have helped the Federal Republic achieve sovereignty and economic recovery. The Free Democrats deliberately attempted to bridge these two conflicting strategies for reunification, by being moderately pro-West but always ready to explore ways of dealing with the East that appeared to present opportunities for reunification. However, the FDP's efforts to gain the "vital center" were undercut on the domestic political scene by both the left and the right, and most important by the Christian Democrats, who preempted the center with their broad and far-flung social and economic programs, and gained a wide and heterogeneous group of supporters.

Most fundamentally, the domestic conflict over foreign policy was polarized because the apparent incompatibility on the international scene between security, rearmament, recovery, and the return of the Saar on the one hand and unification of East and West Germany on the other posed basic and painful choices of priority. The core issue in this framework was widely perceived to be rearmament versus reunification. At the same time, limited agreements and ad hoc coalitions among the major political parties and interest groups lessened and occasionally obscured this fundamental split. The Socialists shared their fervent commitment to unification, their aversion to a "miniature" Europe, and their pronounced anticlericalism with many groups in the FDP and the DP; they profoundly disagreed with these groups on economic issues, and they abhorred the right-wing chauvinism expressed by some FDP and most DP members. The Free Democrats generally agreed with the Christian Democrats on issues of economic doctrine and shared the apprehensions of the CDU Protestants about clericalism; they were not enthusiastic about Western European integration, which was supported by most CDU members, and they felt that Adenauer was dragging his feet on unification. The Socialists, the Christian Democrats, and the Liberal wing of the FDP shared a fundamental commitment to a democratic political order, even though Adenauer himself was frequently accused of neglecting the spirit of the democratic process by apparently preferring to rule over a "Chancellor-democracy." Clearly, there were overlapping elements of agreement among these groups and their supporters. Strong disagreements on some issues were counterbalanced by agreements on others, and all political parties agreed at least partially on some foreign policy issues.

It is the polarization of viewpoints on how to achieve unification, combined with the overlapping patterns of preference on related "sub-issues" that characterizes the domestic consensus pattern before 1955. The polarization in the domestic contest over rearmament and reunification was essentially imposed by the polarization in the international system, even though its meaning derives from the conflicting blueprints that the contending parties advanced for the nature of German society. The important changes that took place in the post-1955 international system provided a significantly different international backdrop for the domestic dialogue over foreign policy, and produced corresponding shifts and realignments in the domestic patterns of consensus. These new patterns of compatibility and consensus shall concern us in the following chapters.

Part II: 1955-1963

5. *The International System and the Pursuit of Goals, 1955–1963*

Although the events of 1955 marked the end of a distinct phase in West German foreign policy, they did not mark a specific turning point in the postwar international system. Major transformations in a political system can rarely be pinpointed so concretely. But it is a basic assumption of this study, and a major reason why it is divided chronologically, that the international system was undergoing far-reaching, though gradual, changes by the middle 1950's. Thus it is to be expected that the three major projects of West German foreign policy began to meet with different sets of restraints and possibilities. The compatibility between foreign policy aims and the attributes of the international system changes with transformations of the system.

At this time, the system's most apparent evolving characteristic was an increasing complexity, which contrasted with the more clear-cut patterns of the preceding decade. It has become commonplace to suggest that the dominant theme of this transformation was the shift from an essentially bipolar international system to a polycentric or "multipolar" one, with increasingly fragmented patterns. But this rather facile description obscures more than it reveals, and appears particularly inadequate for an examination of compatibilities between systemic conditions and Bonn's foreign policy aims.

The difficulty with describing the pre-1955 international system as "bipolar" and the post-1955 system as "polycentric" is not so much the highly abstract nature of these concepts as the fact that it was a *combination* of bipolar and "multipolar" patterns that accounted for the most striking attributes of the post-1955 system. Bipolar patterns on the level of nuclear capabilities were coupled with—and in fact, contributed to bringing about—less cohesive and more fragmented political patterns within the two Cold War alliances. In order to legitimately use shorthand terms like "bipolar" or "polycentric," it is necessary to specify more precisely the relationships that these concepts are applied to. That is, as a summary description of all relational patterns of the system, these terms are too broad; however, they may be useful when applied to only one relational level, for instance nuclear capabilities, conventional force levels, polarization of tension, patterns of alignment, and so forth. As noted previously, the pre-1955 system is often summarily described as "bipolar." But that system, although it showed a pronounced polarization of perceived interests, tensions, and Cold War alignments, was, until its later stages, characterized by an American monopoly of strategic nuclear capabilities. On this crucial level, bipolarity was still absent, even though the anticipation of a nuclear stalemate led to serious reappraisals of NATO strategy.

The most salient features of the post-1955 international system have been cogently summarized by George Liska:

> As regards capability, the contemporary system is a mixed one. In the last resort—represented by strategic nuclear weapons—it is still bipolar. . . . The stalemate on the nuclear-strategic plane increases the political significance of the second plane, that of diplomatically and militarily more readily usable capabilities—chiefly conventional-military and economic. In that regard, the international system is now finitely multipolar, that is, it consists of a limited number of powers with substantial capability, whose dealignment or realignment would significantly affect the global balance of readily usable power. And finally, strategic-nuclear inhibitions on a free employment of even the usable capabilities heighten the significance of a third plane in the inverted pyramidal structure of world equilibrium. On the broadest but not any more solid plane, the international system is infinitely multipolar in political-diplomatic influence: a great and growing number of states, and groups within states, behave as if they were independent "poles" in the politics of the state system. To sum up, the system is quasi-multipolar in behavior and mixed bipolar-multipolar in the structure of capabilities; the pattern of behavior predominates over the pattern of capabilities whenever a balance neutralizes conflicting capabilities on one or the other level.[1]

Liska's exposition obviously meets the need to distinguish more carefully between different levels or planes of systemic relationships; it is especially useful because it separates patterns of power from patterns of purpose and behavior. Still, important systemic relationships intrinsically and simultaneously combine bipolar with multipolar attributes on the *same* level of relationship. For example, the developing bipolar nuclear stalemate induced the superpowers to pursue the Cold War on levels that appear less volatile because they are largely nonmilitary. This development has given the unaligned nations a significance—far outstripping their physical power—which has allowed them to serve a mediatory function between the Cold War antagonists. To put it another way, it has enabled them to significantly fragment bipolarity. The United Nations began to serve as an important and convenient forum for this mediatory activity. In their attempt to enlist UN support for their respective national policies—a process that was resisted by the unaligned countries—the two superpowers traded economic aid and support on colonial issues for the unaligned nations' support, expressed primarily in voting, on Cold War security issues.[2] The preconditions for this "balancing" reflect systemic patterns that are simultaneously bipolar and multipolar; they rest on the assumption that at least one bloc retains an interest in obtaining the symbolic value of United Nations support for security policies—an interest stemming from the Cold War polarization—and that the rival bloc and the balancing bloc resist these efforts—thus creating a relationship that necessarily involves at least three poles. The real significance of this interaction cannot possibly be expressed in either bipolar or multipolar terms alone. The essence of the relationship is not simply tripolar; that term would imply a similarity of power and purpose among the three blocs reminiscent of a classical balance-of-power system. The relationship derives its meaning from bipolar patterns of tension and power, combined with tripolar patterns of bargaining postures.

In order to convey with a shorthand term this peculiar pattern, which recurs on a variety of relational levels in the post-1955 system, I have elsewhere proposed the concept of "heterosymmetry."[3] Although somewhat forbidding at first sight, this term serves to describe briefly the fragmented nature of bipolarity after 1955. It appears particularly relevant when applied to the two major factors of systemic transformation—the developing Soviet-American nuclear stalemate, and the emerging regionalism in Western Europe and elsewhere in the world. A heterosymmetrical relational pattern is similar to the one illustrated in the United Nations example. Two poles predominate in an essentially symmetrical relationship; but this predominance is qualified by the presence of additional components, which need not upset the balance between the bipolar blocs.* Crucial relationships in the post-1955 international system exhibit this "bipolar-tripolar" or "bipolar-multipolar" or "heterosymmetrical" structure.

One of the most important changes brought about by the gradual emergence of a nuclear stalemate is the change in the credibility of using weapons of such destructive dimensions. In effective deterrence three elements are essential. First, the nation or bloc that makes the deterrent threat must have the *power* to carry it out. Second, the *will* to use this power must exist. And third, the adversary who is to be deterred must be aware of the first two factors.[4] Given an extreme asymmetrical (monopolistic) distribution of nuclear power, the credibility of the monopolist's threat is high. The risks of retaliation on the same level are nil, and the monopolist can credibly extend the protection of nuclear deterrence to cover his allies. Furthermore, aside from ethical and other nonphysical restraints, the threshold of provocation for a nuclear strike can be set low because there is no risk of retaliation. An attack with conventional means may be effectively deterred by the threat to meet it with a nuclear response. What Robert Osgood calls "active deterrence" falls roughly in this category:

> Active deterrence refers to the deterrence of military aggressions upon allies and other powers. If it depends upon strategic nuclear reprisals rather than upon local resistance, it requires convincing a potential aggressor that one will counter aggression with a first strike . . . which

* Components added to the basic symmetrical relationship may, of course, upset the balance between the two superpowers or between their alliance blocs. Thus the relationship would be rendered "hetero*a*symmetrical."

will inflict unacceptable costs in relation to the aggressor's anticipated benefit.

Exercised against an aggressor with a substantial counterstrike capability, active nuclear deterrence clearly puts a premium upon the *credibility* of a first strike, not just upon the *capability* to inflict great damage. . . . The growth of Soviet striking power has seriously diminished the credibility of America's willingness to deliver a first strike on the Soviet Union and its allies in response to their aggressions upon America's allies. . . .[5]

As the pattern of nuclear capabilities moves toward a duopolistic "standoff" or stalemate, the most credible type of deterrence is what Osgood calls "passive deterrence." This is

the deterrence of a direct offensive assault upon one's nation. Essentially, it requires convincing a potential aggressor that one can inflict unacceptable damage upon him with a second-strike attack. . . . Since the *credibility* of a massive second strike in response to an all-out attack could hardly be discounted by the aggressor, passive deterrence puts a premium upon one's *capability* to inflict unacceptable retaliatory damage.[6]

The immediate consequence of a duopolistic distribution of nuclear capabilities and the type of deterrence it makes credible is that a superpower's threat to extend nuclear protection to its non-nuclear allies becomes less convincing. Aware of this and of their nonetheless increasing dependency on the superpower they are allied with, the allies are tempted to seek indigenous nuclear capabilities. That is, in light of the diminishing credibility of the superpower's active deterrence, the allies are tempted to establish a credible passive deterrence of their own.

The concepts of active and passive deterrence are "ideal" analytic types; the realities of the post-1955 international system cannot be summarily categorized within them. But there is no doubt that the credibility of American active deterrence diminished. In August 1957, the Soviet Union fired an ICBM; this was followed by the dramatic launching of Sputnik. Although the Western powers responded in December 1957 by announcing the decision to deploy IRBM's in Europe, the overall pattern of nuclear capabilities in the international system was moving toward a nuclear standoff. The mutual dependency of the United States and its Western European allies, which had rested on the assumption that their ultimate security interests coincided, slowly began to erode. These tensions became especially noticeable within NATO. At a time when distance still protected American territory from attack, the United States suspected that the Western Europeans were dragging their feet in participating in the common defense. But even then some Europeans expressed the opposite fear: a Soviet attack on a NATO power not considered "vital" to American interests might not bring forth an American nuclear response.[7]

European NATO members responded to the developing nuclear stalemate in essentially two ways. Although the United States consistently opposed the spread of nuclear weapons, France began to demand an independent national nuclear arsenal, and Great Britain sought air-to-ground missiles to counteract the obsolescence of its major delivery instrument, long-range bombers. The conflict culminated in the Skybolt controversy of December 1962, which will be discussed on pp. 160–61.

Other NATO members, notably West Germany, either rejected, or were prevented from developing, independent national nuclear forces. Instead, those powers sought to counteract the waning credibility of America's active deterrence posture by seeking a share in NATO's nuclear planning and control, in the hope that this would convincingly reinforce America's protective umbrella over its non-nuclear NATO allies. To put it another way, in trying to gain a voice in the decision whether to employ nuclear retaliation in case of an attack upon themselves, the allies attempted to link themselves more directly to the credible passive deterrence posture of the United States.

Neither alternative—an independent nuclear arsenal for France, or control sharing of American nuclear power by other NATO members—became a reality between 1955 and 1963, although France was well on its way to becoming an independent nuclear power. But the trend toward these developments, and the underlying apprehensions and political calculations, clearly reflected a heterosymmetrical pattern. In the first place, the pattern created by the threats and counterthreats of the United States and the Soviet Union, and their respective allies, was heterosymmetrical. In light of the developing nuclear deadlock, the two major Cold War powers moved toward an essentially symmetrical mutual deterrence posture based on their passive deterrence capabilities. But the Soviet threat to Western Europe, brought about by the diminishing credibility of American active deterrence, injected an asymmetrical element in this relationship. At the same time, the United States continued to pose an implicit nuclear threat to the allies of the Soviet Union, especially Communist China. Hence the overall pattern of nuclear threats and counterthreats presents a clear example of heterosymmetry: the essentially symmetrical passive deterrence posture of the United States and the Soviet Union was coupled with either superpower's nuclear "side-threats" against the allies of the other.

On the political level, the patterns of tension and alignment in the post-1955 international system were also moving toward heterosymmetry. First, as already noted in the United Nations example, a large number of the nations that gained independence during the 1950's chose to remain unaligned. Although the power of these new nations was very limited, the ideological dimensions of the East-West conflict and the fact that these new nations occupied strategically important parts of the world led to a sustained contest over their allegiance, or at least neutrality, in the Cold War confrontation. A new Cold War front opened up, and while the East-West positions in central Europe began to harden considerably, the conflict between the United States and the Soviet Union was extended to every part of the world and to every conceivable area of competition, ranging from the space race to the Olympic games. The determination of the nonaligned nations to maximize the benefits of a neutral stance led to an overall international political pattern that was still bipolar in terms of fundamental tensions, but was qualified by the emergence of a group of neutral nations.

Second, the two Cold War camps were losing a good deal of their internal cohesion. The tensions that developed within the

Western alliance because of the shifting Soviet-American power relationship were soon aggravated by the emergence of economic and political regionalism in Western Europe. Although Western Europe did not exactly become a distinct "third force," there was a noticeable increase in European self-assertion. This was enhanced by economic reconstruction and by sociopolitical stability, and was buttressed institutionally by the establishment of the Common Market of the Six. Factors such as an increasing spirit of self-confidence, the rejection of American diplomatic tutelage, the conviction that the cultural potential of Europe was far from exhausted, and the less readily expressed expectation that a strong and reasonably united Europe could perhaps play a decisive role in old-fashioned power politics were clearly felt, no less real because of their often intangible quality. With respect to European political and economic interests in the world at large, United States policy during the Suez crisis painfully reminded many Europeans how much the pursuit of their interests outside of Europe had become dependent upon their transatlantic protector's response to Moscow's nuclear blackmail. The allies' awareness of their own military weakness was coupled with an increasingly assertive diplomatic posture, especially on the part of France, and caused troublesome fissures in the Western alliance.[8]

Similar trends toward "polycentrism" developed in the Soviet bloc.[9] The Soviet alliance system in Eastern Europe and the Sino-Soviet relationship felt divisive pressures, which pointed out that the Soviet bloc was not immune to centrifugal forces. Both Cold War blocs were undergoing a process of gradual attrition, and the tight polarization of purpose and alignment that had characterized the international system in the decade following World War II began to loosen considerably. Still, patterns of political heterosymmetry were coupled with fundamentally bipolar Cold War conflicts of purpose—temporary détentes notwithstanding—and on the crucial level of nuclear capabilities the Soviet-American relationship was becoming more symmetrical.

SECURITY AND REARMAMENT

Shortly after the Federal Republic joined NATO in May 1955, the changes in the power relationships of the international system, and their implications for West German security, were poignantly illustrated by the SHAPE atomic exercise Carte Blanche. During this exercise, which simulated 335 atomic bombings on German soil, casualties were estimated to have exceeded five million. Aside from its domestic political repercussions, Carte Blanche unmistakably pointed to the potential risks that a NATO partner would have to face now that the Soviet Union possessed nuclear weapons and delivery systems—risks that were to be avoided, according to the Bonn Government, precisely by German membership in NATO. In the wake of the political uproar over Carte Blanche, the Government intended to salvage the rationale for its rearmament policy by arguing that nuclear bipolarity had restored a place of decisive importance to conventional armaments, and that even if nuclear war were to occur, regular forces would still be called upon to fulfill important tasks.[10]

This line of reasoning was seemingly contradicted in Washington by the Eisenhower Administration's "new look" strategy, which stressed massive retaliation against conventional provocation and envisaged drastic reductions of American conventional force levels. Actually, the Pentagon's assessment of the forces that were needed for the defense of the West was not really at odds with Adenauer's. The question was not so much what forces were required as who would provide them. Washington spokesmen were quite candid about this. Admiral Radford, for example, who was closely identified with the "new look," argued for a global "balance of forces" and suggested that

> this balance can best be achieved by each nation contributing to the pool those forces and facilities that it is most proficient in and best capable of developing.
>
> In view of our industrial capacity, technological ability, and limited manpower, we believe that the most effective contribution which the

United States is capable of making consists of complex technical weapons and equipment, modern air and naval power, and highly mobile offensive combat forces backed by ready reserves.

On the other hand, we feel that the other free nations can most efficiently provide in their own and adjacent countries the bulk of the defensive ground forces and local naval and air power.[11]

This theme of a strategic division of labor among the Western alliance partners had already been taken up by British government spokesmen, who held that the American argument also applied to the British situation. The SPD's argument that German forces were intended to become NATO's foot soldiers now began to appear quite credible.

The anticipated economic saving, which was an important reason for the United States and Great Britain to return to a pre-Korea deterrence strategy, had in 1954 led NATO to decide that conventional attacks in Europe would be countered with tactical nuclear weapons—especially since the conventional force goals advocated at Lisbon in 1952 had not been met. But the expected saving did not materialize, and the danger of escalation from tactical to strategic nuclear war now had to be reviewed in the context of bipolar nuclear capabilities. In Western capitals, there were already doubts as to whether a full-blown American response could be relied upon in light of Soviet nuclear retaliatory power. Since a strategic nuclear response to a conventional provocation was no longer fully credible, the credibility of a tactical strike that might escalate into an exchange of strategic strikes also had to be reexamined. NATO was now faced with the question of whether tactical nuclear weapons should be viewed primarily as instruments of *defense* or as a component of strategic nuclear *deterrence*; that is to say, whether their primary function was to stop invading enemy forces, or to provide the psychological restraint that would deter an attack in the first place. As noted in Chapter 2, the requirements of these two functions were not altogether reinforcing or necessarily complementary.[12] The problem was further complicated by the Soviet Union's prompt response—a decision to deploy tactical nuclear weapons on the other side of the Iron Curtain. The differential advantage that NATO planners had hoped to gain was quickly called into question.[13]

It has been convincingly argued that the West should at that time have organized a deterrence posture with which to confront the Soviet Union on *all* capability levels, and that establishing sufficient conventional forces was essential for a credible strategic nuclear deterrence posture.[14] But because of its forward position, the prospect of "deterring" Soviet ground forces with Western ground forces had little attraction for West Germany. Whether it was rational or not from the perspective of the overall East-West nuclear power relationship, the American plan to deploy tactical nuclear weapons in Europe—which was publicized as reinforcing deterrence rather than as serving as an instrument of defense—held significant attractions for Bonn. The Eisenhower Administration's strategy was in part based on the reasoning that the implicit threat of immediate nuclear responses, which was created by denying the likelihood of conventional responses, would deter a Soviet conventional attack. As long as it was reasonably credible, this deterrence posture was highly attractive to Western European powers, especially the Federal Republic. It was widely believed in Germany and elsewhere in Europe that preparation for a conventional response would increase the likelihood of war by undermining the credibility of massive retaliation, and would in fact encourage American "nuclear disengagement" from Europe. Since even a limited engagement with conventional forces would make Germany a battlefield, from Bonn's perspective it seemed better not to extend the range of retaliatory options because this seemed to weaken the "automaticity" of a nuclear response.[15]

This was the interest calculation of a power interested in deterrence rather than defense; a "limited" engagement of East-West forces in West Germany would most likely mean total war for the Federal Republic. From the viewpoint of Washington, which actually had to plan for both deterrence *and* defense, the decision to rely heavily on tactical nuclear weapons in no way reduced the necessity for conventional forces, especially in West Germany. Moreover, in order for NATO to employ tactical nuclear weapons efficaciously, the enemy would have to be forced to attack in concentration; this would require a powerful "forward" shield of NATO's troops.[16] German rearmament, which heretofore had been viewed primarily as part of NATO's overall conventional capabilities, now became a crucial element in the Pentagon's nuclear strategy for Europe. At the same time, NATO's overall defense planning—for the contingency that deterrence had failed—began to conflict with West Germany's primary interest in deterrence, because the requirements of effective defense did not altogether coincide with the military and psychological stance required for a credible deterrence posture.

By 1956, the Bonn Government began to reappraise its security policy. In the summer, when the original conscription bill was presented to the Bundestag, the Government still argued for the buildup of conventional forces with determination and apparent conviction. Adenauer warned against a relaxation in confronting post-Stalin Communism, and stated that West Germany could not afford to disappoint the Western powers because this could lead to an understanding between the United States and the Soviet Union on the basis of a divided Germany. In other words, the Government explicitly viewed rearmament not only as an instrument for defense against attack from the East but also as an instrument for increasing the Federal Republic's political leverage within the Western alliance. Whatever Adenauer's private misgivings about the changing East-West nuclear power balance may have been, in his public pronouncements he interpreted American military policy as stemming primarily from Washington's dissatisfaction with the Europeans' slack performance of their defense obligations. Nevertheless, Adenauer called the strategic change of emphasis from conventional forces to atomic arms a mistake, and stressed the need for localizing conflicts by employing conventional responses.

The Government now shifted from arguing that German rearmament would help deter Soviet aggression to stressing that German force levels would aid in deterring *atomic* war. Most likely, "this shift in emphasis corresponded to a modification of general apprehension. In the early fifties, at the beginning of the rearmament debate, German politicians had to deal with the fear of Soviet aggression. In 1955 and 1956, this fear had abated, and had been replaced by the fear of nuclear weapons."[17]

In September 1956, the first indications of a change in policy became apparent. The Cabinet announced the reduction of the conscription period from eighteen to twelve months; this meant that West Germany's total force goal would be reduced from 500,000 to 325,000. In October, Franz-Josef Strauss, previously Minister of Atomic Affairs, replaced Theodor Blank as Defense Minister. In October and November, the change in the East-West power relationship was forcefully demonstrated by the West's failure to come to the aid of the Hungarian revolutionaries and by Khrushchev's threat to employ missiles during the Suez crisis. At the end of the year, Adenauer and Strauss came out in favor of obtaining some measure of German control over nuclear weapons.

To explain this shift in policy, Adenauer argued that a non-nuclear NATO response to a Soviet attack was no longer likely in view of the ramifications of the Radford Plan, the French transfer of troops to Algeria, British reliance on nuclear defense, and Belgium's reduction of the period of conscription. In effect, Bonn implied that the West could continue to rely on nuclear deterrence, and that Western Europe's conventional capabilities were now so depleted that NATO had no choice but to use tactical nuclear weapons to respond to a Soviet attack.[18]

Behind these somewhat oversimplified announcements were a persuasive strategic rationale and a fundamental lack of confidence in NATO's ground forces. There had been consistent opposition in Bonn, especially on the part of the Socialists, to having West Germany provide the bulk of NATO's conventional forces. But the Government felt that for political reasons the Federal Republic should faithfully fulfill her treaty obligations. Now even the Government began to doubt the value of a large German conventional contingent because this would provide NATO, and the Pentagon, with precisely the wider range of choices of response that seemed to undermine nuclear deterrence and increase the risk that Germany would become a battlefield in a conventional war. Such misgivings were reinforced by reductions of conventional forces in other NATO countries. These reductions further emphasized the existing functional separation between Germany's conventional force responsibilities and America's nuclear obligations to NATO—the less West Germany's allies were involved in the early stages of a Soviet attack, the less likely, or the more delayed, would be the trip-wire response that was supposed to trigger American nuclear retaliation. Because Germany could not accept a substitute for a "forward strategy," it consistently aimed to fully engage its allies at the periphery of the Eastern bloc. A German voice in nuclear councils was expected to reinforce the Western nuclear presence at the East German border by extending Washington's nuclear commitments more unequivocally to cover the Federal Republic.

Strategic and military calculations were reinforced by political considerations. In January 1956, East Germany's armed forces were officially integrated in the Warsaw Pact military structure, and the Soviet Union began to advocate a reduction of troops and the prohibition of atomic weapons in the two parts of Germany. These proposals, antecedents of the Rapacki Plan of 1957, threatened to destroy the clear-cut military dividing line in central Europe, which Bonn wanted for reasons of deterrence. The proposals also held out the danger that military disengagement would be coupled with a more specific de facto, or even de jure, recognition of East Germany. By incorporating both East and West Germany in one international agreement, the Ulbricht regime would have gained at least the de facto recognition that Bonn sought to deny it at all costs. In November 1956, Khrushchev proposed to withdraw Soviet troops from East

Germany if NATO would reciprocate by pulling out of the Federal Republic. Against this background of Soviet maneuvering, a German share in nuclear control or planning now seemed to provide Bonn with a veto power in Western councils, which could prevent a possible American military disengagement in central Europe.

The international repercussions of this change in Bonn's defense policies were immediate. On September 28, the same day the Cabinet announced the reduction of service time, the British, Belgian, Dutch, Danish, and Norwegian representatives at the NATO Council in Paris severely criticized what they considered a crippling reduction of the German contribution to the common defense effort. In the following month, similar objections were voiced when the Consultative Assembly of the Western European Union met in Strasbourg.

Bonn's ideas on the sharing of nuclear control met with even less enthusiasm. As late as the middle of September, when the WEU Council of Ministers met in Paris to discuss the implications of the Radford Plan, Bonn's concern was apparently still confined to seeking a solution on the level of conventional armaments. But soon thereafter, Adenauer intimated somewhat vaguely that he favored some type of "third force" European atomic confederation, and in October he broached the question of nuclear arms sharing in the context of the Western European Union. But the WEU, in addition to suffering from organizational inadequacies (it lacked the authority and supranational instrumentalities of either NATO or the defunct EDC), was annoyed by the simultaneous announcement that service time in Germany would be shortened, and limited itself to emphasizing the importance of conventional forces. The question of nuclear armaments was shelved for further study. In December, the Bonn Government was saved from a politically embarrassing situation when the British carried the brunt of the argument, and proposed in the NATO Council to institute nuclear sharing by providing European forces with American tactical nuclear warheads. The United States agreed to provide tactical nuclear weapons and warhead stockpiles, although under the legal restraints of the McMahon Act Americans had to retain exclusive custody of the warheads. But this proposal, with its long-run inadequacies, meant that the European allies would become increasingly dependent on weapons over which they exercised no control; and it could not obscure the fissures that were beginning to plague NATO. France, in particular, was interested in ultimately developing her own strategic nuclear capability, which would permit her to join the special Anglo-American atomic entente as an equal partner. Some type of atomic consortium between France and Germany was in fact created through the EEC's March 1957 Euratom agreement on nuclear research, but the German Government stressed that it did not seek the lifting of the limitations placed on West German armaments through the Paris treaties of 1954.[19]

In the spring of 1957, West Germany began to receive a variety of dual-purpose missiles and atomic artillery units as part of the 1954 plan for relying on tactical nuclear capabilities to reinforce the credibility of strategic retaliation. West Germany's defense structure now became even more dependent on nuclear weapons over whose control and planning Bonn exercised no specific or contractual influence. In December 1957, after the Soviet Union launched its first ICBM and Sputnik, the United States decided to deploy IRBM's in Europe. Germany had been permitted to receive these missiles under a NATO agreement, but they were vulnerable to attack and could have been readily overrun in a Soviet invasion. Bonn showed no interest in having them installed on German soil and stressed instead its desire to become a full and equal partner in NATO's tactical nuclear planning.[20] After De Gaulle returned to power in 1958, France and Germany reportedly discussed the establishment of some type of nuclear partnership between the two countries. It is not certain whether France was unwilling to be sufficiently generous in sharing control and secrets, or whether Bonn felt that the time had not yet come to ask for a dispensation from Germany's armaments restrictions.[21] At any rate, nothing came of the discussions, and Franz-Josef Strauss complained later in the year that if France continued in her development of an

H-bomb, the Federal Republic might have to follow suit. Bonn now began to show interest in IRBM's, which were to be installed as soon as they could be deployed on mobile launching sites.[22]

Throughout these developments, there were significant political limitations on Bonn's nuclear policy. On the domestic scene, the furor caused by Carte Blanche and by the Government's nuclear ambitions provided a check that could not be neglected entirely. Internationally, the reaction ranged from lack of enthusiasm to outright suspicion and antagonism. But Germany's location on the front line of the Western alliance and its commitment to tactical nuclear deterrence of a conventional attack provided Bonn with convincing reasons for participating equally in the decision to use nuclear weapons. The waning credibility of the American nuclear commitment and the failure of the West to intervene decisively in Hungary in 1956 seemed to provide Bonn with a strong incentive for seeking a voice in the nuclear decision making of the Western alliance. And the awareness that independent French nuclear capabilities, even as a Franco-German *force de frappe,* would not be strong enough to protect West Germany and Berlin also moved Bonn to prefer participating with NATO in nuclear decision making to any other alternative.

In light of such considerations, in the fall of 1960 Adenauer began to advocate an integrated NATO force de frappe as an alternative to the national force de frappe favored by De Gaulle. The conclusion De Gaulle drew from the changing nuclear circumstances—namely that European nations needed independent nuclear deterrents—could not be implemented by West Germany because of political and contractual restrictions and strategic considerations. At the same time, Bonn viewed with increasing misgivings the trend toward expansion of the nuclear club, since the Federal Republic was apparently to be excluded. The logical middle course between independent capabilities and no control sharing at all was a tightly integrated nuclear alliance with equal control sharing. West Germany now aimed to increase her military and political influence not so much on the basis of a "special understanding" with the United States, or through the quest for an independent nuclear arsenal, but rather by stressing the need for the political and military integration of the alliance and for a larger German share in the control of nuclear weapons.[23] Bonn was very conscious of the maneuverability that would result from Germany's increased bargaining power, both within the Western alliance and vis-à-vis Moscow. As early as 1957, Strauss had explained that

> in all negotiations about reunification, risks and chances must be weighed against each other. The risks will diminish, the chances will improve, the more Germany herself has to throw in the scales. . . . A policy of strength in the age of the hydrogen bomb means in no case that one wants to use military pressure, with the risk of a third World War, in order to bring about some territorial changes. . . . A policy of strength means rather that one's own freedom of decision cannot be influenced by pressure from hostile or unfriendly quarters. . . . Germany . . . must become so indispensable to her Western friends, and so respectable for her potential adversary, that both will value her presence in the negotiations.[24]

An increasing number of proposals for a jointly controlled NATO nuclear force were put forth in the late 1950's and early 1960's, posing a delicate problem for American policy in Europe. The United States had consistently sought to prevent nuclear proliferation, and the most that Washington was willing to concede was the establishment of nuclear control arrangements that would allow NATO members to decide jointly about use, reserving a veto for the United States. In December 1957, at the same time the U.S. announced that IRBM's would be deployed in Europe, the NATO Council agreed to allow bilateral agreements between the United States and other member countries regarding IRBM deployment, with the understanding that the warheads would be under exclusive American control. The ally would actually operate the missiles, thus making for a joint decision. Ultimately only the United Kingdom, Turkey and Italy availed themselves of this offer.[25]

Other attempts to restrain proliferation on a national basis, such as the British plan for a WEU arms pool and the gradual relaxation of United States supervision over Euratom, also proved ineffective, particularly with respect to France. Although the McMahon Act, as amended in 1958, made it possible for the United States Government to transmit more information to its allies, the provisions pertaining to the custody of warheads remained the same. Germany was excluded in any event because of her WEU restrictions. But the provision that nuclear information could only be shared with nations that had already made "substantial progress" could only give France an incentive for accelerating her development program so that she might qualify as soon as possible.[26]

In March 1960, General Norstad suggested the establishment of a highly mobile, multinational NATO force, which would consist of a brigade each from the United States, Great Britain, and France equipped with both nuclear and conventional weapons, and which would preferably be commanded by a non-American. The Norstad plan was officially endorsed in Washington, but American officials stressed that control of warheads in the multinational units would still be exercised by the United States. Franz-Josef Strauss then indicated that West Germany was not interested in participating in these units, perhaps partially because participation would have obscured French and British objections against a full integration of NATO forces. Because of the objections voiced by the United States Congress and the Soviet Union—which warned that this proposal might jeopardize the forthcoming Summit meeting—nothing came of the plan in any case. In April, the United States proposed the deployment in Europe of several hundred Polaris missiles on flatcars and barges. Great Britain showed interest, but De Gaulle balked, and reportedly told Norstad that France would be willing to accept Polaris installations only if one-third of them were made available to France for use with her own nuclear warheads.[27] In September, Spaak, Norstad, and Adenauer began negotiations to establish NATO as a nuclear power, and such an arrangement was publicly endorsed by Bonn in October. In December, the United States offered NATO five submarines equipped with eighty Polaris missiles, to be delivered by 1963, provided that the NATO powers agreed on a multilateral system of control. The Allies were expected to purchase one hundred IRBM's for deployment at sea, at a cost of about $1 million each. But in view of the impending change of administration in Washington and the fact that the approval of the United States Congress was still required—which would most likely mean that warheads would continue to remain in American custody—the NATO Council issued a noncommittal communiqué in response to the American proposal.[28]

The revamping of American strategy by the Kennedy Administration soon presented Bonn with an even more troublesome set of circumstances. The new administration was intent on reversing the trend toward reliance on tactical nuclear weapons that had characterized NATO planning since 1954, and began to stress a more flexible and credible "graduated" scale of responses to a corresponding array of contingencies. This Law of Requisite Variety (to borrow a phrase from cybernetics) postulated that only variety could deter or destroy variety, and that the West should be fully prepared on all capability levels—in order to avoid the dilemma involved in choosing either a nuclear strike with the attendant risk of a counterstrike, or the politically disastrous consequences of doing nothing at all. The level of provocation had to have a credible retaliatory counterpart.

Even more clearly than the implications of the Radford Plan, the so-called McNamara doctrine seemed to reduce the chances of escalation—which Bonn sought to strengthen for reasons of deterrence—and increase the chances that conventional aggression would be met with a conventional response. From the European perspective, a "graduated response" by Washington "came to be regarded exclusively as a defense against escalation, against the spread of hostilities to Soviet and American territories, rather than being regarded *at the same time* as a means designed to restore psychological *plausibility* to the American deterrent."[29]

It may well have been true that "those Europeans who believe[d] that emphasis on local defense reduce[d] the credibility of the deterrent [were] confusing cause and effect," but

Government circles in Bonn generally reacted negatively to the McNamara doctrine.[30] Washington consistently pressed Bonn to increase the strength of West German ground forces at a time when Strauss and Adenauer were apparently convinced that the West was unable to offset the conventional capabilities of the Soviet Union. Ever since the rearmament program triggered by the Korean War, American strategy had gradually moved toward mobilizing conventional forces to strengthen nuclear deterrence. Not even the Eisenhower Administration's "new look" had reversed this trend substantially—it merely tried to shift the burden of providing conventional forces to the European allies. When the Lisbon force goals could not be achieved, Washington attempted to fill the gap with tactical nuclear weapons deployed in Europe, coupled with more precise verbal commitments and the threat of dire consequences if they were challenged.[31]

Initially, the Kennedy Administration was so strongly opposed to nuclear proliferation that it pigeonholed all proposals for a NATO nuclear force. When it became clear that European demands for a share in nuclear control could not be ignored, Washington reluctantly began to support multinational nuclear control ventures.[32] From the American point of view, the task was to "give Europeans as much of the appearance of nuclear participation and as little of the substance of nuclear decisions as will persuade them not to adopt policies that are incompatible with American strategic doctrine."[33] In May 1961, Secretary of State Dean Rusk announced at the NATO Foreign Ministers' meeting at Oslo that the United States would be willing to assign Polaris submarines to NATO, and in the following week President Kennedy considered the possibility of establishing a multinational seaborne missile force "if this should be desired and found feasible by our allies once NATO's non-nuclear goals have been achieved."[34] In essence, Kennedy repeated the offer made by the Eisenhower Administration, and promised NATO five Polaris-equipped submarines, with more to come, if NATO could agree on a multilateral control scheme and if NATO members would meet their conventional force goals. Although no agreement on a control arrangement had as yet been reached, the U.S. announced in May 1962 that it would transfer five submarines to NATO. But this was merely a change on paper, since the crews were American, their firing orders came from the President, and their immediate control was transferred from Admiral Dennison as Commander of the United States Atlantic Fleet to Admiral Dennison as Commander of SACLANT.[35] In October 1962, the United States offered to sell France a Nautilus-type attack submarine, without long-range ballistic missiles, and a dozen aerial tankers to permit in-air refueling of the French Mirage IV bomber, which Paris intended to make the major French nuclear delivery instrument.[36] Again, this was hardly more than a gesture since the submarine without missiles could not provide even part of the independent deterrent that France was aiming for.

By December the entire NATO nuclear armaments issue had come to a head over the Skybolt controversy. Because of the improvement of antiaircraft missiles, the Skybolt missile, to be carried by raiding bombers, had been planned as a "standoff weapon" that would give Great Britain a nuclear striking power without ground-to-ground missiles. The scrapping of the Skybolt development program by the United States thus meant in effect that Britain would have to either abandon plans for an independent nuclear capability because of lack of an adequate delivery system or carry on the development independently at exorbitant costs. The Polaris "compromise" made at Nassau provided that the United States would sell Britain Polaris submarine missiles, on the condition that Britain would assign her Polaris submarines to a NATO command, whenever established, as the nucleus of a NATO atomic force.

Bonn, in addition to facing the political dilemma that arose because France rejected both the immediate Polaris arrangement and the ultimate NATO force, was not reassured by the strategic-military implications of the Nassau agreement. The agreement had two distinct components, and each had a somewhat different implication for Bonn's strategic-political interests in a NATO nuclear force. The American component looked to the establishment of a multinational seaborne force, under a multilateral authority in NATO, consisting of the British contribution of four or five Polaris submarines, an equal or larger American contribution, a French contingent, and a contingent of NATO-owned surface ships to be manned and financed by the NATO non-nuclear members willing to accede to it. However, paragraph six of the agreement, drafted by the British, called for a more immediate solution by combining R.A.F. bombers with American submarines under a NATO nuclear command in which non-nuclear NATO powers would participate. The American component of the agreement, with its provision for the multinational staffing of surface ships, in a sense merely underlined the distinction between nuclear and non-nuclear NATO powers because it retained the specifically national contingent of American and British submarines. The British component, with its emphasis on joint planning and control, was more pragmatic, and held somewhat greater attractions for Bonn because it implied more influence over the deployment and use of atomic weapons.[37]

The full exploration of these developments, and an assessment of the strategic and political implications of the possible choices, fell upon Adenauer's successor. They were postponed in any event because of the French refusal to participate in a multinational venture. But in the remaining days of his administration, Adenauer was faced with an increasingly complex and troublesome strategic situation, in which the repercussions of the Nassau agreement were only one problem. Since Bonn's policy of seeking a share in nuclear control remained essentially unchanged, it began to conflict increasingly with the independent nuclear ambitions of De Gaulle. At the same time, De Gaulle's faithful support of Adenauer on the Berlin question, which I shall consider more fully below, implied to Adenauer that vital German interests were more fully appreciated in Paris than in Washington or London.

This line of thought was strengthened by the disquieting revamping of Washington's strategic thinking. By 1962, President Kennedy and Defense Secretary McNamara had presented a fully articulated and partially implemented "doctrine of flexibility," which involved contingency planning that tacitly admitted the feasibility and acceptance of a limited war in Europe. In December 1962, McNamara suggested that because of the shifting nuclear balance of power, nuclear arms had become NATO's *shield* and conventional forces NATO's *sword*, and implied that a nuclear counterstrike following conventional provocation might be "delayed."[38] But the most credible response to conventional attack, a response with conventional forces, held little attraction for Bonn because it meant total, if non-nuclear, war for West Germany. The deterrence posture that would serve Germany best—the threat of an immediate strategic or at least tactical nuclear retaliation—was undermined by waning credibility and was officially hedged in Washington. The possibility of a "conventional pause," during which Washington would determine whether an attack would be appropriately countered by nuclear retaliation, necessarily made Bonn nervous.

Changes in the deployment and tactical disposition of NATO's defenses added to Bonn's security concerns. The emphasis of NATO's defense planning gradually began to shift to a tactical doctrine of "fluid defense" and mobility, with designated but not otherwise prepared defense positions. This defense doctrine required not only time to assess the opponent's major thrusts and to direct counterforces to critical sectors of the front, but also space—and both commodities would be at a premium for Germany in case of an attack, because time and space would determine the extent of destruction on German territory. Bonn's misgivings were aggravated by the Kennedy Administration's decision not to deploy tactical nuclear weapons too close to the front.[39] From Washington's perspective, this reversal of NATO practice was complementary to the doctrine of fluid defense and a "conventional pause," and in addition tightened control over nuclear weapons by removing them from forward positions. But Bonn strongly resisted a thinning-out of NATO's nuclear presence at the East German border, because it seemed to increase the likelihood of a conventional response and because it undermined NATO's forward strategy even more than the doctrine of flexibility and a conventional pause. The more the Pentagon's emphasis appeared to shift from deterrence to defense, the more German security interests seemed threatened.

Even on the level of deterrence itself—aside from the perceived conflict between the requirements of deterrence and the requirements of defense—conflicts of interest developed within NATO. Important in the Kennedy Administration's reappraisal of nuclear strategy was an effort to strengthen the credibility of the nuclear deterrent by stressing the feasibility of controlling a nuclear war and of preventing "spasmic," irrational nuclear exchanges. Again, this created a conflict of interest in the alliance because the European powers believed they could gain most by "emphasizing the uncontrollable nature of nuclear war, in order to preserve the credibility of such deterrent power as [was] available on the continent. . . ."[40] Furthermore, the Cuban missile crisis and the test ban treaty—the latter negotiated after Adenauer left office—strongly pointed to a Soviet-American common interest on nuclear questions. The treaty was the first formal acknowledgment of this common interest. To many Europeans the test ban treaty, following the Allies' exclusion from Washington's deliberations on the Cuban confrontation, symbolized the possibility that in the case of a major European crisis the two nuclear superpowers would settle the issue bilaterally, and that Washington would complement the Pentagon's doctrine of strategic flexibility with a diplomatic counterpart of political flexibility.[41]

POLITICAL AND ECONOMIC RECOVERY*

The decision to establish the Common Market of the Six, and Adenauer's acquiescence to Britain's exclusion from membership in 1963, were the most important aspects of the Federal Republic's international economic policy between 1955 and 1963.

* With the restoration of West German sovereignty in 1955, the legal dimension of the goal of political recovery had been accomplished; hence it seems unnecessary to continue treating the goal of political recovery under a separate heading. Political aspects of this goal continued to pose some serious problems, however, and will be treated in the next chapter.

Their political implications went far beyond their specific impact on the goal of economic recovery, and by the end of the Adenauer era posed some of the most difficult and divisive problems for Bonn's foreign policy.

When the Six, already joined in the ECSC, met at Messina in June 1955, their joint communiqué specifically acknowledged that the proposed European Economic Community was intended by the signatories to be the next phase in the building of a united Europe. Attempts to unite Europe militarily had failed with the EDC; now economic integration was to prepare the way for political union. Adenauer's cherished dream of a united Western Europe had proceeded one step further, and the political aspirations reflected in the Treaty of Rome of 1957 suggested that crucial and perhaps painful measures of economic integration would be assessed by the participants in light of the larger promise of political union. Before turning to the political implications that were soon to emerge from the EEC's economic structure, it is helpful to briefly mention relevant aspects of the German economy.

During 1956, West Germany further reduced tariffs and other import restrictions, but continued to enjoy a considerable balance-of-payments surplus, especially with countries of the European Payments Union. The Bonn Government had already begun to restrain internal demand by enforcing a tighter monetary policy, and it was mainly the increasing foreign demand that kept the economy in full swing. Although seasonal employment fluctuated greatly, unemployment was no longer a major problem, and Bonn initiated a campaign to recruit foreign labor, primarily for agricultural and construction work. The Federal budget continued to show a heavy cash surplus, in large part because the funds allotted for the establishment of the Bundeswehr were not called upon. While imports from the dollar area rose faster than exports, goods and services supplied to American troops in West Germany more than equalized the dollar-area import deficits. There was no serious inflationary trend, but the Government felt obliged to admonish business and labor to exercise self-restraint on profit margins and on demands for wage increases.[42]

These generally favorable economic conditions, which also prevailed in other countries of the Six, began to level off somewhat by 1957. This was the major reason why the Rome treaties for the Common Market were drafted in some haste and with a feeling of urgency—they were to be safely executed before adverse economic conditions in the member states would bring on second thoughts about dropping traditional protectionist devices.[43] During 1958 and 1959, the German economy again showed a large growth rate, although different sectors of industry were developing unevenly. Coal mining in particular suffered from reduced demand and high inventories, and the Government felt it necessary to deliberalize ECSC coal imports.[44] Steel production also fell somewhat, and this aggravated the structural malaise of the coal-mining industry. But exports continued to remain high, and during the first half of 1960 they showed an increase of 21 per cent over the comparable period in the previous year, with a particularly marked increase in exports to Germany's Common Market partners. Imports rose 25 per cent, and import restrictions were further liberalized.[45]

On the whole, the West German economy was well equipped to operate within economies-of-scale such as the EEC, especially with respect to industrial products; the major trouble spot was agriculture, having been traditionally shielded from foreign competition through direct and indirect subsidies. At the same time, the belief of German industrialists and economists that West Germany could well hold her own in international markets, integrated or not, led these circles and their spokesmen in the Government, especially Ludwig Erhard, to warn that grave dangers might arise from the economic and political separatism of the Six. These warnings mainly took the form of suggestions that Britain be given membership in the EEC, and that her accession be made as easy and inviting as possible.[46]

The Bonn Government insisted throughout that it favored a broader EEC membership, and that West Germany would especially welcome the inclusion of Britain. Nonetheless, Britain's own misgivings, both political and economic, made her accession unlikely in the foreseeable future, and De Gaulle, who had returned to power in 1958, was known to be highly critical and suspicious of British (and American) influence in the realm of the Six, since he counted on the leader's role for France. Although Adenauer continued to stress that Bonn did not oppose extending an open-ended invitation to European countries, new developments soon threw grave doubt on Adenauer's determination to enlarge the Common Market.

Great Britain, having failed in its attempt to organize a seventeen-nation free trade area—an issue that divided the Six for a long time—had agreed with Norway, Sweden, Denmark, Austria, Switzerland, and Portugal to form the European Free Trade Association (EFTA), which would go into operation in May 1960. During the fall and winter of 1958, there were intricate negotiations on whether to allow an expansion of the Common Market to accommodate a free trade area, and if so, under what conditions.[47] At that time Franco-German tensions were already developing, and they foreshadowed the dilemma that confronted Bonn in 1963 when De Gaulle vetoed British accession to the EEC. During 1958, Adenauer, and especially Erhard, had made attempts to mediate between London's proposals for a free trade area and De Gaulle's insistence that the EEC be kept pure by the exclusion of Britain, a country that might water down EEC provisions right from the beginning. Although important industrial and commercial circles in West Germany were becoming uneasy about the impending economic split of Free Europe, Adenauer's overriding concern with nurturing Franco-German reconciliation and a Western European union finally led him to throw his support behind De Gaulle. Soon thereafter, De Gaulle reciprocated by endorsing Adenauer's determined stand on the developing Berlin crisis of November 1958, during which the Anglo-American powers showed a much more flexible attitude and a greater willingness to negotiate than did Bonn and Paris.[48]

When Britain led the negotiations for the creation of EFTA in the summer of 1959, it apparently expected the support of the United States. But Washington was not enthusiastic, and in the fall Douglas Dillon, then Undersecretary of State, advised Britain against the establishment of EFTA on the grounds that it would create further difficulties for the already precarious American balance-of-payments situation. However, the United States continued to support the EEC—which also created problems for the American balance of trade—for the express reason that the Common Market served fundamental political purposes, such as encouraging close cooperation between France and Germany. At the same time, Washington urged American and Canadian participation in an organization that would succeed the OEEC, subsequently established as the OECD, in which the now affluent European nations would share the burden of aid to underdeveloped countries and throw fewer obstacles in the way of American attempts to remedy payments difficulties.[49]

As the members readily admitted, their primary purpose in finally establishing EFTA was to pressure the EEC into acceding to a larger free-trade arrangement in Europe along the lines of the OEEC. Although the United States did not approve of establishing yet another economic group for this purpose, the intended outcome was strongly favored in Washington. An economic split of free Europe would be avoided, and American and Canadian membership in the OECD would help lay the economic foundations of Washington's political "grand design" for the Atlantic community.

The possibility that the Common Market could be watered down by pressures for wider membership was effectively obviated by the so-called Hallstein Plan for accelerating certain provisions of the Treaty of Rome. Germany had made important unilateral tariff reductions (between 20 and 25 per cent below the January 1957 base rate) during the summer of 1957. These cuts would have allowed the Federal Republic to make almost no additional tariff changes within the EEC until the end of 1961, and from a psychological point of view, Germany would not have yet fully experienced the reciprocal nature of her dependence on her EEC partners. Since both the Common Market and EFTA had scheduled tariff reductions for July 1960, this early unilateral reduction would have strengthened EFTA's ability to apply economic and political pressure on other Common Market countries, because Germany would have suffered the least and could have remained on the sidelines. Hence, in March 1960, Hallstein—a confidant of Adenauer, and the president of the Common Market's Brussels commission—suggested accelerating the realization of Common Market goals by doubling the planned 10 per cent July reduction of customs duties. He also suggested that this be coupled with the imposition of the common external tariff, which had not been anticipated until January 1, 1962.[50]

Apparently this step was proposed not only to strengthen the economic position of the EEC vis-à-vis EFTA, but also to prevent a possible dilution of EEC provisions by potential applicants, especially Britain. The acceleration plan would strengthen the EEC as an organization, and for all practical purposes make its integrative features irrevocable. Furthermore, a common external tariff would create a more cohesive and impenetrable shell for the EEC, and in that respect, would support French policy. The plan clearly favored French political objectives, and it has been suggested that acceleration was first proposed by Olivier Wormser, director of the economic section in the French foreign ministry.[51] The United States expressed approval of the acceleration plan, but pressed again for a "reconstituted OEEC" that would include the United States and Canada.

> By a master stroke of diplomacy, Professor Hallstein and the Quay d'Orsay were able to adopt a totally new strategy. . . . The balance of payments of the United States was just beginning to give serious concern. The Americans were therefore all the more reluctant to countenance any new larger areas that would discriminate against them. The move to convertibility, in December 1958, played right into their hands, for with the dissolution of the European Payments Union, the larger Europe of the fifteen or eighteen could be argued to have lost its economic relevance. The whole problem could thus be placed into an Atlantic framework: And there the United States could be relied upon to support the Community for political reasons, and to oppose British schemes for economic reasons.[52]

As could be expected, the Hallstein Plan, which was generally well received in the Community on its economic merits, met with considerable opposition in West Germany because it required rapid increases in German tariffs against non-EEC markets. The final program, which was approved in May 1960, provided as a concession to German industrial interests that only half of the unilateral German tariff cuts would have to be restored during 1960, the other half by the end of 1961.[53]

Britain's hopes of inducing the EEC to consent to a wider and presumably more diluted European economic community had clearly faded by 1961. Early in the year, Britain began to show interest in forming a commercial link with the Six, and proposed a "harmonized" common tariff between the Six and Britain, with the proviso that Britain would not be required to apply the common tariff to its EFTA partners and to the Commonwealth states. Agricultural products were to be excluded from the arrangement entirely. By midyear, however, London applied for full membership, realizing that De Gaulle would probably veto a purely economic association and that Britain would have little to fear from the political evolution of the Community in light of De Gaulle's rather contemptuous attitude toward supranational institutions. Apparently the most pressing reasons for Britain's decision were the hope that she could deal more successfully with her serious economic problems, and the fact that the new administration in Washington strongly urged British membership.[54]

The American and British expectations that the EEC could be turned from a "little Europe" construct into a less exclusive organization were the very things that reinforced De Gaulle's already substantial and deep-seated misgivings. There may have been weighty factors that contributed to the stiffening of French demands and attitudes on British accession, such as the "misunderstanding" of intentions between De Gaulle and Macmillan when they met at Rambouillet in December 1962, the Labour Party's swing against the Common Market, the bracing pro-De Gaulle plebiscite in France, or the increasingly tense negotiations at Brussels. Most important, perhaps, were the scrapping of the Skybolt missile program and the Nassau agreement between President Kennedy and Prime Minister Macmillan.[55]

The timing of this important event was almost unbelievably

maladroit. De Gaulle suspected that a decision with such fundamental ramifications must have been considered by both sides for a considerable time—with the implication that Macmillan had been less than candid at Rambouillet—and the ultimate support for the British nuclear posture was now specifically dependent upon the United States at a time when Britain was expected to cast her lot wholeheartedly with the European cause. The dowry of atomic capabilities and secrets that Britain might have presented to her future Common Market partners now was indefinitely committed to Washington and NATO, and her political inclinations still seemed primarily "Atlantic-oriented" rather than "pro-Continent."

It is apparent that the members of the Atlantic community were forming delineations of economic, political, and military interests that confronted Adenauer with unpleasant alternatives in the remaining days of his administration. France sought to shut out Anglo-American influence in Western Europe by tightening the outer shell surrounding the Six—politically, economically, and militarily. Given his fundamental commitment to Franco-German reconciliation and a Western European union, Adenauer was determined to avoid jeopardizing Franco-German collaboration in political and economic matters. At the same time, security considerations and their political ramifications propelled the Bonn Government toward the United States and NATO—especially since French efforts to obtain independent nuclear capabilities threatened to make Germany a "first satellite" of France rather than her equal partner.

Before January 1963 it was still possible for Bonn to equivocate about the tug-of-war between France and the Anglo-American powers. Though Adenauer stood firmly behind the Hallstein acceleration proposals, the Government also agreed to make substantial contributions to the West's foreign aid programs and to coordinate its bilateral aid programs in Latin America with the Alliance for Progress. Bonn also sought to ease the American balance-of-payments problem by advance repayment of debts and by taking measures designed to return

American capital to the United States. Bonn also made compensatory gestures to Britain, agreeing to prepay debts, increase German purchases of British armaments, and liberalize drawing rights on Deutsche Mark deposits with the International Monetary Fund. In addition, in 1961 the Government appreciated the Deutsche Mark, and West German gold and foreign exchange reserves gradually began to decline.[56]

But by early 1963 the choices confronting Adenauer allowed little equivocation. In the fall of 1962, De Gaulle and Adenauer had drafted a Franco-German friendship treaty, which contained no provisions of great practical importance, but must have looked to Adenauer like the capstone of his policy of reconciliation with France. A few days before Adenauer was to arrive in Paris for the official signing of the treaty, De Gaulle held his famous press conference of January 14, 1963, in which he explained his reasons for excluding Britain from the EEC. No doubt only the intervention of Adenauer on behalf of Britain could have induced De Gaulle to reconsider. But for Adenauer this would have meant that the friendship treaty, the most striking symbol of Franco-German reconciliation, might fall by the wayside or become meaningless.

For De Gaulle, proper timing was crucial. Adenauer was a lame-duck chancellor and his successor could not be expected to show equal understanding toward De Gaulle's ambitions in Western Europe. In fact, Adenauer and his unswervingly pro-French policy had become increasingly isolated both on the domestic scene and on the international scene. Adenauer's relations with the Kennedy Administration were much less cordial than his relations with the Eisenhower Administration had been, largely because of disagreements over the West's policy vis-à-vis the Soviet Union. And relations with London had been strained for some time because of Adenauer's support of French interests and his suspicions that the British were willing to negotiate a Cold War détente with the Soviet Union on the basis of some measure of disengagement in central Europe.

On the domestic political scene, Adenauer's foreign policies and his increasingly authoritarian manipulations had split his own Cabinet and were drawing sharp criticism from many quarters. By that time there were in effect two German foreign policies, not one. The first was Adenauer's, which allowed De Gaulle to blackball Britain's membership in the EEC with Adenauer's implicit acquiescence, and which resulted in the Franco-German friendship treaty. The second was that preferred by Erhard and Foreign Minister Schröder, who advocated a more flexible course, and tended to support the Anglo-American position not only on matters pertaining to the Common Market but also on a more imaginative Eastern policy.[57]

REUNIFICATION

By 1955, the Soviet Union appeared more and more reconciled to the division of Germany and the existence of two German states. Although it is an exaggeration to say that "the Geneva Summit Conference of 1955 in fact marked the end of the Cold War in Germany,"[58] from 1955 until the Berlin crisis of 1958, Moscow's German policy was limited to proposing a variety of disengagement and neutralization plans, which were designed to portend unification, but in fact sought to pry West Germany from the Western military alliance. The Soviet Union seemed prepared to accept and consolidate the political status quo in central Europe, and after the Bantung Conference the strategic preoccupations of the Soviet Union turned primarily to other Cold War fronts, especially the Middle East and Asia.[59]

The Soviet Union's willingness to accept the existence of two German states and to solidify the partition of Europe was most specifically reflected in its decision to establish diplomatic relations with the Federal Republic. For Bonn this posed a painful dilemma. It tended to underline the division of Germany, and in effect lent it a certain de jure recognition. But the Bonn Government also believed it could not afford to block diplomatic channels that were so important to the unification question; it therefore felt obliged to allow a unique dispensation of the Hallstein doctrine—according to which the Federal Republic withholds or withdraws formal recognition of governments that recognize the East German regime.[60]

In the fall of 1955, Adenauer went to Moscow to explore the chances for a solution of the unification question and to obtain the release of German prisoners of war still being held in the Soviet Union. Nothing was accomplished on the unification question, and Khrushchev told Adenauer that West Germany had been explicitly warned that the Paris Agreements would stand in the way of German unification and that the Soviet Union could not be expected to take the chance that a united Germany would join the Western alliance. After Adenauer returned, there was a series of exploratory exchanges between Moscow and Bonn, and in November 1955 the Soviet Union again proposed the establishment of an all-German council based on direct negotiations between East and West Germany. But the Geneva Foreign Ministers' Conference in November, which was to translate the generalities of the Geneva Summit into concrete programs, made no progress on the German unification question. The West's decision to rely primarily on tactical nuclear weapons now made it seem imperative that the forward position of NATO be kept intact; the Western powers now implied in effect that a united Germany should be free to join NATO. To be sure, this was coupled with a proposal for a tight security system that would have mobilized every signatory in case a united Germany became threatening. But the prospect of a united Germany's joining NATO was obviously unacceptable to the Soviet Union, even with the promise that her security concerns would be fully accommodated. John Foster Dulles chided the Russians for "balking" whenever they "came face up to what [unification] involved," but at the same time suggested that "obviously, if Germany were reunified by free elections this would mean the end of the puppet regime which the Soviet Union has installed in East Germany. This in turn would almost surely have serious repercussions upon the other satellite countries in Eastern Europe."[61]

The events of 1956 in the Soviet bloc tended to remove the spotlight from the German question. Still, after the Hungarian uprising Moscow again showed some interest in the unification issue, and letters from Bulganin to Adenauer hinted that West

Germany's secession from NATO might make a difference in Moscow's attitude on the matter. The Soviet Union now began to lay heavy emphasis on questions of disarmament, and Bonn was becoming somewhat nervous about what Foreign Minister Brentano called "a certain readiness in the free world to come to an understanding with the Soviet Union on the basis of the status quo."[62] Nonetheless, in light of Soviet suggestions that Adenauer "needed" a failure in disarmament negotiations, the Government made it a point to impress upon both the Western allies and the Soviet Union that Bonn would not stand in the way of disarmament, even if it were not accompanied by unification.[63]

Nonetheless, Bonn firmly rejected all the suggestions for partial disarmament and nuclear disengagement in central Europe that were proposed in a variety of quarters. Bonn's ambition to share nuclear control—undoubtedly one reason why disengagement proposals multiplied rapidly—seemed threatened, and the general relaxation of international tensions posed the danger that the West might recognize the German status quo.[64] Adenauer viewed the military and political neutralization of Germany as a pseudo-solution without lasting value, and thought disengagement would create a power vacuum, a political no-man's land that could not be expected to maintain itself in the conflict between the two hostile blocs. Disengagement would have ended Adenauer's plans for a Western European union, and by prying Germany from the Western alliance would have undermined NATO's "forward strategy." Bonn's suspicions of Moscow's motives appeared not unjustified, since the Soviet proposals were never specifically linked with the question of unification, but seemed primarily designed to prevent the Federal Republic from obtaining a share in controlling nuclear arms. Furthermore, all Soviet proposals started with the assumption that two German states existed and that they would participate in negotiations as sovereign equals. Acceptance of even the initial stages of the Soviet plans would have implied Western recognition of the Pankow regime, which then could have sabotaged all further progress. Also, Adenauer distrusted Western interest in disengagement proposals because it seemed to be based not so much on a desire to see Germany reunified as on the need to bring about a lessening of East-West tensions and to explore all possibilities for disarmament and arms control.[65]

In 1957, the connections between disengagement, the nuclear balance between East and West, and German access to nuclear weapons became crucial.[66] The day after the Soviet Union launched its first Sputnik, Polish Foreign Minister Rapacki announced his plan for a nuclear-free zone to include Germany, Poland, and Czechoslovakia. When the United States decided in December to deploy IRBM's in Europe, Bulganin sent a letter to the leaders of all NATO powers, suggesting that the atomic arming of West Germany would block even the last chance for unification that was still open, namely the chance for an agreement between the two German states.[67] Bonn in fact showed no interest in receiving IRBM's at this time. But the Soviet-American exchange of notes early in 1958 indicated that Moscow was primarily interested in the prohibition of nuclear weapons and the withdrawal of troops in central Europe; its attitude on German unification was not changed. Khrushchev, who replaced Bulganin as Prime Minister in March, proposed a disengagement program that combined Eden's 1955 plan for the creation of a demilitarized zone with Rapacki's suggestion for a denuclearized central Europe; but only Britain was willing to enter negotiations on that basis.[68]

A decade after the blockade of 1948, Berlin again became the focal point of the Cold War in Germany. The Berlin crises that began in 1958 were not the result of sudden shifts in Soviet tactics or strategy but rather were the logical culmination of 1955–58 Soviet policies. In the three years after West Germany joined NATO, the Soviet Union had persistently attempted to solidify the political lines of division in central Europe by following a two-Germanies policy and by seeking to gain Western recognition of the East German regime. At the same time, Moscow tried to blur the military boundaries running through Germany and to deny West Germany access to nuclear control sharing by proposing disengagement and demilitarized zones.

Having failed thus far, the two-pronged Soviet interest

pointed almost inevitably to Berlin. Politically, Berlin was a constant source of embarrassment for the Pankow regime and was the last symbol of the Four Powers' responsibility for all-German questions; circumstances seemed propitious for pressuring the West into a de facto recognition of East Germany and for freezing out West Germany's presence in West Berlin. Militarily, the access routes to Berlin were the vulnerable point of the Western defense line; the Soviets enjoyed local superiority of power, and could apply pressures and engineer provocations with fine and ambiguous gradations. In contrast to the more clear-cut trip-wire situation along the East-West German border, West Berlin was a spot with ambiguous thresholds of provocation.[69]

Even before the Soviet Union demanded the end of Western occupation of West Berlin and the creation of a "free city," the East Germans had prepared the way by announcing that the Western powers had forfeited their right to maintain garrisons in Berlin by allegedly violating the Potsdam Agreement. The famous Soviet note of November 27, 1958, did not as yet threaten to conclude a separate peace treaty with the East German regime, or impose any time limit on the withdrawal of Western troops or the recognition of East Germany. But it was obvious that the Soviet Union was preparing to press the West harder to "clarify" the political situation in Berlin and East Germany before the East-West military demarcation was underlined by West German access to nuclear control. The Soviets noted that the unification of Germany "on a militaristic basis" would be intolerable, and proposed again the establishment of a German confederation in which the social and political structures of the two German states would have at least equal standing. In fact the Russians now stressed that the problem of unification should be approached "primarily from class positions," and that in light of its social achievements East Germany was fully justified in raising the question of liquidating the order existing in the Federal Republic.[70]

For the Federal Republic, Soviet pressures on Berlin had a twofold implication. First, the establishment of a free city, perhaps under some form of United Nations supervision, would have removed the last vestige of Four Power responsibility for German unification by abrogating the Four Power Agreement. Equally important, it would have severed the already tenuous political-constitutional link between West Berlin and the Federal Republic. The Western powers had never been enthusiastic about a too specific and visible integration of West Berlin into the Federal Republic (this was reflected in the special provisions made for Berlin in the Basic Law) primarily because they wanted to preserve the legal fiction that West Berlin was under the authority of the occupying powers. Although there was a de jure separation between West Berlin and the Federal Republic, there was a de facto economic, political, and symbolic connection that Bonn was determined to preserve at all costs. The creation of an isolated miniature state of West Berlin thus would have undercut the Western position in two ways: it would have shut out the Western powers by abolishing the Four Power Agreement, and it would have excluded the political influence of the Federal Republic. A major political ambiguity standing in the way of the Soviet two-Germanies policy would have been clarified and resolved in Moscow's favor.[71]

Although Bonn and the Western powers agreed that no illusions could be entertained about Soviet willingness to yield anything of substance on the unification question, they drew somewhat different conclusions from this realization. This led to a significant difference between the Anglo-American attitude and the Franco-German attitude. London and Washington were convinced that the Soviet Union was primarily interested in the political solidification of the status quo, and were prepared to lessen tensions in central Europe by "de-fusing" the Berlin question through negotiations. Bonn advocated a much more rigid line, which found the support of De Gaulle—who could count on Adenauer's gratitude at no cost to French interests, and who was in Adenauer's debt for support in the EEC-EFTA controversy.

Prior to the Geneva Conference of May 1959, Macmillan went to Moscow, where he apparently tried to sound out Khrushchev on the concessions the Soviet Union might be willing to make in return for Western agreement on troop reductions on both sides of the Iron Curtain. Bonn was not happy about Macmillan's mission, but some disengagement features were presented in a Western peace plan at the conference in May. This so-called Herter Plan attempted to link unification with a European security plan, and contained a genuine concession to the East, not only because it envisaged a limitation of armament levels in central Europe, but also because it relegated the demand for free elections to the third stage of a four-stage unification program, which was to be capped by a peace settlement.[72] It became clear, however, that the Soviet Union simply was no longer interested in entertaining unification projects. Moscow wished only to solidify the political division of Germany by rendering it more explicit in the contractual provisions of disengagement schemes that would, at the same time, keep West Germany from sharing nuclear control.

Adenauer, in addition to intrinsically objecting to disengagement, considered such Western proposals unwise not so much because the Soviet Union might accept them, but because once they were presented as concessions they would become the basis and starting point for further Soviet demands at the next stage of East-West discussions. From the perspective of Bonn, these proposals implied a willingness to water down the Western position—leading to a gradual de jure recognition of the German status quo. Adenauer's concern was by no means unjustified. Even such a close and determined Cold War ally as John Foster Dulles had at one time said that free elections were not the only way to negotiate unification, and had toyed with the idea of accepting the so-called "agent theory," according to which the West could officially deal with East Germans through the fiction that Soviet authority had been "delegated" to them as Soviet "agents." There was also a feeling in Bonn that nothing was to be gained by going through the motions of yet another elaborate unification plan that would imply a weakening of the Western stand, and then proceeding with what everybody knew was the business of the day, the Berlin question.

In any event, the Herter Plan was doomed from the beginning because the Soviet Union insisted on including East Germany as a full-fledged participant at all stages. The Western powers argued that they could not negotiate on the basis of a two-Germanies concept, since this would signify the end of Four Power responsibility for all-German questions; furthermore, there would have been no incentive for the Pankow regime to make any concessions, because it would "get exactly what it wants, namely, the formal recognition of the East German regime as a separate sovereign state."[73] And, although the conduct and policy of the East German Government would ultimately be directed from Moscow, the three Western powers would in effect be eliminated from the subsequent negotiations between the two German governments. On the Berlin question, however, the Western powers seemed not averse to an interim agreement that would have included the "symbolic" reduction of their occupation forces and the curtailment of propaganda activities in both East and West Berlin. Although there was some difference of opinion on whether such an arrangement should last two or five years, the real stumbling block that finally precluded even a Berlin agreement was the Western claim that in case a final solution was not forthcoming, their rights would still be secured by the Four Power Agreement, whereas the Russians argued that in that case Western rights would be void.[74] Discussion continued at the Eisenhower-Khrushchev meeting at Camp David—with Eisenhower in effect admitting that the Berlin situation was abnormal—but no specific agreements could be reached.

The Soviet Union now began to threaten more insistently that it would conclude a separate peace treaty with East Germany, and it generally stepped up its propaganda campaign against West Germany, prior to the Paris Summit Conference of May 1960. Moscow now played down its demands for withdrawal of Western troops from Berlin, and attacked instead the political presence and "interference" of the Federal Republic in West Berlin. Khrushchev accused Adenauer of sabotaging reunification by refusing to admit that two Germanies existed, and argued that he, Khrushchev, was speaking about German unification as a private individual because this was a question to be settled not by third states but by East and West Germany.[75] The campaign of mutual recrimination grew worse: the Soviet Union implied that Adenauer had himself affixed the swastika which appeared over his signature in the guest book of the National Gallery in Washington, and Bonn accused Moscow of "obvious untruthfulness."[76]

The abortive Summit meeting, which was overshadowed by the U-2 incident, could not obscure the fact that Soviet policy on Berlin had failed. On a stopover in East Berlin, Khrushchev again announced that the Soviet Union was not going to wait much longer before it eliminated "the remnants of World War II" by negotiating a peace treaty with East Germany, and that the "social achievements" of the Ulbricht regime would be fully protected by the Soviet Union.

During 1960, Soviet pressures on Berlin abated somewhat. Moscow was apparently waiting to assess Eisenhower's successor before renewing its prodding, and toward the end of the year Bonn and Moscow held trade negotiations, which reflected a general improvement in the tone of Soviet-German diplomacy. It was not until after June 1961, when Khrushchev met Kennedy in Vienna, that the Soviet Union renewed its squeeze play on Berlin—which culminated in the erection of the Berlin Wall in August. The building of the wall, however, had antecedents and causes that were not entirely under the control of Moscow.

Soviet pressures on Berlin had in the meantime contributed to developments that threatened a serious weakening of the East German state. Since 1958 the question of Berlin had received increasing attention in the East bloc's diplomacy and press. As rumors grew that the last exit from East Germany to the West might be blocked permanently, refugees poured into West Berlin; this drew needed manpower from the shaky East German economy and posed embarrassing political problems. By July 1961, the number of refugees entering West Berlin had reached ten thousand a week; it was apparently at a meeting of East-bloc leaders in Moscow at the end of the month that the decision was made to stop this flow by erecting the wall. On August 13, units of the People's Police and the National People's Army occupied East Berlin and began to block transit between East and West Berlin.[77]

In addition to closing the last door between East and West Germany, this step destroyed the last remnant of the unity of Germany and that of Berlin, and abrogated the Four Power Agreement that had been designed to preserve unity. The East had forcibly achieved a tightening and clarification of the political line running through Germany; and the Soviet Union had taken measures that for all practical purposes anticipated important aspects of the separate peace treaty it had threatened the West with for so long. By "delegating" its rights in East Berlin to the Ulbricht regime, the Soviet Union had completed the division of Germany.

Following the erection of the wall, Britain and the United States pressed even harder for a solution of the Berlin issue, with the formal but pessimistic concurrence of Adenauer. In the fall of 1961, Dean Rusk and Andrei Gromyko explored the possibilities for agreement, but reached no conclusions; and when Adenauer went to Washington, he and President Kennedy agreed that the anticipated East-West talks would be limited to the question of West Berlin. By narrowing the discussion to Berlin, Adenauer hoped to forestall further Western concessions on such far-reaching topics as disengagement, possible recognition of the Oder-Neisse line, or West German access to nuclear control. But limiting talks to West Berlin implicitly conceded the Russians' right to confer on the subject, whereas the Soviet Union categorically denied the Western powers any rights in East Berlin. This tended to support the Soviet argument, consistently advanced since November 1958, that there was no longer a Berlin question but only a "West Berlin question."[78]

Exploratory discussions held early in 1962 and during the later Geneva disarmament conference brought to light a Soviet attitude much tougher than it had been before the erection of the wall. Moscow now returned to its previous demands for the withdrawal of Western troops from West Berlin, and noted that even their replacement by United Nations contingents or a "symbolic" Soviet garrison could only be regarded as an interim solution. Nevertheless, Britain and the United States were apparently prepared to offer a four-point program for the establishment of an international access authority to West Berlin. This proposal was allegedly leaked to the press by the Bonn Government to assure that it would never get off the ground.[79]

This incident, which caused great annoyance in Washington, was only the symbol of some larger reasons why the relations between Bonn and Washington grew strained toward the end of Adenauer's chancellorship. Late in 1961, the Soviet Union mentioned to Bonn the feasibility of bilateral discussions; this raised in some minds the possibility of a second Rapallo.[80] The Bonn Government scrupulously avoided giving the impression that it was in any way interested, and called Soviet proposals in that direction "unrealistic and reactionary."[81] At the same time, Bonn viewed with increasing misgivings the seemingly conciliatory Anglo-American attitude on some aspects of the German question. Although Bonn had consistently demonstrated its wholehearted loyalty to the Western cause, Adenauer was haunted by the fear that overriding American interests would lead Washington to a modification of its German policy. I have already noted the repercussions of the revamping of American strategy on West German security interests; Washington's complementary "flexibility" with respect to the German question could only add to Bonn's concern. The Kennedy Administration, in its attempt to free itself from what it regarded as the stale and entrenched international positions of the Eisenhower Administration, was determined to regain for America the ability to exploit the changing circumstances of the Cold War. This willingness to explore new approaches to East-West tensions contrasted sharply with the Adenauer Government's lack of new ideas.

In part, the frictions developing between Bonn and Washington may have been a question of personalities. Adenauer probably viewed the pragmatism of Kennedy and his "bright young men" with a certain measure of alarm, and according to all accounts, would have preferred to continue dealing with a Republican administration. The Kennedy Administration in turn must have felt that the Adenauer group represented the outdated remnants of an intransigent and unimaginative Cold War posture that could not be expected to be appreciative of the ways of flexibility and sophistication.

But the divergence of views had more fundamental causes, which rested on realistic assessments of national interest. The global perspectives and responsibilities of the United States allowed and required Washington to view the German question and the Berlin issue in the overall context of East-West dealings. From Bonn's perspective, any conciliatory approach to the Soviet view on central Europe threatened vital interests of the Federal Republic. This also explained Bonn's lack of initiative on the German question; given the tightening of the line running through Germany and the rigid Soviet insistence on a two-Germanies concept, there remained no meaningful alternatives that could be pursued without granting a measure of legitimacy to the Soviet Union's demands that the German question be "stabilized" by Western recognition of the East German regime.

6. *Goal Compatibilities and the International System, 1955–1963*

The increasing complexity of the post-1955 international system brought new strictures and opportunities for the pursuit of West German foreign policy goals. The compatibility between international conditions and foreign policy aims had shifted considerably since the postwar period. The combination of nuclear symmetry with political heterosymmetry had a fundamental impact on West German security aims. On the level of military capabilities, Germany was obliged to reevaluate her security policies against the background of the symmetrical East-West nuclear balance that had evolved from the previous American nuclear monopoly. Politically, the goal of security had to be reassessed in the context of the heterosymmetrical relationships that resulted from regionalism and the strains nuclear symmetry put on the Western alliance.

From Bonn's perspective, the military-strategic ramifications of nuclear symmetry were very serious. West Germany's entire security policy was based on the threatening posture of the Soviet Union and her satellites, and *any* appreciable increase of power in the Eastern bloc would necessarily be viewed with apprehension by the Federal Republic. A change in the East-West power balance as fundamental as the evolution of nuclear symmetry could not help but throw a different light on West Germany's strategic and tactical security requirements.

After 1955, the Soviet military threat in central Europe appeared perhaps less immediate and menacing, due to the apparent Soviet preoccupation with solidifying the status quo in Europe. But the Bonn Government's overall view of the nature of international politics inclined it toward strategic assessments of the enemy's capabilities rather than his intentions. Since West

Germany's defense planning had chiefly relied on the protective umbrella of American nuclear capabilities, the diminishing credibility of "active deterrence" required a reappraisal of the goal of security. To be sure, the American commitment to West Germany's defense was based on a reliable American national interest, and Washington's prestige was almost irrevocably tied to the inviolability of the territory of the Federal Republic. Also, nuclear bipolarity did not ipso facto negate a determined posture of active deterrence—it rendered it less credible, and raised the threshold of provocation for a nuclear counterstrike. Yet the balance of power had been fundamentally altered by the Soviet Union's acquisition of nuclear capabilities, and the Western alliance now confronted an opponent whose power had increased enormously. On the whole, the changing power distribution placed the Federal Republic's security efforts on a much more complicated and tenuous footing.

In contrast to other NATO members, the Bonn Government refrained from publicly voicing its apprehensions about the diminishing credibility of active deterrence. Up to the fall of 1956, the Government's faith in the efficacy of a conventional German military contingent was apparently unimpaired. Even when Bonn came out for equipping the Bundeswehr with nuclear arms, the Government's explanations did not in any way refer to the serious liabilities nuclear symmetry was placing on the United States. It would have been possible, of course, to defend the continued buildup of West German conventional forces on strictly military grounds. Because of nuclear bipolarity, which rendered a nuclear response to an attack on West Germany less credible, confronting the East with strong conventional forces would provide more credible deterrence. But this deterrence posture would have implied acquiescence in the possibility of a "limited" war in Europe—limited from the viewpoint of the United States, but total from the perspective of Bonn. West Germany was interested in deterrence, not defense.

The fundamental German interest in a precisely defined East-West military line of demarcation, which, if crossed, would bring American nuclear retaliation or at least a local tactical nuclear response, explains in part Bonn's persistent rejection of proposals that envisaged military disengagement in central Europe. Although Eisenhower and Dulles were prepared to extend at least tactical American nuclear presence to the periphery of the Eastern bloc, the "new look" strategy already threatened an overall division of functions—between the strategic nuclear obligations of the alliance superpower and the conventional force responsibilities of West Germany.[1] These disquieting developments were reinforced when the Kennedy Administration introduced strategic and political concepts of flexibility that undermined NATO's forward strategy and implied a "conventional pause" on German territory. Germany's interests seemed to call for a Maginot-line concept of deterrence.

Bonn was reluctant to air its security concerns in public, in part because Adenauer had, on both the international and domestic fronts, such a heavy political investment in close American-German cooperation. The efficacy of this cooperation would have been called into doubt by the open admission that nuclear bipolarity had lessened the congruence of American and German security interests. But the recurring Berlin crises, during which Adenauer seemed to detect a dangerous weakening of Anglo-American resolve in confronting the Soviet Union, only strengthened Bonn's determination to share in the control of Western nuclear power. Hence Bonn wished to engage the United States and NATO more fully in the security concerns of West Germany: the Western nuclear presence was to be extended unequivocally to the Eastern borders of the Federal Republic by making West Germany a full partner in NATO's nuclear planning and control.

At times, Adenauer must have felt that some vital German interests were finding a more understanding and sympathetic ear in Paris than in Washington, especially after De Gaulle lent his wholehearted support to Bonn's inflexible Berlin policy. The "Washington-Bonn axis" of the Eisenhower Administration was gradually being replaced by a Franco-German understanding, at a time when De Gaulle was in need of an ally within NATO and when Adenauer required support for his intransigent Eastern policy.[2] But the military dimensions of Bonn's foreign policy were necessarily anchored to the overwhelming might of the United States. Moreover, French efforts to become the European nuclear protector gave Bonn political doubts that stood in the way of a viable Franco-German security partnership. At the same time, "the strategic changes put into effect by Kennedy and McNamara enhanced . . . French diplomatic leverage. For the conventional, or even the tactical-atomic defense of Europe (as against deterrence by the threat of strategic nuclear strike), [was] hardly conceivable without French cooperation. And France's interests here pointed in a very similar direction to Germany's."[3]

The political crosscurrents that began to affect Bonn came chiefly from the heterosymmetrical political alignments in the Western alliance rather than from nuclear symmetry—although symmetry and heterosymmetry are intimately related. Hence we must now turn to the second range of systemic contingencies that affected West Germany's security goals after 1955.

No doubt there was a close connection between the growth of nuclear symmetry and the ensuing divisions within the Western alliance. Nuclear bipolarity and the waning credibility of active deterrence, added to regional self-assertion and the reassessment of an apparently diminishing Soviet military threat, presented vexing problems for the Atlantic alliance. In particular, the Franco-American disagreement over conceived interests, purposes, and policies complicated the political solidarity and the effective coordination of Western defense in the NATO framework.

The friction developing between Washington and Paris put Bonn in a most difficult position. From the very beginning of his administration, Adenauer had sought to build West Germany's entire foreign policy on the assumption that Franco-American solidarity would continue, or that an integrated Western Europe would stay welded to the Atlantic community. The political and socioeconomic recovery of West Germany within a Western European union made a close relationship between France and

Germany indispensable, and was to be underpinned by the wider Atlantic power complex, which would provide the ultimate guarantee of security for West Germany. Clearly, the foundations of this congruence were shaken by the emerging fissures between France and the United States.

The developing Franco-American divergence also posed specific security concerns for the Federal Republic. For one, it tended to undermine the effectiveness of NATO as an instrument of deterrence. Bonn was convinced that its most fundamental security interests lay in a closely knit Western defense posture. When Bonn finally requested a share in nuclear control, one anticipated effect was a strengthening of the collective control organs of NATO, if for no other reason than to supervise Germany. A similar strengthening of NATO, which changed it from a guaranty pact to an integrated alliance, had taken place at the time of Germany's accession to membership in 1955.

By supporting a multinational nuclear force in the framework of NATO, Bonn also hoped to close the status gap between NATO's nuclear and non-nuclear powers—the Federal Republic was threatened with indefinite or permanent exclusion from a nuclear directorate. The strenuous French efforts to obtain nuclear arms further underlined NATO's dual-status membership policy, while Bonn, because of political and contractual restraints, could not compensate for the inequalities developing between France and Germany by creating independent nuclear capabilities for Germany. Consequently, the Federal Republic supported NATO on proposals for the sharing of nuclear decisions. Clearly, German security interests, which ultimately derived from the East-West nuclear balance, pointed in the same direction as the political ramifications that developed from the heterosymmetrical loosening of bipolarity—namely, toward a support of NATO and, implicitly, of the United States.

Thus, the West German Government was induced to take sides with Washington rather than Paris. To be sure, Bonn's advocacy of some degree of nuclear control sharing within NATO did not coincide with Washington's preference for avoiding *any* control sharing. But compared to the distasteful possibility of a fragmentation of the alliance, which might be triggered by independent national efforts to obtain nuclear arsenals, the possibility of a NATO-coordinated sharing of nuclear control must have appeared at least tolerable to the United States. Consequently, the Federal Republic's interest in multinational nuclear arrangements dovetailed with an at least second-choice set of American objectives. It would be an exaggeration to say that Bonn's security policy and its pro-NATO dimensions were specifically anti-French. Still, to use the more positive indicator of support, it is clear that Bonn's choices furthered the interests and position of the United States and NATO rather than those of France. Yet it was no unmixed blessing to lean too closely on the American power complex. American concepts of strategic and political flexibility began to make Bonn wonder whether vital German interests were securely anchored in Washington; and De Gaulle's force-de-frappe planning was probably not entirely unappealing. In any event, the blurring of common interests among the NATO partners left Bonn with serious strategic and political problems, which necessitated painful choices among allies without allowing a fully satisfactory resolution of the security issue.

West German aspirations to political recovery were necessarily affected by these developments. In the early years of the Federal Republic, the pursuit of political and economic recovery benefited importantly from the international system's bipolarity, which provided the West with strong incentives for building up the Federal Republic. At that time, the efforts of the Adenauer Government necessarily focused on the gradual restoration of sovereignty, although political recovery had a much broader if less tangible meaning for Adenauer and those close to him in the CDU. The restoration of sovereignty was viewed primarily as a preliminary legal step, which would allow West Germany to join a fraternal European community as an equal partner. One must remember this distinction between the legal and psychological aspects of political recovery, because the legal manifestations of political recovery had been essentially achieved by 1955, whereas its political-psychological components were still an active aspiration.

As long as the Western alliance was not subject to divisive cross-pressures, the blueprint for a fraternal Western Europe and a "grand design" for a wider Atlantic community were entirely complementary. Adenauer viewed these two groupings as mutually reinforcing. But with the developing French ambitions for a "third" European force in world politics, and for a position of French predominance in this third force, both the smaller and the more inclusive groupings were exposed to abrasive encounters. These divisive tendencies—which of course were not merely due to irrational French nationalism but which reflected the divergence of real national interests—created difficult problems for West Germany's political recovery goal. With the erosion of the solidarity of the Atlantic alliance, Bonn's principle of close and loyal attachment to the "West," as a political and cultural abstraction, had to be applied in specific political contexts that necessitated choosing not only between the United States and France, but also between France and other EEC and WEU partners. For a Government that sought so self-consciously and deliberately to win the good will and respect of *all* its alliance partners as the prerequisite of psychological and political recovery, this situation presented a genuine dilemma. In particular, the crucial and sensitive relationship between France and Germany needed to be carefully protected from disruptive influences.

The primarily legal elements of the sovereignty gained by the Federal Republic in its early years were largely achieved with the support of the United States, in the face of French reluctance if not outright objection. But in the pursuit of the less tangible aspects of political recovery—Germany's return to the fold of the international community—the Bonn Government needed to make no specific distinctions among alliance partners when it expressed general allegiance to the Western cause. This situation changed in the middle 1950's, both because of the erosion of the Western alliance and because Bonn's concerns shifted to different aspects of political recovery now that sovereignty had been restored. The United States had run out of sovereignty payoffs, and Adenauer's ambitions for Germany's political recovery in the context of a Western European union necessarily had to be addressed to France, whose good will was the prerequisite. With the elimination of the Saar problem and the frictions over restoration of sovereignty, Bonn could concentrate on further cementing the Franco-German reconciliation; and reconciliation was symbolically capped by the friendship treaty of 1963. This entailed a tacit ordering of priorities, which British membership in the Common Market may have fallen victim to.

De Gaulle's exclusion of Britain from the Common Market, with Adenauer's consent if not his advice, posed a particular problem in the pursuit of Germany's political and economic interests.* West Germany's international economic policies tended to accentuate the divisions that developed in the Western alliance. By contributing to the economic success of the Common Market, Germany helped to bring about the institutional regionalism that was an important factor in the loosening of postwar bipolarity. Although the United States chose to give priority to political-strategic considerations and supported the EEC rather than EFTA, the exclusion of Britain from the Common Market was a serious setback for American policy. It prevented the intended relaxation of economic tensions between the EEC and other alliance members, and it vetoed the economic solidarity that Washington sought as part of its political "grand design" for the Atlantic alliance. British membership would have softened the outer shell of the EEC, and would have lessened the economic and political pressures that were building up within the Western alliance.

Tensions between Washington and Bonn thus developed on

* One hesitates to apply any longer the term "recovery" to describe Germany's aspirations and policies in the field of international economics. Whatever the proper label may be for the affluent conditions of the German economy in the late 1950's and early 1960's, there was no longer any incentive or need for the Western alliance or the United States to programmatically aid the German economy. In that respect, no direct connections can be drawn between the conditions of the international system and Germany's economic well-being.

two levels. The first, and probably less serious, involved an essentially economic conflict between West Germany as an EEC member and a United States concerned about its balance-of-payments difficulties. Secondly, American attempts to bridge the economic fissures in the Western alliance by sponsoring British membership in the EEC were repelled by De Gaulle with the implicit consent of Adenauer. Since De Gaulle viewed Britain's application as an attempt to solidify the Anglo-American foothold on the Continent, Adenauer's acquiescence strengthened Western European separatism not only on the economic level but, mutatis mutandis, on the political and strategic plane. In this overlapping of issues the Bonn Government was of two minds in more than one sense. Giving support to American rather than French nuclear policies seemed in Germany's interest in any case, and by doing this, Adenauer counterbalanced his support of De Gaulle on the political-economic plane. Bonn was also speaking with two voices because of the increasing opposition to Adenauer in the Cabinet and the Bundestag, caused in part by the general trend of events but also because there was considerable doubt that the exclusivist structure of the EEC was in the long run beneficial to German economic interests. (For example, because of its tariff restrictions, especially on agricultural products, some German businessmen tended to view the EEC as an obstacle to more trade with Eastern Europe.) This point of view was presented even by the Government's own economic spokesman, Erhard, the patron saint of West Germany's economic miracle. Aside from the personal hostilities that had developed between Adenauer and Erhard in the course of time, the controversy in the Cabinet reflected fundamental differences of opinion not only on the political aspects of Adenauer's Europe policy but also on its purely economic consequences. It is difficult to know whether the German economy would have benefited more from a more inclusive European economic arrangement than it gained from the EEC up to 1963. But this was the subject of serious speculation. In contrast with the pre-1955 situation, it could by no means be taken for granted that the political dimension of Adenauer's Europe policy complemented Germany's economic aspirations.

This raises the question whether the pursuit of political recovery was compatible with the pursuit of economic recovery after 1955. This is a highly speculative matter because the unquestioned economic benefits Germany gained through the EEC would have to be weighed against the unknown advantages that could have been obtained through a larger European economic union or free trade area. It is impossible to say whether Adenauer's Europe policy was directly incompatible with German economic aspirations: the economic and political aspects may no longer have been reinforcing, but at least they were not patently conflicting. Yet, as already noted, political recovery was by itself becoming more complex because of the erosion of the Western alliance. Adenauer's overriding preoccupation with a Western European union and a Franco-German rapproachement led him to support Paris rather than Washington or London, as was exemplified by the Hallstein acceleration plan and Britain's exclusion from the Common Market. There are thus two speculative sequences in assessing the compatibility between economic and political recovery: if the German economy would have been better served by a larger European economic construct, then economic interests were slighted by Adenauer's way of pursuing political recovery. If the German economy would *not* have gained substantially from a larger European economic grouping, then economic interests were not incompatible with the way Adenauer pursued political recovery, although there were tensions between the aspects of political recovery that focused on Franco-German reconciliation and those that were addressed to the U.S. and the Atlantic alliance at large.

In any event, in the post-1955 international system the goals of political and economic recovery were no longer as harmonious and reinforcing as before. The shifting of these relationships was further complicated by the fact that although Franco-German cooperation was the indispensable keystone to Bonn's Europe policy, other EEC members also had to be taken into account. The Benelux countries and Italy were on the whole not enthusiastic about a restrictive interpretation of the EEC, especially because this would result in an unshakable Franco-German economic hegemony and its attending political implications.

I have already noted the changes in the compatibility of political recovery with the goal of security. Because of the blurring of compatibilities between political and economic recovery, there were also shifts in the relationship of economic recovery to security. Bonn was convinced that for both strategic and political reasons Germany's security interests lay within the wider framework of NATO, but this conviction strained the compatibility of security policies with France-oriented policies of political recovery. Again, provided that German economic interests would in fact have been better served by a wider economic grouping than the EEC, West German security interests seemed strongly complementary to economic aspirations. This connection was not overlooked by some elements in the CDU, by important business interests, or by the opposition. The possibility that economic, political, and strategic interests could be compatibly pursued in a wider institutional framework of a Western alliance, rather than in the "little Europe" context desired by De Gaulle, held powerful attractions for these groups, and formed the basis for a significant, if perhaps tenuous, consensus among them.

Because of their continued lack of success in the post-1955 period, it is tempting to dismiss Bonn's unification policies as patently incompatible with the contingencies of the international system. But this dismissal would obscure the degree to which the goal itself underwent important changes and would prevent an examination of the shifting relationships between unification and other foreign policy goals.

The major unification efforts made by the Bonn Government after 1955 were not directed toward bringing about unification on terms acceptable to the West (for that there was little hope) but rather sought to prevent the legitimization of the established status quo in central Europe. Under the weight of necessity, Bonn had apparently accepted the fact that unification had become unfeasible in the foreseeable future, and that its remote nature did not even permit the formulation of a meaningful policy for its achievement. This lowering of the aim itself had important implications for Bonn's "unification" policy within the Western alliance. It meant, for one thing, that the actual function of the Western powers, especially the United States, Great Britain, and France, was limited to denying the Soviet Union and East Germany a de jure recognition of the German state of affairs. In a paradoxical fashion, to legitimize the status quo would have been to *change* the status quo.

This was not the only paradox in the unification issue. Bipolarities of interests, tensions, and power were not conducive to unification: that was the lesson to be drawn from the conditions of the pre-1955 period. But the nuclear bipolarity that developed after 1955, and its corollary political heterosymmetries, gave the nuclear superpowers a certain community of interests, which seemed equally unfavorable to prospects for unification. It was inconceivable by now that a show of strength could pressure the Soviet Union into allowing unification; and in addition, the sobering specter of mutual annihilation created an important Soviet-American common interest in avoiding cataclysmic war. This realization was forcefully demonstrated by the Cuban missile crisis, and found its symbolic recognition in the test ban treaty. However, any lessening of tensions or intimations of Western flexibility posed the threat that East-West conciliatory arrangements would be made at the expense of the German question. This was the fundamental paradox of the unification issue: without an abating of East-West tensions neither side could afford to allow German unification on the opponent's terms; yet an East-West détente contained the possibility that the German status quo might get not only a tacit but also a legal blessing.

Strategic aspects of nuclear symmetry posed an additional problem for unification—this one of an essentially psychological nature. For the reasons already noted, Bonn demanded a voice in nuclear councils, and aimed to reaffirm NATO's nuclear presence at the periphery of the Eastern bloc. Nuclear control sharing and a forward strategy would serve Germany's security interests and could conceivably strengthen Bonn's ability to restrain American willingness to recognize the status quo in Germany. But this Maginot-line strategy underlined militarily the division of Germany, even though it may have helped avert the possibility of its formal recognition. Such objections were in fact raised by German military planners with political sensitivities.[4]

If nuclear symmetry added to the unification dilemma, the relaxation of the international system's political structure was hardly more propitious. On the surface it seems that internal fissures in the Cold War blocs would have enhanced Bonn's chances to move the system toward conditions more conducive to unification. The gradual diminishing of Moscow's domination over its satellites and the emerging Sino-Soviet crises seemed to provide openings for Western probing actions, and the conflicts in the Western alliance helped to make West Germany a pivot whose support was solicited by both Washington and Paris. In fact, however, the Soviet Union's Eastern European satellites looked toward Moscow as the ultimate protector against any threat that a united Germany might pose to the territorial status quo in central and Eastern Europe. The unresolved German question served as an effective bond in the Eastern bloc, and symbolized an important common interest. Most likely, Moscow viewed East Germany not only as a crucial forward bastion, but as reinforcing Soviet control in Poland and Czechoslovakia. The Pankow regime was the shield of the Warsaw Pact countries. (On the other hand, it could of course be argued that the reunification of Germany would push Eastern European countries closer to the Soviet Union.)

In Bonn and elsewhere there was no lack of advisers and critics, who urged upon Adenauer a more flexible and imaginative Eastern policy that would take advantage of the breakup of the Eastern monolith. In particular, they repeatedly suggested a more flexible application of the Hallstein doctrine and a reappraisal of Bonn's adamant refusal to recognize the Oder-Neisse line. But such counsel assumed a genuine interest in unification on the part of the Soviet Union and its satellites—a supposition for which there was slight evidence. Since there was little reason to think the Eastern bloc would consent to unification on terms acceptable to Bonn and the West, Adenauer clung all the harder to his legalistic position, which would have been compromised seriously by shelving the Hallstein doctrine and recognizing the Oder-Neisse line. The apparent futility of political action made Bonn even more determined to keep its legal claims pure and rigid.

Western disunity also affected the German question in a way that gave Bonn ambivalent thoughts. To be sure, Bonn's leverage in Western councils was increasing because of the Washington-Paris split. But the unavoidable taking-of-sides in Franco-American disagreements carried unpleasant implications for Bonn's unification policy. Again, it is necessary to distinguish between the two aspects of the unification issue that began to diverge sharply in the post-1955 period: unification itself, which became an increasingly distant and unreal possibility, and Bonn's efforts to prevent the West from legitimizing the division of Germany. Although De Gaulle had recognized the Oder-Neisse line, Bonn had every reason to seek and anticipate the collaboration of France on the issue of legitimization, especially on the Berlin question. On the other hand, De Gaulle could hardly be expected to work enthusiastically for German unification itself. Walter Lippmann has argued, for example, that "the hard line that France takes about Berlin and the Soviet Union is founded . . . on a basic French national determination not to have to live with a large united Germany. At bottom the hard policy is directed not against the Russians but against those Germans who want to make an opening to the East."[5] On the other hand, the United States and Great Britain appeared less reliable in unconditionally supporting Bonn's aim to deny legitimization to the status quo, but could perhaps be counted on to show less aversion to unification itself. In any event, although the goal of unification looked as distant to Adenauer as to anyone else, he could not foreclose avenues of approach that necessarily led to the United States, because the United States was the only Western world power with global interests sufficiently far-flung to arrange the East-West "deal" that could conceivably result in unification. Yet here again Bonn had to fear that it was precisely a global deal that would usher in, or reflect, an East-West détente at the expense of Germany.

This line of thought held even larger implications. In seeking a sympathetic American attitude toward unification, the Federal Republic would need to compensate the United States by wholeheartedly supporting the overriding American aim for a united Atlantic alliance. But if successful, a united Western posture would hardly provide the Soviet Union with incentives for risking German unification. Furthermore, it must have appeared unlikely that the United States, in attempting to cement the Western alliance, would be willing to arrange, or even advocate, a global deal that would alienate such other alliance members as France and Great Britain.

Whether or not such speculations had any place in Adenauer's thinking, it is clear that the double aspect of the German question—unification itself, and the danger of Western legitimization of the status quo—were underscored by the fissures in the Western alliance. Short-run attempts to prevent the solidification of the status quo were incongruent with long-range planning for unification, although the distant nature of the goal rendered such speculations dubious and extremely hypothetical.

This circle of limited and at times ambivalent alternatives exemplifies the dilemmas that faced the Adenauer Government in its last years. The shifting and blurring of compatibilities among foreign policy goals confronted the Government with troublesome choices, but their causes in the increasingly complex international system were essentially beyond Germany's control.

7. *Patterns of Consensus and the Domestic Political System, 1955–1963*

By the end of the Adenauer era in 1963, the bitter and uncompromising contest over foreign policy that had divided the major political groupings of the Federal Republic since 1949 had given way to a significant, if limited, measure of consensus. As in the pre-1955 period, it was primarily the international environment, with its shifting restraints and opportunities for Bonn's foreign policy projects, which set the boundaries for the domestic political discourse on foreign affairs, and which produced a corresponding shift in domestic political alignments on foreign policy questions. Most important, the priority choice of security, recovery, and democratic freedoms on the one hand, or unification on the other—which had been the keystone of the domestic quarrel over foreign policy—had become largely a moot issue. Since 1949, the domestic polarization of viewpoints on foreign policy questions had reflected the tensions and incompatibilities between the goals of security-recovery and unification on the international scene. Hence, the inescapable realization that there was no longer a reasonable chance for unification, on terms other than those of the Soviet Union, partially freed its most ardent champions from their preoccupation and permitted them to assess other foreign policy issues on their own merits and with more detachment. The "great debate" over unification versus security and freedom, which had underlain all major foreign policy contests in Bonn, was largely cut off by the realization that the strictures of the international system suspended the possibility of unification for the time being. Among the major political parties and interest groups, this development strengthened and enlarged the partial and ad hoc points of agreement that had existed before 1955; it was further enhanced because important shifts of power within the CDU/CSU and the SPD increased the influence of the more flexible elements in both parties, and thus allowed a significant measure of agreement between them.

SECURITY AND REARMAMENT

In the area of rearmament and military-strategic policy, these shifts in attitude did not come about until the late 1950's, when it had become obvious that not even the most conciliatory overtures to the Soviet Union, as embodied in the SPD's 1959 Germany Plan, would elicit responses that could be interpreted as portending unification. In fact, the long contest over rearmament that had taken place before West Germany's accession to NATO in 1955 was intensified in the following years by the Government's policy on atomic weapons and its plans to share in the control of nuclear capabilities. The implications of the SHAPE atomic exercise Carte Blanche in 1955, which ultimately ushered in a searching reappraisal of the Government's security policy, had equally serious repercussions on the domestic political scene.

Throughout the prolonged and heated rearmament debate, which began in 1950, the Socialists had insisted that a West German military establishment's only value was to counterbalance East German forces. The SPD had argued all along that rearmament would freeze the division of Germany, and that both Cold War camps were trying to exploit Germany's power potential at the expense of German unity. With the developing nuclear stalemate in the middle and late 1950's, these objections were powerfully reinforced by the fear that rearmament and membership in NATO would increase Germany's chances of becoming a battlefield in a "hot war." In this context, Carte Blanche convinced the opposition not only that unification had been endangered by Germany's membership in the Western military alliance, but that the promised security benefits were hollow if not entirely nonexistent.

Nonetheless, the SPD's criticism of Carte Blanche was not based just on a strategic assessment of the deterrent effect of nuclear capabilities, or on the military implications of tactical nuclear weapons; rather, it focused primarily on the consequences for the civilian population in case a nuclear war should break out in Europe. The opposition accused the Government of keeping the German people in the dark about the realities of nuclear warfare, and caustically reminded Adenauer of his frequent arguments that it was precisely Germany's accession to NATO which would obviate the danger that Germany would become an atomic battlefield. The Socialists were especially annoyed by the prospect that German contingents would become NATO's foot soldiers, and were sharply critical of apparent American readiness to resort to nuclear retaliation in case of a Soviet attack. American threats of "massive retaliation" were viewed as particularly maladroit in view of the internal changes in the Soviet Union after Stalin's death and Moscow's insistence that atomic weapons be banned. In addition, at least in their public statements, the Socialists again questioned the efficacy of having a German army, since NATO seemed prepared to meet conventional attack with nuclear counterstrikes. As in the pre-1955 period, the Socialists found it difficult to arrive at a logically consistent viewpoint on the question of Bonn's military policy: on one hand, the SPD objected to the buildup of German conventional forces, but on the other, party spokesmen rejected the only possible alternative, namely, American strategic nuclear deterrence. The Socialists now argued that conscription would be unnecessary and that a small army of volunteers would fill West Germany's security needs because it would make no difference in the nuclear age whether the Federal Republic had twelve divisions or six thousand volunteers under arms.[1]

During 1956, the recruitment method and the makeup of West German armed forces became the major point of contention. The Socialists had on many occasions expressed concern over a possible revival of German militarism. Since this danger would presumably arise from a professional army with long-term service, it came as a surprise that the SPD spoke out so strongly for a volunteer rather than a conscript contingent. The entire issue hinged on the size of the German contribution to NATO. The Social Democrats' preference for a volunteer army stemmed from their objections to having a contingent as large as 500,000 men—a figure that SPD spokesmen considered a ceiling, rather than an obligation—imposed upon West Germany by her treaty commitments. The Socialists sought to keep the size of the German contingent to a minimum in order to reduce its adverse effects on unification; most likely, they also hoped for political gains in the 1957 elections because conscription was very unpopular and promised to be a profitable campaign issue.

Length of service and recruitment methods also caused dissent within the Government and the CDU/CSU. In March 1956, the Bundesrat confronted the Government with a recommendation for twelve rather than eighteen months of service time, and even CDU deputies, among them the chairman of the Defense Committee, came out in favor of the shorter term. When the conscription bill came up in the Bundestag in July, in order to insure its passage it did not refer to length of service at all. The Free Democrats, who abstained from voting on the bill, had already indicated their preference for a conscripted contingent, and the German Party also opted for conscription, although the DP's military expert had initially favored a professional army.[2]

The Government in fact now called for a reduction in service time, which, as noted in Chapter 5, caused a good deal of consternation among the Western allies. But at the end of 1956, the Government's announcement of its nuclear ambitions—which, from Adenauer's perspective, was a logical corollary to the cutdown of conventional capabilities—reinforced all previous objections to rearmament with the fear that West Germany would become even further involved in the Cold War. In May 1957, the first major Bundestag debate on the question of nuclear armaments took place, focusing on the military and political aspects of nuclear testing and the storing of atomic arms on German territory. The SPD condemned the arming of German forces with atomic weapons, and called for a comprehensive international agreement, combined with an effective control system, to ban and eventually abolish nuclear arms. During the summer, prior to the forthcoming elections, the SPD generally stepped up its campaign against German rearmament, and accused Adenauer of having sabotaged a bill designed to regulate nuclear energy used for peaceful purposes because he wanted to keep the road open for the production of nuclear weapons.[3]

The 1957 election, which provided the CDU/CSU with an absolute majority of Bundestag seats, was widely regarded as a popular endorsement of Adenauer's foreign policies.[4] After the election, the Socialists renewed their efforts to stir up popular opposition to nuclear weapons, and demanded that the people be fully informed of the consequences of nuclear war. Following the launching of Sputnik and the announcement of the Rapacki Plan, the SPD also called for an atom-free territory and military disengagement in central Europe, and urged the Government to refuse nuclear arms for the Bundeswehr in light of the new developments. Generally, the Socialists and Free Democrats endorsed the disengagement proposals that were being advanced on both sides of the Iron Curtain—the FDP itself had presented similar plans in 1952 and 1956—in the hope that these proposals would not only slow down the nuclear armaments race but also improve, or at least preserve, the remaining slim chances for unification.[5]

In January 1958, Adenauer and Foreign Minister Brentano went to great lengths to explain their objections to the Rapacki Plan, which had been endorsed by Premier Bulganin, but they refused to divulge more specifically what plans they entertained for equipping the Bundeswehr with atomic arms. By March, however, Government spokesmen were ready to defend their plans. They now argued that since West Germany's security depended on NATO, and since NATO necessarily had to be equipped with the most modern weapons owing to Soviet capabilities, supplying the Bundeswehr with tactical nuclear arms would be unavoidable in the long run. Defense Minister Strauss stated that although the Government did not really want tactical nuclear weapons, it was driven to this decision by the need for being armed adequately; and Adenauer suggested that if a major member of NATO did not possess weapons equal to those of its opponent, it would have "neither significance nor importance."[6]

The strategic and political motivations that had led the Government to reappraise its security policy found little sympathy in the ranks of the opposition. The March Bundestag debates on atomic armaments were the most heated in the short parliamentary history of the Federal Republic. Deputies used terms such as "mass murderer," "liar," "tramp," and the SPD attacked the Government's entire foreign policy and accused Adenauer of preferring to involve a divided Germany in the nuclear arms race rather than seek an all-German peace treaty. The opposition asked the Bundestag to resolve that the Government refrain from arming the Bundeswehr with atomic weapons, and to insist that atomic missiles not be stationed in Germany.[7]

The Free Democrats, whose political fortunes had seriously declined since the "Young Turks" revolt split the party in 1956, and who had been excluded from the CDU/CSU-DP coalition after the 1957 elections, had become increasingly critical of Adenauer's foreign policy, which they considered dangerously inflexible and unimaginative. The FDP now joined forces with the SPD and declared that although freedom had to be defended with all means available, the nuclear balance between the superpowers made atomic weapons for West Germany unnecessary, especially since the other side offered, with the Rapacki Plan, to renounce nuclear capabilities. Although the relationship between the FDP and the labor movement had been less than cordial in the past, the Free Democrats now joined forces with organized labor to attack the Government's armaments policy. At the end of March 1958, after an emergency meeting in Hamburg, the executive body of the Trade Union Federation (DGB) decided to organize demonstrations throughout Germany, and demanded that the Government hold a national referendum to decide the atomic issue. In April, the FDP parliamentary group and the DGB issued a joint statement that again called for a referendum on the grounds that most Germans were opposed to placing atomic weapons in the hands of the Bundeswehr.[8]

The Bundestag debates ended with a majority of deputies empowering the Government to continue West Germany's armaments program within NATO. The FDP deputies abstained, and the Socialists now felt obliged to make more dramatic efforts to carry the issue directly to the people. Länder governments were urged to hold popular referenda, but such attempts were stopped by a Supreme Court injunction in May; and the SPD launched a "Fight Against Atomic Death" campaign, which enlisted scientists, theologians, publicists, and politicians. The Socialists argued, with a good deal of justification, that the CDU had tried to keep atomic armament from being discussed during the election campaign of 1957, and that the people should now be given the opportunity to express themselves on an issue of such magnitude.[9]

No doubt the public was extremely concerned, and there is every indication that a majority was strongly opposed to nuclear armaments. In public opinion surveys throughout 1957 and 1958, almost three quarters of the respondents were opposed to equipping the Bundeswehr with atomic weapons, and less than 20 per cent were in favor. The reaction against storing atomic bombs and munitions was similarly strong.[10] Nevertheless, when the Social Democrats made nuclear armament the chief issue in the North Rhine–Westphalia elections of July 1958, and the CDU based its campaign on the support of NATO, the CDU received an absolute majority. But the inference drawn by independent observers that "a representative segment of the population had indicated that it will no longer oppose atomic armament" does not appear to be entirely justified.[11] Even though a large number of West Germans apparently opposed atomic arms on German soil under any kind of control, approximately half the respondents canvassed in opinion polls supported West Germany's membership in NATO. An even higher percentage, which had been increasing since 1951, wanted American troops stationed in Germany. Apparently West Germans, although opposed to atomic arms, were becoming increasingly aware of the complexities of defense requirements and were not prepared to reject German participation in the Western defense effort merely because they found atomic arms distasteful.

It is necessary at this juncture to briefly discuss the tensions that were developing within the CDU/CSU and the SPD in the late 1950's. By 1958, serious disagreements on foreign policy questions and arguments on other issues had developed within the CDU/CSU. A number of CDU deputies had become more and more restive under the firm personal regime of Adenauer, who tended to exclude from consultations not only the opposition but also the leaders of his own party. His authoritarian ways were increasingly attacked, and disagreements among CDU leaders regarding the course of West German foreign policy were aired more openly. Bundestag President Eugen Gerstenmeier and other leading CDU members found considerable support when they advocated a more flexible Eastern policy, a more sympathetic consideration of the Rapacki Plan, and other proposals for military disengagement in Europe. Tensions in CDU ranks were further aggravated by the conflict within the administration—particularly between Adenauer and Erhard—over the Common Market and the possible economic split of free Europe that could follow the establishment of EFTA.

These fissures foreshadowed the crisis that Adenauer precipitated in 1959 by vacillating about whether he wished to succeed Theodor Heuss as President of the Republic. Adenauer's display of cynicism and his power plays during that episode—which were obviously designed to perpetuate his influence on foreign policy in the event of his retirement as chancellor—had a disconcerting effect not only in political circles but on the public at large. For the first time a *fronde* in the CDU stood up against the chancellor, and, although it was fragile, demonstrated the degree of opposition to him that had developed within his own party. This marked the beginning of the deterioration of his political and personal authority.[12] After the 1961 elections, these developments came to a head.[13] The FDP had made a significant comeback—at the expense of the CDU/CSU, since the Socialists had also gained—and now made Adenauer promise to relinquish the chancellorship by 1963 as a precondition for rejoining the governing coalition. Fragile to begin with, the 1961 coalition collapsed after a year in the wake of the uproar caused by the so-called *Spiegel Affäre*. During this unsavory episode, leading staff members of the weekly magazine *Spiegel*, which to the Government and especially Franz-Josef Strauss had long been a gadfly, were arrested for publishing allegedly secret evaluations of West Germany's and NATO's military strength and efficiency. The arrests were carried out in ways reminiscent of Nazi methods, and led to the forced resignation of Franz-Josef Strauss, who had worked behind the scenes to engineer the clamp-down on the *Spiegel*.

The political repercussions of the *Spiegel* affair were only the symbol of a more fundamental and widespread restiveness and dissatisfaction among the coalition partners and within the CDU/CSU. There was general concern over Adenauer's inflexibility and his increasingly authoritarian and tactless political manipulations, and it became apparent that he was losing his grip on his own party. The FDP was finally persuaded to rejoin a reshuffled Cabinet after Adenauer had threatened to create a "grand coalition" between the CDU/CSU and the SPD; but while the Free Democrats were restrained for the time being, the internal cohesion of the CDU/CSU had been shaken fundamentally. Adenauer was a lame-duck chancellor and in 1963 could not even prevent the chancellorship from going to Ludwig Erhard—a candidate whom Adenauer had opposed and openly humiliated all along, saying he was insufficiently astute in international affairs and lacking in political acumen, vision, and experience. The CDU/CSU elements that were less committed to Adenauer's unswervingly pro-French policy and generally more open-minded and flexible on foreign policy issues had finally wrested control of the party from Adenauer and his supporters.

During the same period, the SPD went through an internal crisis of its own.[14] Ever since the demoralizing election defeat of 1953, which was aggravated by the discouraging showing in 1957, the SPD was rent by factional struggles. It had developed a "right" wing, made up largely of younger members who hoped to revamp its orientation and image and change it from a doctrinaire instrument of the "class struggle" into a broadly based party that would have appeal for a wider and more heterogeneous constituency. The changes proposed by these reformists not only affected policy issues — they favored acceptance of the EDC, German membership in NATO, and dropping the demand for the nationalization of basic industries—but also entailed a reshuffling of the party power structure. The SPD's "left" wing, composed mainly of older members and party functionaries, strongly resisted these pressures, and for a time managed to exclude such reformists as Willy Brandt and Fritz Erler from important positions within the party.

At the SPD's Stuttgart Congress in 1958, the tensions that had been building up for a number of years became a full-fledged struggle for control of the party. The contest was essentially between the party's functionaries—who generally supported Schumacher's successor, Erich Ollenhauer—and the SPD politicians in the Federal and Länder parliaments. The conflict, with its important implications for SPD policy, was not entirely resolved in 1958. But the Stuttgart Convention paved the way for the famous Bad Godesberg Program of 1959, in which the SPD jettisoned most of its Marxist ideological outlook and turned toward the party's more flexible "liberal" wing, which had for some time fought the functionaries' doctrinaire conceptions of domestic and foreign policy. The Bad Godesberg Conference not only dissociated German Social Democracy from Marxism, but solidified and brought out into the open the takeover by the party's "liberals"—Willy Brandt, Carlo Schmid, Fritz Erler, Karl Mommer, Waldemar von Knoeringen, and Herbert Wehner. The party as a whole went through a reappraisal of its policy stands, and by 1960 Willy Brandt had brought to the SPD's political activities a new style and vigor, which contrasted sharply with the lackluster image of Ollenhauer. Although Brandt did not become chairman of the SPD until after Ollenhauer's death in 1964, he was selected as the party's candidate for the office of chancellor, and the major planks in the SPD's 1961 election platform had been strongly shaped by Brandt and his supporters. The SPD was trying hard to create a new image, and although the party's electoral gains in 1961 were not spectacular, it seemed to have overcome its doctrinaire paralysis, and was obviously willing to reorient itself in order to offer the voters a "modernized" and attractive program.

Subtle changes in the Socialists' military policy were already noticeable at the 1958 Stuttgart convention. To be sure, they persisted in accusing the Government of having intensified East-West tensions and of having abetted Germany's division, and they called for a "democratic" defense policy based on the recognition that a reunited Germany should abstain from the military alliances of both Cold War camps. But while the Social Democrats still denounced a conscripted army, they also declared that the military establishment should be an integral part of a democratic society, and that a relationship of mutual trust should exist between the army and the democratic forces of a nation. By the end of the year, Socialist leaders had become increasingly concerned with the "estrangement" between the armed forces and the SPD, and expressed fears that the armed forces might come under the "ideological influence" of the Government, with the danger that the army would be turned into the propaganda instrument of one party. In an ironic reversal of positions, the SPD now called upon Social Democrats to volunteer for careers in the Bundeswehr.[15]

At the 1959 Bad Godesberg Conference, the SPD for the first time expressed a genuinely positive attitude toward national defense, and began to support a full-fledged German defense effort within the context of the Western alliance.[16] No doubt the change in party leadership and the hopelessness of the German question, which was reflected in the abortive SPD Germany Plan of 1959 (to be discussed later), permitted this open reversal of the Socialists' defense policy.

Step by step, the Social Democrats began to narrow the gap between their outlook on German rearmament and military policy and that of the Government. In January 1960, a party spokesman warned against oversimplifying the complexities and difficulties of foreign policy problems, and explained that because of the "impenetrable international situation," the SPD did not intend to question West German membership in NATO.[17] The entire style of the Socialists' dialogue with the Government on defense issues began to change. The previous harangues gave way to a more sophisticated exchange of opinions on strategic problems, and the SPD began to offer positive suggestions about ways to enhance the deterrence posture of the Western alliance. Ollenhauer proposed the development of a foreign policy on which the "responsible political forces" of the Federal Republic could agree, a policy based on the understanding that the SPD would no longer question West German membership in NATO and that Berlin would be defended at all costs. In June, Herbert Wehner, who had for years been castigated by the Government as a leftist radical, spoke in strikingly conciliatory tones of a "positive" stage in the effort to reach "the highest degree of agreement on the vital questions concerning Germany," and suggested a "joint stock taking" of points of agreement.[18] There was some hope that the party's new mobility could be exploited in the election campaign of 1961.

At the November 1960 Hanover Convention, which chose Willy Brandt as the SPD candidate for chancellor, the Socialists declared that Germany needed the protection of NATO, "to which she contributes in loyal fulfillment of her obligations," and that developments in world politics had proved the wisdom of changing the SPD's attitudes on foreign and military policy.[19] Even the issue of atomic armaments, which the SPD had not stressed very much since 1958, had apparently lost its starkest terror. SPD spokesmen now emphasized the importance of achieving a "sensible distribution of tasks" within NATO to ensure its maximum effectiveness, and underlined Germany's dependence on NATO's deterrence capabilities. The Socialists warned the Government not to pursue a policy that would deviate from NATO strategy, and rebuked Adenauer for giving the impression that Germany might plan more defense preparations than those provided for in the NATO Council's decisions. At the same time, Willy Brandt called for the strengthening of NATO, and for better political coordination in particular. Clearly, the Socialists primarily objected to the possibility of an independent West German nuclear policy, but were not averse to increasing German influence over nuclear policy in NATO councils.

After the fall elections, in which the Socialists had made some gains, Willy Brandt declared that "our nation has a natural interest in the fact that decisions concerning the life or death of our nation cannot be made without consulting our own Government," but counseled a "certain reserve" to protect the reputation of the fledgling German democracy; he suggested that the question of furnishing NATO with nuclear weapons should be decided on the basis of "political prudence and military expediency."[20] Early in 1962, SPD spokesmen again urged the meticulous fulfillment of Germany's treaty obligations, and supported the extension of the basic military service time. In addition, Fritz Erler rebuked Strauss for "going it alone and coming out with demands for nuclear weapons," which had served neither the interests of the Federal Republic nor those of the Western alliance. By now the SPD regarded itself as the true champion of NATO, and the Socialists urged the Government to resist with more determination the "separatist tendencies emanating from Paris," which would endanger the alliance.[21]

By 1963, the SPD even found it possible to express its sympathetic understanding of the problems Washington faced in trying to retain the credibility of the American nuclear deterrent through a doctrine of flexibility. Although the Bonn Government reacted negatively to the McNamara doctrine, Raymond Aron thinks the Socialists apparently understood fully that "the United States was forced to give up the doctrine of massive retaliation," and that

> European nations acquiring national deterrents—i.e., limited and vulnerable forces—will have to follow suit for identical and even more compelling reasons. Mr. Erler and the Social Democrats seem inclined towards this view, the practical implementation of which points toward Western reinforcement in conventional arms—that is, parity at all levels.[22]

In fact, the Socialists now argued that an effective Western deterrence system required the strengthening of conventional forces. They also called for German participation in the strategic planning of the Western alliance and a tighter integration of

NATO so that the United States, NATO, and individual members would avoid the gaps and overlaps in planning that a lack of unity might cause.[23] The Socialists had come very close to supporting the American position which necessarily put them in opposition to the separatist nuclear ambitions of De Gaulle. Apparently they were primarily concerned that De Gaulle would succeed in persuading Adenauer to place Germany's security under the protection of the French rather than the American nuclear umbrella, even though the Government was already on record as favoring a coordinated Western deterrence posture rather than independent national nuclear arsenals.

The Free Democrats, who had emerged as the real victors of the 1961 election and who had joined the CDU/CSU in the uneasy coalition of 1961, also began to recant, and rejected the go-it-alone approach they had toyed with previously. The 1962 FDP Düsseldorf Conference came forth with what amounted to an unconditional endorsement of NATO, and called for the closest collaboration between NATO and West Germany's defense planning.[24] In essence, all the political groups that were extremely wary of De Gaulle and a "little Europe" under the protection of a French force de frappe—the SPD, the FDP, and the liberals of the Erhard wing of the CDU/CSU—cautioned Adenauer to stay close to the NATO line and to resist French pressures for a militarily more independent Europe. Furthermore, the developing consensus on the major strategic line for Bonn was apparently supported by public opinion. Surveys indicate that by 1962 the public's confidence in NATO as a protective shield against the Soviet Union had significantly increased, and there was evidence that the popular attitude on the presence of American troops in West Germany was even more positive than it had been in 1958. Half of the respondents, however, rejected nuclear arms for the Bundeswehr, and only 28 per cent indicated approval. Nonetheless, the comparable figures five years previously had been 72 per cent and 13 per cent.[25]

On the whole, the debate over rearmament and large strategic questions had run its course. But it was ironic that at a time when Adenauer began to entertain serious misgivings about strategic developments and became increasingly uneasy about the flexibility displayed by the Kennedy Administration, his former acceptance of NATO's strategic guidelines was gaining the support of his most vociferous critics. By 1963, it could be argued that

> Today the Government is chided by the opposition if it fails to support the Western alliance and its leading power, the United States, or if it does not extend to them the proper measure of confidence. Were one to look for differences among the parties' security policies it might perhaps be found only in the fact that the Social Democrats place greater hopes on measures of arms control and therefore call for a more active participation of the Federal Republic in this field.[26]

POLITICAL AND ECONOMIC RECOVERY

Before turning to the political conflicts that developed because of the Government's policy on the European Economic Community, we must briefly review some of the critical responses to the Government's general economic policy. West Germany's increasing prosperity made it difficult for the opposition to attack the Government's economic policy on any fundamental grounds. Criticism was frequently directed against what seemed to be attempts to restore or preserve remnants of the old social order, but the Government's social policy went much further than the Socialists had expected, and their theory of the impoverishment of the masses collapsed due to the widespread satisfaction with socioeconomic developments.[27] In the main, the Socialists' criticism was limited to attacking the rising price level, which they attributed to the excessive profits of industry and the permissive pro-business attitude of the Government. SPD spokesmen viewed the rising wage level as an inadequate compensation for the reduced purchasing power of the Deutsche Mark, and defended the labor unions against charges that irresponsible wage demands had caused the wage-price spiral. Siding with Ludwig Erhard, the Socialists advocated the abolition or reduction of tariffs and the liberalization of import restrictions as a means of increasing imports and thus of lowering the domestic price level.[28]

During the 1957 election campaign, the Socialists were careful to point out that they intended to make no "economic experiments" if they gained a parliamentary majority, and the question of socialization and state ownership of the means of production received only perfunctory mention in their election program. By 1958, the SPD's opposition to the Government's economic policy had turned almost entirely from issues of economic doctrine to those of economic growth and an equitable distribution of the national income. At the May 1958 Stuttgart Conference, which anticipated the more fundamental and explicit programmatic revisions of the 1959 Bad Godesberg Program, the Social Democrats advocated a "free economic system." They said that this system could be created only "if we preserve as many forms of enterprise and economic units as possible, and if we keep the influence of the state and its bureaucracy within bounds."[29] The economic order that the SPD advocated at Stuttgart was distinguishable no longer in principle, but only in degree, from the Government's "social market" economy. The Socialists agreed that public control of the economy would only be necessary in sectors where competition was restricted, and public ownership was deemed desirable only in situations where other means of control were insufficient. Although they had continued to call for public ownership of the coal mining industry, by the fall of 1959 even that demand was dropped. They now suggested that the coal crisis should be attacked by controlling production and by organizing social programs, and that these measures should be taken in consultation with the High Authority of the Coal and Steel Community.[30]

In the 1961 election campaign, the Socialists focused on the need for a wider distribution of property and income, and argued that because of the Cold War it was especially desirable that the Federal Republic become the model of a socially enlightened economic order. A "middle class" policy, to be coupled with a more progressive income tax structure, was to improve the conditions for small and medium-sized firms and allow them to compete against big concerns. The Socialists called for a program of "suitable" taxation of big business and suggested that the proceeds, which were to be paid in stocks, should be put up for sale in the form of People's Shares. In other words, the SPD no longer emphasized the demand that labor be given a voice in the economic decisions of management, as it had under the much-touted "codetermination" program, but rather called for an arrangement whereby labor and low-income groups would serve as the "employers" of management in a stockholder status.[31]

This shift of emphasis, which eliminated the SPD's time-honored theme of the class struggle, reflected a general trend in the aspirations of lower-income groups. I have already noted in connection with the labor movement's attitude on the establishment of the ECSC that the trade unions gradually extended their concern with economic issues to issues of social respectability and equality, and that labor circles anticipated to gain on the international level the social acceptability denied them domestically. The gradual scrapping of the Socialists' doctrinaire attitudes permitted them to come closer to the labor movement's psychological orientation, from which sprang the effort to tone down the element of class interests in union demands. In the affluent setting of the "economic miracle" it had become somewhat gauche and embarrassing to advance economic demands in the name of "working class" interests. The preoccupation of lower-income groups with respectability and upward social mobility demanded that class distinctions be blurred and underplayed.*

This general economic and social background called for extreme caution on the part of the Socialists when it came to as-

* In February 1962, the SPD's economic expert touched upon considerations of this nature and stated that "for a period lasting several decades, we have been involved in an extensive and historical process characterized by a steadily increasing assimilation of the employee into the governmental and social structure. Thus, the employees (workers, salaried employees, etc.) are not only becoming citizens with equal rights but also citizens who enjoy equal respect and equal rights in all economic and social walks of life." SPD Executive Committee, *News from Germany*, XVI, no. 2 (Feb. 1962), p. 1; for a summary of the sociopolitical orientation of the Trade Union Congress of October 1962, see *Gewerkschaftliche Monatshefte*, no. 12 (Dec. 1962), pp. 710–17. See also Klaus Bölling, *Republic in Suspense* (New York: Praeger, 1964), Chapter 3.

sessing the implications of the EEC. During the Bundestag debates on the EEC in the spring of 1957, the opposition carefully weighed each critical step. The Socialists believed that the EEC was insufficiently integrative on functional levels and too restricted geographically, and they voiced the concern that German membership in the Common Market could further deepen the division of Germany. They pointed to the advantages that the EEC would give France, by increasing her export trade and by solidifying her relationships with her overseas territories, and they emphasized the disadvantages for the German economy that would result from the projected rise in the common external tariff. Erhard was criticized for objecting to the full equalization of social service payments among EEC members, which would have benefited German recipients, and for sabotaging the proposal that the Six should pursue a common economic policy.[32] Although the Socialists were already rethinking their economic doctrine, they were nonetheless attracted to the possibilities the EEC offered for some measure of economic *dirigisme.* Although the SPD and the Erhard group in the CDU shared misgivings about the exclusive nature of the proposed economic structure, they were on different sides of the fence when it came to assessing the value of common economic planning among the Six.

The SPD's position was a difficult one, and was subject to cross-pressures that did not allow for an unequivocal reaction to the EEC. On one hand, the Socialists had little interest in further strengthening a "little Europe" construct that would give power to the conservative elements in Western Europe and highlight the division of Europe and the split of Germany; on the other hand, it was politically risky to attack the Government's proven economic policy, and the SPD entertained hopes that the EEC could be turned into a supranational organization for economic planning. In the end, the Socialists announced that they welcomed extension of the ECSC common market beyond coal and steel, provided (1) that the inclusion of overseas territories for which other states were actually responsible would not saddle the Federal Republic with a colonial policy;

(2) that the border between East and West Germany would not become a customs border creating an even deeper division of Germany; (3) that the German tariff level would not be raised excessively, so that German exports and domestic price stability would not be endangered; (4) that membership in the Common Market would be opened to all countries in order to avoid a further division of Europe; and (5) that Euratom would exclusively serve the peaceful uses of atomic energy, and that property rights of all fissionable material would remain attached to the Community.[33]

Some of the Socialists' economic objections were shared by important German commercial circles. The German business community was far from united in assessing the implications of the EEC. One element saw great opportunities in exploiting a large "internal" European market in the context of the EEC, while another group, for whom Ludwig Erhard became the spokesman, feared the loss of markets outside the EEC that was to be expected because of the higher common external tariff—which would primarily benefit France. Nevertheless,

> A dominant element in the Federation of German Industries . . . backed the Common Market from the start. . . . There is in German business a tendency towards bigness as such, which has been taking the form of both horizontal and vertical industrial combinations in the Federal Republic, and this tendency . . . found a new outlet in the formation of powerful industrial amalgamations across Europe. Above all, West Germany [had] the capital to assure her a favorable position in the European combines and alliances that have been mushrooming among the Six.[34]

Some of the business groups that were less favorably disposed toward the EEC tended to lean politically toward the FDP. These groups were not as impressed with the political dimensions of a Western European union as they were concerned about the economic consequences of the EEC's restrictiveness, which, regardless of the open-ended invitation for other countries to join, seemed to portend that Great Britain and the Scandinavian countries would be excluded indefinitely. There was also the question of social security costs, which would increase as a result of their standardization among the Six, and which would add to the contributions that German entrepreneurs were making already. Furthermore, prominent commercial interest groups were suspicious of the Common Market because of its possibilities for economic dirigisme, and some opposed it because it included the loss of tariff protection. Agricultural interests were particularly alarmed by the threat of losing the tariff protection that had traditionally shielded them from foreign competition.[35]

The cross-pressures felt by industrial interests, and the fears of agricultural interests, raised some intricate political questions. For one, Erhard's supporters in the CDU/CSU, who were not overly enthusiastic about the restrictive nature of the EEC, came very close to the FDP on this issue, and the dividing line between the FDP and the CDU's Erhard group became more ambiguous. Agricultural interests had a powerful spokesman not only in the Bavarian CSU but also among some elements of the fragmented FDP, and moreover, they were being courted by the Socialists, who were seeking to overcome their traditional handicap in rural areas. These complex, overlapping, and at times contradictory interest calculations became even more pronounced during the late 1950's, especially after the establishment of EFTA. Again, the SPD, the FDP, and the Erhard supporters in the CDU/CSU—a somewhat incongruous "coalition" —reiterated their objections to the exclusivist nature of the EEC, and pressed for a less restrictive European economic organization. After the establishment of EFTA, the Socialists—acting as spokesmen for a conglomeration of otherwise diverse political orientations—warned again that the reduction of tariffs within EFTA and the EEC, coupled with the common external EEC tariff, would lead to an increasing alienation between the two economic groupings, and would, in addition, push up the price level in Germany.[36]

By now the SPD's international economic policy, and its political implications, were clearly approximating the American position. Although the United States had supported the EEC rather than EFTA for political-strategic reasons, Washington nonetheless favored a less exclusive economic organization, because an economic split of free Europe would aggravate American balance-of-payments problems and undermine the economic foundations of the political-strategic "grand design." The following remarks by Fritz Erler could well have originated in Washington:

It is . . . important to reach a reasonable basis for cooperation between the Common Market and the . . . EFTA Seven or Eight, or however many they may become. It is therefore important that instead of erecting a common high-tariff wall around Europe, we should make the trade relations with the rest of the world as liberal as possible. This applies in particular to the United States and to Canada, both of which did a great deal for European economic cooperation after the war and also helped us very much in rebuilding our own industry. We should not drive them from our markets today.

This was the subject of a conference in Paris in the middle of January, and it was decided there to improve and strengthen the organization that was especially successful in supporting European cooperation in the years after the war, namely the Organization for European Economic Cooperation.

This is progress of a kind. The West German Bundestag . . . agreed to the Common Market treaty in 1957 only in the expectation that it would be superseded by a larger community, which would include all the countries in free Europe. Reservations about a common import tariff were set aside in the hope that this tariff would be waived within a large European area so that intra-European trade would not be affected. The existence of two economic associations in Europe may have serious disadvantages for the total economic area of Europe, unless it develops into a wider association. The Federal Republic will have to guide its flow of goods into new channels; thus it will be forced to carry the heaviest burden, because it has greater obligations to the Outer Seven than the other Common Market countries have.[37]

The Social Democrats by now were not only echoing the American position, but found themselves in partial agreement, at least on this issue, with Ludwig Erhard and the German industrial interests that supported him. The most ardent European integrationists—the group around Adenauer, Brentano, and Hallstein—found themselves beleaguered from many quarters, including their own party. In fact after the 1961 elections one of them, Brentano, had to be sacrificed to FDP pressures as a symbolic gesture to prove that the Government would follow a broader European and Atlantic course. The Hallstein acceleration plan now became the target of the heterogeneous group of Government critics. Hallstein, who had previously been chided by the Socialists for his romantic *Europasehnsucht,* was criticized for ignoring the threatening economic division of free Europe and for creating faits accomplis that would favor the interests of De Gaulle but leave an agreement with the EFTA Seven to an indefinite and uncertain future. The Socialists prodded Erhard, who resisted the acceleration plan, to show more political backbone, and admonished the Government to revise its "cold shoulder" attitude toward Great Britain. The SPD pointed to the concern expressed by German consumers, industry, and farmers over the increase in tariffs and its effect on prices, and demanded that efforts be renewed to prevent the impending economic split of free Europe.

Erhard, who had led the fight against acceleration within the Government and who took the credit for having won the six-month delay, kept stressing the need for a less restrictive European economic association, and there is considerable evidence that he was right when he said German economic interests were solidly behind him. Although German industrial interests managed to view the threat posed by EFTA with a certain measure of self-assurance, they nevertheless expected reprisals from EFTA, and feared that a general increase in the price of raw materials would result from the movement toward a common external tariff.* Even the Federation of German Industry (BDI)

* See Leon Lindberg, *The Political Dynamics of European Economic Integration* (Stanford: Stanford University Press, 1963). In 1958 over a fourth of West Germany's exports had gone to EFTA countries, and it appeared that this market would be severely curtailed if Britain should gain preferential treatment under EFTA tariff arrangements. But Scandinavian tariffs were low to begin with, and Germany's location and traditional trade relations with Switzerland and Austria

and the Trade Union Federation began to see eye to eye on such far-reaching economic issues, and both organizations emphasized the need to prevent the economic split of non-Communist Europe.

Nonetheless, the German labor movement had much to gain from strengthening the EEC. The Common Market produced increased social security benefits, high employment levels, and a higher standard of living; and labor leaders were not willing to see actual and potential gains watered down by an overly accommodating expansion of membership. As already noted, the same cross-pressures were impinging on industrial interests. Although they were uneasy about EFTA, German industrial and commercial circles did not feel fundamentally threatened by Great Britain's preferred position among the Seven, and the benefits brought by the EEC were generally acknowledged to have been substantial. Trade unions, important business interests, and the political parties all expressed a generally positive attitude on European economic integration, but were worried nonetheless about its divisive consequences.

The Socialists generally considered Western unity inadequate and thought it was specifically threatened by the EEC-EFTA split. They now called for the "closest Western solidarity" on economic matters, and welcomed the establishment of the OECD and the possibility that Great Britain would join the EEC. They were careful, however, not to give the impression that the SPD did not identify with EEC objectives—as long as they did not preclude a union with larger membership. When the EEC decided to proceed to the "second stage" of the Common Market in January 1962, the SPD supported this progression, but at the same time urged EEC members not to aim at an "inexpedient autarchy" that might jeopardize British accession. The Socialists called for the further functional expansion and

---

seemed to compensate for the advantage EFTA might give the United Kingdom. This may have allowed the Government and German industry to face EFTA with fewer misgivings than the apparent threat to a major export market may have justified. For the Government, political considerations were overriding in any case, and the Common Market held sufficient attractions for the business community to allay its most immediate fears.

solidification of the economic community, which would be effected by the speedy amalgamation of the EEC, Euratom, and the ECSC, and for a geographical extension, which would be effected by admitting Britain and other interested EFTA members.[38]

By 1962, Adenauer found himself pressed from all sides to come out unequivocally in favor of Britain's admission to the EEC. He was opposed by a heterogeneous group, whose members feared that he would stand in the way of British admission to the EEC or at least give in to De Gaulle's pressures in that direction. But the congruence of viewpoints and interests among Adenauer's opponents was not complete even at the economic level. The Socialists wanted to strengthen the EEC's institutions and extend its membership, because they thought this would help increase the Common Market's authority over economic planning. The prospect of increased EEC authority was viewed with apprehension by some CDU and FDP leaders and their supporters in industrial and commercial circles. Nonetheless, elements from a broad spectrum of political viewpoints and interests combined in opposing EEC exclusiveness, which was advanced by De Gaulle and faithfully supported by Adenauer. In addition, these groups had shared all along a deep suspicion of De Gaulle's designs for a Western Europe under French hegemony. They refused to make gracious allowances for De Gaulle's manipulations, which seemed to contravene German interests not only on the economic level but, from their perspective, on the political and military-strategic level as well.

REUNIFICATION

Since the early 1950's, SPD spokesmen had insistently warned that the Government's policy of rearming West Germany in the framework of an alliance opposed to the Soviet Union worked against unification. As an alternative, the Socialists proposed to seriously consider a central European collective-security system, coupled with the military and political neutralization of a united Germany, on the assumption that only then would the security interests of both Cold War camps be taken care of, and the reunification of Germany become possible.*

The disengagement plans that proliferated on both sides of the Iron Curtain in the middle 1950's seemed to lend a powerful and widespread support to this line of thinking. To be sure, the Socialists were fully aware—as was the Government—that these proposals stemmed primarily from apprehensions about a German share in the control of nuclear weapons, rather than from a fundamental interest in German unification. By 1957, the Socialists' main efforts to achieve unification centered on suggestions about creating a military détente in central Europe by withdrawing or thinning out conventional forces in Germany; disengagement seemed the only way to remove Germany from the grasp of the two Cold War camps and thus allow reunification without upsetting the East-West balance of power.[39]

The Free Democrats, who had become increasingly disenchanted with Adenauer's inflexible and stagnant policy, were also willing to explore more fully the possibilities for disengagement. As early as 1952, the FDP had sponsored the Pfleiderer Plan, which incorporated features of disengagement; and a sim-

* In April 1956, Fritz Erler presented the SPD argument in considerable detail in an article in *Foreign Affairs.* After arguing that both East and West were attempting to achieve a predominant position in both parts of Germany, and saying "the claim that a reunited Germany should be a member of NATO is as much of an obstacle to reunification as would be a Communist demand that a reunited Germany must be bolshevised," Erler went on: "The view was expressed by George Kennan that the Four Powers would not need to go beyond committing themselves not to enter a military alliance with Germany. One obstacle to reunification might thereby be removed, but that would not be enough. Germany and her neighbors cannot find security by creating a vacuum in the heart of Europe. Germany must be prepared, if attacked, to contribute to her own defense with her own (probably limited) armed forces within the framework of a general security system. But she should not have been already serving in time of peace as a barracks for one bloc against the other. She might allow the West to install a radar line on her Eastern borders and the Soviets to install one on her Western borders. That would be no threat to either and would provide protection for both against surprise attack, as well as compensation to them for having given up strategic positions. By her free choice Germany would be a partner of the free world economically, socially, culturally, and politically, even though—for the sake of liberating 17,000,000 of her people—she would no longer be a formal military ally in NATO." Fritz Erler, "The Struggle for German Reunification," in *Foreign Affairs,* XXXIV, no. 3 (Apr. 1956), pp. 380–93.

ilar plan had been put forth by Erich Mende in 1956. The "third force" role for Germany had always been attractive to some FDP circles; disengagement not only might bring about unification but also might subsequently allow a united Germany to play the role of balancer in European politics. After the 1957 elections, the Free Democrats castigated Adenauer for his high-handed rejection of the Rapacki Plan—he had not even consulted the Bundestag—and called upon the political parties to form a Government under a chancellor who would be willing and able to conduct a more dynamic and imaginative unification policy.[40] During the spring and summer of 1958, at the same time as the anti-atom campaign, the SPD and FDP again pressed for disengagement negotiations; and at the SPD Stuttgart Convention, Adenauer was accused of aiding both Cold War camps in their attempts to use Germany as a military outpost—at the expense of German unity.[41]

Moscow's apparent willingness not only to live with the status quo in central Europe but to solidify it contractually seemed to require even greater efforts to suggest unification programs that might elicit interest in the Soviet Union. Moscow's insistence that the "social achievements" of the Ulbricht regime would have to remain unimpaired, and the Berlin ultimatum of November 1958, brought to light a Soviet attitude that was deeply disappointing to the Socialists. Speaking of the Soviet draft for a peace treaty with Germany that had accompanied the 1958 note on Berlin, Erich Ollenhauer remarked that "the general political impression it conveys . . . makes it unacceptable to German Social Democrats. The draft begins with the division of Germany, contains no provisions for a possible reunification of Germany, and is aimed at isolating Germany politically and militarily in Europe.[42]

These developments seemed to call for a final effort to test Soviet intentions, and in February 1959, Carlo Schmid and Fritz Erler headed a SPD delegation to Moscow to hold discussions with Khrushchev. Their exchange of ideas on unification made it clear that the Soviet Union was unwilling to agree to unification on terms acceptable even to the Socialists, not to speak of the Bonn Government. One week after the return of their delegation, the Socialists once more presented a detailed Germany Plan, which advocated a step-by-step military disengagement, to be coupled with the gradual political and economic integration of the two Germanies. The new plan offered Moscow concessions that even previous Socialist proposals had shied away from. It envisaged, in effect, the withdrawal of foreign troops from East and West Germany even without a prior agreement on the German question, with the exception that the legal and military status of Berlin would remain unchanged. The plan also embraced to a large extent the Soviet idea of a "confederated" Germany, in that it proposed the establishment of all-German institutions which Bonn and Pankow would participate in equally. The issues of free elections and the unhindered activity of political parties in both parts of Germany were relegated to the final stage of a three-stage integration plan.*

With the 1959 Germany Plan, the Socialists offered the last concession they felt capable of making: they would deal with the Pankow regime as an acceptable and equal partner in unification projects.[43] But even this extremely accommodating proposal found no meaningful echo in the Soviet bloc, and a year after its inception, following the negative Soviet attitude on unification at the 1959 Geneva Conference, the Socialists themselves considered it a thing of the past. In March 1960, the Soviet ambassador to Bonn reportedly told Socialist leaders that the Soviet Union's price for unification was the establishment of Communism in all of Germany,[44] and the Soviets' threats that they would make a separate peace treaty with East Germany further dampened remaining hopes for reunification. The Socialists did not immediately scrap their interest in disengage-

* SPD Executive Committee, *News from Germany,* XIII, no. 4 (Apr. 1959). Bonn criticized the plan because it would weaken the West's defense and because East Germany could sabotage it at any stage by not going on to the next; moreover it implied recognition of the Pankow regime, and the holding of all-German elections after the framing of the Constitution could lead to a non-democratic form of state. In March, Brentano said in Washington that no other stages of reunification could be considered prior to free and secret elections. See *Keesing's Contemporary Archives,* XII, 16782.

ment, but SPD spokesmen now saw unification as only a distant possibility, and called for retaining the confidence of the West while attempting to win that of the East, because "anyone who believes this double task to be impossible has practically written off our countrymen in East Germany."[45]

The erection of the Berlin Wall was the Soviet act that finally pushed the SPD toward the resigned and pessimistic attitude on unification that the Government had conveyed for a number of years. During the 1961 election campaign, even the SPD's candidate for chancellor had to admit that "the task of securing the free part of our country seems to have been forced upon us as topic number one, rather than reunification."[46] With this announcement the great reversal of the SPD's policy priorities, which had been in the offing for a couple of years, was now being specifically acknowledged. After the election, Brandt again asked that the German issue not be removed from the political agenda of the West, although it was "at present and for an immeasurable time to come, a hopeless issue," and although Brandt felt that "apart from surrendering our freedom, there is obviously no conceivable price for the reunification of Germany."[47] By 1963, SPD spokesmen admitted that the realities of international power relationships did not allow a fundamental change in the conditions of the oppressed in East Germany.

The developments that led the SPD to reverse its long-held policy priorities had similar effects on the FDP. During the 1961 campaign, the Free Democrats still called for a more "independent" foreign policy for West Germany and asserted that it was the Germans themselves who must ultimately accomplish reunification, rather than the Four Powers. As late as the beginning of 1962, the FDP proposed that Bonn should hold bilateral exploratory talks with the Soviet Union on the German and Berlin question, and some elements of the party were not entirely immune to Soviet enticements designed to raise hopes for a second Rapallo. In March, however, shortly before leaving to visit the United States, Erich Mende declared that his party had reconsidered its foreign policy stand and that it was now opposed to Germany's neutrality and to disengagement projects for central

Europe. The FDP renounced its previous suggestions for bilateral Moscow-Bonn discussions, and at the FDP's conference in the summer the issue of unification remained largely in the background; instead, the need to secure a liberalization of the Ulbricht regime to better the lot of East Germans was emphasized.[48]

Germany's unification was, at least for the time being, a dead political issue, and the FDP's Thomas Dehler, vice president of the Bundestag, regretfully admitted "the Germans' consciousness that unity is a historical task set for them has atrophied," and that the promise to work for national unity, embodied in the Basic Law, was apparently no longer regarded as binding.[49]

Thus the major impediment to a consensus on foreign policy had been overcome. The most fundamental dichotomy that had been underlying the contest over foreign policy since 1949, and the key choice that inevitably colored responses on other foreign policy goals, was rendered essentially neutral. The partial and ad hoc elements of agreement among political parties and major interest groups, which had existed all along, could now move into the foreground and coalesce into an informal and incomplete, but nonetheless significant, consensus. Lines of confrontation had become blurred, and equally important, the two major political elements that had symbolized, and given expression to, the previous polarization of viewpoints—Adenauer and the SPD—had become similarly "neutralized." Adenauer had been removed from power and was replaced by a more conciliatory CDU/CSU group, which had never been completely committed to his particular foreign policy program. The Socialists, of necessity, had transformed their party to such an extent that it also no longer upheld its part of the previous polarization.

Conclusion: West Germany as a "Penetrated" Political System

To a remarkable extent Kurt Schumacher's early prediction that West Germany's foreign policy would ultimately determine the content and direction of the internal social order seemed to be borne out by subsequent events. The necessities and opportunities presented by the international system loomed large over the formative phase of the new domestic order. Charting a foreign policy course that deviated significantly from the major guidelines set down by the Western powers, especially the United States, would have been impossible. As a consequence, the connection between international factors and the allocation of values in the domestic political system was very close. Although the Cold War was highly conducive to success in the goal areas of political and economic recovery—with the meaning and content given them by the Adenauer Administration—the patterns of power and purpose in the international system necessarily placed Bonn's major foreign policy projects in opposition to the interests of the Soviet Union. The reunification of Germany—which could be achieved only with the consent of both Cold War camps—remained the largest unresolved foreign policy task of the Bonn Republic.

Given the intimate connection between the major patterns of the international system and the evolving characteristics of West German society, external events "penetrated" the domestic political "subsystem" of West Germany to a high degree, making for a fusion of national and international systems patterns. In such a "penetrated system," as James N. Rosenau has called it, the national society becomes so permeated by its international environment that the traditional analytical distinction between international systems and national systems is imprecise if not untenable. Such considerations not only lead to the conclusion that cogent political analysis requires a readiness to treat the functioning of national systems as increasingly dependent on external events and trends, but they also suggest the need to identify a new type of political system that will account for phenomena which not even a less rigid use of the national-international distinction renders comprehensible. Such a system might be called the *penetrated political system*, and its essential characteristics might be defined in the following way: A penetrated political system is one in which *nonmembers of a national society participate directly and authoritatively, through actions taken jointly with the society's members, in either the allocation of its values or the mobilization of support on behalf of its goals.* The political processes of a penetrated system are conceived to be structurally different from both those of an international political system and those of a national political system.[1]

In elaborating his proposal with examples, Rosenau suggests that although

no other type of penetrated system can be more all-encompassing than a postwar occupation, it does not necessarily follow that all military occupations constitute penetrated systems. France during the German occupation of 1941–44, for example, would not be classified as a penetrated system since the French did not accept German participation in their affairs as legitimate and therefore resisted being mobilized in support of values that the Germans had allocated for them.[2]

In other words, *consensus* on the value reallocation caused by external events is a crucial element in defining a penetrated system.

For my purposes, Rosenau's definition of a penetrated system is not quite appropriate, since his formal definition focuses entirely on the direct and authoritative participation of nonmembers of a national system in its value allocation. This definition seems unnecessarily restrictive. Its stress on authoritative participation of nonmembers renders it strongly institutional, and it cannot accommodate penetrative processes that take place without the direct and authoritative participation of nonmembers. For example, the "permeability" of the modern nation-state as a consequence of developments in weapons technology[3]—a most important case of penetration by external events and trends —cannot be accommodated by Rosenau's definition although the perception of this type of penetration by national decision makers could plausibly lead to a reallocation of values. In short, penetration may take place without the instrumentality of direct, personal, or authoritative participation of nonmembers in this process.

A more useful and broader definition of a penetrated system would seem to be the following: a political system is penetrated (1) if its decision-making process regarding the allocation of values or the mobilization of support on behalf of its goals is strongly affected by external events, and (2) if it can command wide consensus among the relevant elements of the decision-making process in accommodating to these events.

Two important and directly related analytical consequences follow from viewing the international system and a domestic system as interpenetrated. First, the distinction between foreign policy and domestic policy diminishes substantially because few processes of value allocation can remain isolated from external contingencies. (This is part of the definition of a penetrated system.) The case of West Germany presents an obvious and striking example. This raises the question of how "foreign" policy goals are perceived and formulated by the decision makers of a penetrated system. As a result of the traditionally sharp analytical distinction between international systems and domestic systems, the question whether policy is made in response to domestic impulses or to international restraints necessarily had to be answered in one of three ways: policy is made (1) primarily in response to domestic impulses; (2) primarily in response to international restraints; (3) in response to both.* The third al-

* The literature cited in notes 3 and 12 to the Introduction is much concerned with the relative influence of domestic factors on international policy, but the various analysts arrive at different conclusions. For example, Rudolph J. Rummel tends to deny the influence of domestic factors, whereas Richard N. Rosecrance and Michael Haas confirm it. In the West German case the predominance of international factors is undeniable; at the same time, the West German polity could only become a penetrated political system, within my definition, because

ternative seems to come closest to the line of analysis suggested by the political processes of a penetrated system. But to say "in response to both" does not really fuse the two systemic levels—it actually underlines their distinctiveness. I have argued in some detail elsewhere that it might be useful to categorize goals according to three frames of value reference that national actors (or, more precisely, their decision makers) may respond to.[4] First, policy objectives may derive from *internal* referents. Such objectives do not directly depend for their formulation and realization on forces outside the state. The advocacy of a certain sociopolitical and economic order or devotion to higher living standards, natural law, and peaceful change—these are some examples of goals with internal value referents. Goals are drawn from *external* referents when their realization depends on the behavior of other members of the international system. These goals cannot be formulated or achieved without making specific reference to, or demands on, other states. Territorial revisionism, a crusading foreign policy, colonial emancipation, the advocacy of regional economic integration or of a fundamental change in the world economic system—all such goals emerge from an externally focused value referent because their formulation and achievement requires the specific identification of other nations as "targets." Finally, objectives may stem from *systemic* referents. These goals are highly instrumental because they are not based on tenaciously held value systems but are formulated in response to what national decision makers perceive to be the existing patterns of power and purpose in the international system. Goals and policies derived from systemic referents often reflect survival values of the nation. They are flexible because they change with shifting perceptions of environmental threats;

---

important political and socioeconomic aspirations of the West German subsystem were furthered by acceptance of the "system dominance" of the international environment. (It is interesting to note, however, that the *Primat der Aussenpolitik* has figured prominently among both German policy makers and historians. The term itself is attributed to either Wilhelm Dilthey or Leopold von Ranke and runs like a red thread through German historiography. See Ernst-Otto Czempiel, "Der Primat der Auswärtigen Politik, Kritische Würdigung einer Staatsmaxime," *Politische Vierteljahresschrift*, Sept. 1963, pp. 266–87.

they are frequently implemented by defensive armaments programs, alliances, and so forth. Systemically focused goals are imposed by the contingencies of the international system and represent the nation's "acculturation" to its environment.

In a penetrated political system these three types of goal referents overlap considerably. In West Germany, goals with essentially internal value referents had to be translated into goals and policies that made demands on foreign decision makers—that is, internal and external referents partially coincided. Inevitably, this meant that the internal value referents of some groups had a better chance of realization than those of others. Furthermore, in the postwar international system very few issues could escape the grip of the Cold War. Many nations perceived the system as polarized; their policies stemmed from systemic goal referents that reflected the Cold War tensions of the system. At the same time, because of concrete historical circumstances, systemic referents closely resembled external referents; goals and policies emerging from a polarized systemic backdrop required specific reference to other states or alliance blocs, and their implementation depended on the behavior of specifically identified members of the system. Consequently, there was a continuous linkage and extensive overlap among all three frames of value reference. This overlap may be regarded as typical of penetrated political systems, and is clearly illustrated in the case of West Germany.

There is a second major analytical consequence that follows from viewing the international system and a domestic system as interpenetrated: the factor common to both the concept of compatibility and the concept of consensus—their status as standards of feasibility—begins to coalesce. The conceptual boundaries between the international system and a national system are initially maintained by the application of these two concepts to the external dimension and the internal dimension of policy goals. This allows the analyst to juxtapose the compatibility patterns of foreign policy goals with the consensus patterns, irrespective of the degree to which the national system is penetrated. However, as the allocation of values in the national system becomes strongly affected by external events and as the domestic consensus on the new allocation increases—that is, as the system becomes highly penetrated—analytical concepts (such as compatibility) that relate goals to external strictures necessarily begin to overlap with analytical concepts (such as consensus) that serve as "domestic" standards of feasibility. In a highly penetrated system, the external operational environment extends into the internal domain, and the concepts employed for structuring the two environments begin to blend. In other words, it becomes possible to analyze systems of linkage between international systems and national systems by applying concepts that, although they originate from distinct analytical environments, are sufficiently isomorphic to allow cumulative propositions. In fact, the very notion of a penetrated system is a cumulative proposition that covers both analytical environments: the degree of penetration is established by assessing (1) the perceived impact of external events on value allocation, and (2) the extent of overlap between patterns of compatibility and patterns of consensus.

In West Germany, by 1963 the degree of overlap between patterns of compatibility and patterns of consensus was extensive. West Germany was more highly penetrated then than it had been between 1949 and 1955, since consensus on the acceptability of ongoing external strictures had been increasing significantly. International systemic factors had been predominant throughout; but as the patterns of power and purpose of the post-1955 international system became more heterosymmetrical and less sharply defined, in contrast to the patterns of the polarized postwar international system, they eased the way for a similar depolarization on the domestic political scene. The resulting measure of consensus, although partial and perhaps tenuous, allowed West Germany to become a significantly penetrated political system.

While there can be little question that West Germany had become a strongly penetrated system, it would nonetheless be difficult to say the case of West Germany proves that international systemic factors are in all cases the overriding ones, and that the influence of domestic factors is secondary. It would be ill-advised even to hazard general propositions about other penetrated systems on the basis of the West German case, although obviously the application of the concepts of compatibility and consensus would allow comparative analyses of penetrated systems.[5]

West Germany as a penetrated political system is unique for a number of reasons. First, international contingencies not only overshadowed domestic ones but in effect came to shape and determine them. Second, the West German government emerged from an occupation regime that left a lasting imprint on both the political structure and the economic structure of the new state. Third, the gradual restoration of sovereignty depended on external support and external regulation. This in turn necessitated a "policy of fulfillment" in the context of integrative European economic organizations and the Western military alliance. Fourth, Western European policy makers frequently agreed on major policy concepts, and American policies generally supported the European cause. Fifth, preoccupation with domestic economic welfare invited a policy of fulfillment, with its attending benefits, and hence sanctioned accepting the predominance of international systemic factors. Finally, Konrad Adenauer and his supporters made political choices that significantly complemented the strictures of necessity.

Adenauer was very conscious of the international realities that imposed such stringent limitations on West German foreign policy. He often mentioned that a see-saw *Schaukelpolitik,* balancing East and West, was neither possible nor desirable. To be sure, attempting that would have been preposterously premature in the early years of the Federal Republic because of the close scrutiny of the Western powers and the contractual obligations of the new West German state. Still, a neutralist Schaukelpolitik, like those pursued by Bismarck and during the Weimar Republic by Gustav Stresemann, did not lack supporters in the Federal Republic. However, there can be little question that Adenauer and his closest advisers were sincere in rejecting such proposals as sheer folly. Again, for Adenauer necessity was combined with choice. Both during the Bismarck era and the Weimar Republic, the Russo-German power relationship was much more balanced than it was at any time during the Adenauer era. Flirtations with the prospect of a "second Rapallo Agreement" stemmed not only from false historical analogy but also from overestimating the substance of the Rapallo Agreement. The bipolarization of power after World War II was in part solidified by the integration of the two divided parts of Germany in the two alliance blocs; there seems to be no way the Federal Republic could have extricated herself from the intricate and interlocking treaty provisions that tied her to the Western alliance, or avoided the incalculable risks of dealing with the Soviet Union on her own.[6] Furthermore, the whole idea of a Schaukelpolitik was fundamentally repugnant to Adenauer. As early as 1919 he had been involved in a plan to create a strong Rhenish Republic within a German federation, a plan that would have involved separating the Ruhr and the Rhineland from Prussia and joining them with the Palatinate. Had this scheme succeeded, it could have imposed a pro-Western policy on the Weimar Republic and prevented Stresemann's Schaukelpolitik.[7] Nothing had happened in the intervening years to change Adenauer's mind. His entire foreign policy program, and the new German social order for which it was to pave the way, was based on the unwavering conviction that the Federal Republic—and a reunited Germany—was to be irrevocably tied to the Western cause. For Adenauer, the resulting overlap of internal, external, and systemic goal referents was not only acceptable, but, to a large extent, desirable.

This is not to say that Adenauer was not concerned about the apparent incompatibility between systemic conditions and Germany's unification, or that he was lukewarm or cynical when it came to mapping out a strategy to resolve the unification question. For Adenauer this was simply a question of putting first things first. His overall vision of a desirable German political order could be realized at least in West Germany even under the restrictive circumstances of the international system; in fact, its realization was accelerated by the Cold War tensions that made the allegiance of Germany a coveted prize in the East-West contest. The political genius of Adenauer, who combined the lofty purpose of a statesman with the crafty pragmatism of a politician, was demonstrated by his exploitation of these circumstances and by his creation of the international foundations that allowed him to guide the domestic political order in the direction he favored. Adenauer's foreign policy program became much more problematic and ambivalent when the international system underwent important changes in the middle 1950's and when Adenauer found it progressively difficult to adjust to the new circumstances. The very qualities that made him perform successfully through the middle 1950's—a tendency to see political purposes clearly dichotomized, single-mindedness of purpose, stubborn determination—became handicaps when the relationships of the international system grew more ambiguous, complex, and fluid, and when sides had to be taken in the rift developing between the United States and France.

Because the West German political system was so highly penetrated, the gradual fragmentation of the Western alliance, whose harmony of purpose and concerted action was the prerequisite for Adenauer's overall foreign policy program, not only created fundamental problems for Bonn's foreign policy, but, as a consequence, undermined the cohesion of Adenauer's domestic support on foreign policy issues, even within his own party. As it gradually became necessary to choose either a "little Europe" construct—favoring De Gaulle's interests and close to Adenauer's most cherished vision—or the cohesion of NATO and the Western alliance—favoring Washington's interests—a long-standing incongruence of purpose within the CDU could no longer be contained, and ultimately led to the political isolation of Adenauer and his supporters. From the beginning, the Protestant, liberal wing of the heterogeneous CDU/CSU held values that grew out of internal referents somewhat different from Adenauer's, and it was not enthusiastically committed to the "miniature" Europe of the Six favored by Adenauer. With the United States and France diverging on military-strategic, political, and economic matters, the choices required of Bonn stirred the CDU into a full-fledged controversy, which was aggravated by the rebelliousness of an already restive *fronde* that had long suffered under Adenauer's authoritarian regime. On both the international and the domestic political scenes, these tensions were already noticeable in the pre-1955 period, even though they could still be checked, and were not as pronounced and divisive as they became in later years. Many of Bonn's recovery goals were achieved with the aid of the United States and in the face of French reluctance if not outright opposition; and the occasional uneasiness within the CDU/CSU foreshadowed the open rebellion of the early 1960's. When the circumstances of the post-1955 international system required unequivocal choices between France and the United States, with far-reaching implications for the overall political, military, and economic interests of the Federal Republic, the fissures in the CDU could no longer be ignored. Shifting systemic goal referents sharpened existing disagreements on values derived from internal referents.

Most likely, Adenauer was saved from becoming politically isolated at an earlier date by the doctrinaire rigidity and negative obstructionism of the opposition. The early recognition that foreign policy would decisively shape the nature of the domestic political order necessarily led the SPD to direct its main thrusts against the foreign policy of the Government—that is, against the policies that resulted in readily visible, practical benefits in the field of political and economic recovery. This not only failed to gain votes for the SPD, but it tightened the bond of the heterogeneous elements within the CDU/CSU. The polarized foreign policy alternatives imposed by the polarization of the international system made for a sharp domestic confrontation over foreign policy priorities.

This sharp confrontation began with the personal animosity between Adenauer and Kurt Schumacher, and culminated with the SPD's Germany Plan of 1959. At a time when the CDU/CSU was going through a most serious internal crisis as a result of Adenauer's cynical manipulations of the presidential succession, the SPD had separated itself more than ever from the parliamentary majority by proposing a unification program that was so accommodating to the Soviet Union it could not even marshal the support of all elements in the SPD. At the height of the "succession crisis," one commentator said:

> The CDU's automatic instinct to support at once the foreign policy arguments of the man who had just dealt it a severe blow—in spite of the party's rebelliousness and disenchantment—seems to be the immediate and necessary consequence of the procrustean policies of the leading opposition party. The more radically the opposition alienates itself from the "Adenauer state," the more it relinquishes the opportunity to exploit the fragmentation of the groups that consider this state their own. . . . All thrusts against the chancellor hit a void, as long as there is a suspicion that these thrusts are aimed not only at his domestic political regime but also at the core of his foreign policy conception—the insoluble bond between the Federal Republic and the Western alliance.[8]

The shifting of power patterns in the post-1955 international system—an important factor in the Western alliance's difficulties, which, in turn, exacerbated the conflict within the CDU and the governing coalition because it required taking sides with either the United States or France—had a similarly profound effect on the opposition, and was a major reason for the reversal of the SPD's long-held priorities on foreign policy issues.

From the beginning, the Socialists were handicapped by the gap between their internal value referents and systemic referents that became increasingly hard to ignore. Over the years, this gap narrowed considerably. After the abortive SPD Germany Plan of 1959, the "great debate" that pitted reunification against rearmament and German membership in the Western alliance had essentially run its course. The SPD realized that unification could not be achieved on acceptable terms in the foreseeable future. Thus, its preoccupation with unification was replaced by the concern that Adenauer would prove himself insufficiently firm in resisting De Gaulle's separatist tendencies, and that the chancellor might support French nuclear ambitions and De Gaulle's apparent desire to keep the Common Market "pure" by setting up exacting conditions for Great Britain's accession. On both counts, the Socialists' position placed them on the side of the United States and Great Britain. The opposition was now led to champion West Germany's wholehearted allegiance to NATO and the wider membership of the EEC: the Socialists in Bonn became the ardent supporters of the "grand design" put forth in Washington.

The Socialists' apprehensions about French nuclear ambitions and the threatening disintegration of the Western alliance were aggravated by the fear that the Bonn Government—and especially the highly suspect Franz-Josef Strauss—could conceivably join the quest for independent national nuclear capabilities. The SPD now saw the collective restraints of NATO as a check both on De Gaulle and on the elements in Bonn that might toy with the idea of mapping a more independent military-strategic and political course for the Federal Republic. The unfeasibility of unification, which dampened the Socialists' enthusiasm for military disengagement in central Europe, now made it possible for them to support NATO as a means of keeping a tight rein on the military, political, and economic separatism of De Gaulle and his sympathizers in Bonn.

The Socialists began to approach the Common Market with a similar purpose in mind. They not only called for a wider membership to avoid the economic split of free Europe and to counterbalance the influence of the "little Europe" supporters in Paris and Bonn, but also pressed for a strengthening of the Common Market's internal authority. Both dimensions—in addition to improving the chances for supranational economic planning—were expected to have a restraining effect on France and solidify the economic foundations of the Western alliance.

Domestic political developments intensified the pressure on the opposition to adjust values derived from internal referents and to reverse its foreign policy stand. The 1957 elections made it clear that the Socialists had not succeeded in translating the desire for reunification, and the general aversion to rearmament and nuclear arms, into votes for the SPD. On the issue of rearmament they were faced with a fait accompli; their desire to prevent the Bundeswehr from engaging in the political meddling of the Weimar Reichswehr, or from harboring the professional militarists of the Wehrmacht, required them to participate in supervising the Bundeswehr. This could not be accomplished with an entirely negative attitude toward the armed forces.

On the issues of political and economic recovery, the Socialists also had to shift gears. By 1955, the legal aspects of political recovery had essentially been resolved by the restoration of sovereignty to the Federal Republic. The opposition now focused its criticism on the exclusivist construction of the developing Western European community and on its anticipated detrimental effects on reunification, Cold War tensions, and the unity of free Europe. But the "economic miracle" had made the Government's socioeconomic program almost unassailable, and Adenauer had apparently succeeded in convincing German voters that economic recovery rested on the international foundations he had laid with his pro-Western foreign policy. The Socialists were faced with a troublesome political dilemma, since important aims of *economic* recovery were being realized in the context of the Six—wherein Adenauer pursued his version of *political* recovery. It became more and more difficult and politically hazardous to attack the combined political and economic dimensions of a "little Europe"; the German voter seemed considerably impressed with at least the economic results of Western European cooperation, and Adenauer managed to underline the connection between his entire foreign policy program and socioeconomic progress and political stability. The constant intrusion of the unification question became a serious political handicap, especially after the 1957 elections.

By the late 1950's, international developments—especially the threatening economic split of Europe after the establishment of EFTA—led the domestic consensus on economic policy to change, and brought the Socialists powerful support. The Free Democrats, the Erhard wing of the CDU, and the influential industrial and commercial circles supporting both, had from the beginning been somewhat uneasy about the exclusivist structure of the Common Market, and had even less enthusiasm for a "little Europe" with an ultramontanist tinge. The establishment of EFTA, and French manipulations to tighten the outer shell of the EEC, brought the opposition to Adenauer's Europe policy fully and unabashedly into his own party. In addition, many CDU parliamentarians openly rebelled against Adenauer's high-handed methods, and were already looking toward Ludwig Erhard as the next candidate for chancellor; hence, Erhard was not only the spokesman for the less restrictive economic integration of Western Europe, but also became the rival of Adenauer's personal choices for the chancellorship.

The Socialists now found themselves in respectable company in their opposition to Adenauer's pro-French Europe policy. Even more important, the political and economic considerations that motivated the combination of anti-Adenauer elements in Bonn tended to complement and reinforce the NATO-oriented security policy that these elements began to share. By seeking to give Western collaboration a larger framework, which would not rend the Atlantic alliance, this informal partnership was at least implicitly directed against De Gaulle. On the military-strategic plane, their line was followed by Adenauer himself, although with growing apprehensions occasioned by Anglo-American diplomatic flexibility on unification and the Berlin question, and because of the shifts in American strategy implicit in the McNamara doctrine. On all grounds—political, economic, and military—the partial agreements in Bonn leaned in a pro-American direction. Clearly, the diverse elements that opted for a united Atlantic alliance and a less exclusivist European political and economic collaboration did not have to face the dilemma Adenauer faced. The Chancellor's commitment to political recovery in a Europe of the Six necessarily led him to accommodate De Gaulle as much as possible, although at the same time he felt that security interests obliged him to support NATO and to prevent France from posing as the nuclear protector of Europe. Though incompatibility was developing between West German security interests and Adenauer's view of recovery, the conception of political recovery entertained by the anti-Adenauer "coalition" dovetailed with its NATO-oriented security policies. On most foreign policy issues, patterns of compatibility began to be reflected in patterns of consensus, making for an increasingly penetrated political system.

The gradual depolarization of the domestic contest over foreign policy and the developing overlap of internal, external, and systemic value referents was accompanied by the attrition of opposing political ideologies. To be sure, the CDU, and to a lesser extent the FDP, had from the beginning eschewed a precisely defined political ideology because it would only have been a handicap in appealing to a large and heterogeneous group of supporters. Still, Adenauer had presented a generally well-articulated blueprint for West German society, and had taken special pains to spell out how his foreign policies were to lay the international foundations for it. While not purporting to be an ideology in any real sense, this was nonetheless a coherently structured conception of the public good. The Free Democrats also based their socioeconomic and political program on philosophical foundations, primarily those of nineteenth-century liberalism and its laissez-faire economic corollary. The Right, although it was heterogeneous, consistently relied on the organismic mystique of "blood and soil," at times coupled with a strident nationalism with neo-Nazi overtones. The Left, preempted by the Socialists after the political and legal demise of the Communist Party, retained its Marxist programmatic outlook well into the 1950's, though with diminishing conviction and growing reservations.

By the early 1960's, if there was not an "end of ideology," at least there was a notable deemphasis of ideological aspects in the political programs advanced by West German parties. Especially after the scrapping of dogmatic Marxism by the Socialists, political parties tended to become primarily functional instruments for the attainment of power rather than spokesmen for political ideologies or consciously structured value systems for political and social action. There is little doubt that the more pragmatic politics resulting from this "rationalization" of the political process helped in blurring the dividing lines among the major political parties. The articulation of interests increasingly required no specific justification by, or reference to, consistently structured value systems; what Butterfield has called "embattled systems of self-righteousness" were giving way to a political dialogue with more modest claims to virtue and certitude.[9]

For the purpose of my inquiry, the "success-oriented" mode of politics that grew up in the early 1960's is important because the shifting patterns of power and purpose in the international system had a profound, if subtle and indirect, impact on it. The major political parties and interest groups believed that foreign policy set the limits of domestic policy and ultimately determined the kind of social order that would prevail in Germany; hence, the strongly ideological political discourse of the early and middle 1950's was necessarily reflected in, and reemphasized by, the contest over foreign policy. When the limits of what could be accomplished in the international system became more clearly visible and incontrovertible, the system forced a more pragmatic and rational assessment of foreign policy projects. The previously much sharper disagreements over foreign policy had frequently been brought about by competing political value systems, whose proponents saw foreign policy as determining the chances for realizing their sociopolitical and economic programs. The growth of consensus on foreign policy thus contributed to the erosion of the ideological content of the political dialogue.

The uncompromising struggle between the Government and the opposition during the first decade of the Federal Republic also rested on different perceptions of the international system and, consequently, on different systemic value referents. The Socialists constantly pointed to the glaring incompatibility between joining the Western Cold War alliance and earnestly pursuing reunification. This incompatibility undoubtedly existed, but it is questionable whether the Socialists' policies could have overcome it, given the stringent limitations imposed on West German foreign policy by the Western powers and the apparent designs of the Soviet Union. But since history does not disclose its alternatives, the Socialists' claim that their foreign policy program might have achieved unification cannot be conclusively refuted. Their foreign policy proposals rested on the assumption that although the conditions of the international system posed stark incompatibilities between foreign policy goals, they would nonetheless allow the Bonn Government to choose between mutually exclusive alternatives. This perception of the international system was patently at odds with Adenauer's, and was probably sustained more by wishful thinking than by a realistic assessment of the Cold War. The Socialists' determined commitment to unification, and to the kind of German society for which it seemed a precondition, most likely came from a psychological stance that expected incantations to yield tangible results. This perception of the international system became untenable when the Socialists realized that the Soviet Union was no longer interested in negotiating unification on terms acceptable to them. In time, systemic restraints were more clearly and widely perceived, and the resulting systemic value referents became more acceptable, even though they required adjustment of internal value referents. The concomitant de-ideologization of the SPD program contributed to this revision. It is to the opposition's credit that it engaged in this truly agonizing reappraisal, and turned to a more constructive participation in the making of foreign policy.

The impact of the shifts in the international system on the de-ideologization of the political process should not be exaggerated. A number of additional factors, perhaps of greater importance, combined to bring about a more pragmatic orientation in West German politics. Social barriers and class differences were diminishing, and the absence of a recognized ruling elite made for a more flexible and tolerant environment for social and political thought.[10] Affluence brought with it a certain hedonistic utilitarianism that had little use for ideological exertions, especially because the demise of the Nazi regime had left most Germans with an ideological hangover. The majority of voters seemed to prefer a policy of caution and stability, and the electoral system promoted appeals to the middle-of-the-road majority by penalizing small political parties through weighted representation of parties with larger followings.

Still, the developing overlap between patterns of compatibility and patterns of consensus reinforced and reflected the de-ideologization of the political process. At the same time, the content and direction of West Germany's social order could now be discussed without constant reference to the international system—precisely because the restrictive parameters of the external environment had become essentially acceptable. It is in this connection, however, that the crisis of political imagination, which resulted from the rationalization and de-ideologization of the political process, took on its most serious meaning. The shifting structure of the international system, and the wider domestic acquiescence in its strictures, to some extent liberated the participants in the political process, and allowed them to consider sociopolitical issues on their intrinsic merits. But the freedom to engage in dialogues about the nature of the Good Society without constant intrusion of extraneous factors could be put to little use in a political order that had shelved the quest for a public philosophy. To the extent that the conditions of the international environment contributed to this development, they helped to create a political-philosophical vacuum whose consequences cannot as yet be foreseen. External necessity had impoverished the meaning of internal choice.

Notes

Notes

Introduction

1. For typical examples, see Morton A. Kaplan, *System and Process in International Politics* (New York: Wiley, 1957); George Liska, *International Equilibrium* (Cambridge, Mass.: Harvard University Press, 1957); Morton A. Kaplan, Arthur L. Burns, and Richard M. Quandt, "Theoretical Analysis of the 'Balance of Power,'" *Behavioral Science,* July 1960, pp. 240–52; Maurice A. Ash, "An Analysis of Power, with Special Reference to International Politics," *World Politics,* Jan. 1951, pp. 218–37. For a critical examination of this approach, see Stanley H. Hoffmann, *Contemporary Theory in International Relations* (Englewood Cliffs, N.J.: Prentice-Hall, 1960), p. 47; and Ernst B. Haas, *Beyond the Nation-State* (Stanford: Stanford University Press, 1964), pp. 57–59.

2. See, for example, Richard C. Snyder, H. W. Bruck, and Burton Sapin, *Decision-Making as an Approach to the Study of International Politics* (Princeton, N.J.: Princeton University Press, 1954); and the early essay by Snyder, "The Nature of Foreign Policy," *Social Science,* Apr. 1952, pp. 61–69. See also Gabriel A. Almond, *The American People and Foreign Policy* (New York: Harcourt, Brace, 1950); Otto Klineberg, *Tensions Affecting International Understanding* (New York: Social Science Research Council, 1950). For critical assessments of this perspective, see Hoffmann, pp. 52–53; and Arvid Brodersen, "National Character: An Old Problem Re-examined," *Diogenes,* no. 20 (Winter 1957), pp. 468–86.

3. Harold and Margaret Sprout suggest that "in analyzing a particular outcome, performance, or state of affairs, it is generally possible to identify certain elements of the total environment that appear to be strategic (that is, very immediate and important). These specific elements constitute the *operational* environment of the actor in that situation. The operational environment (the factors which an outside observer judges to be relevant and significant in explaining an event or state of affairs) should be distinguished from the environment as it appears to the actor in the situation. His image of reality we shall call his *psychological* environment." *Foundations of International Politics* (Princeton, N.J.: Van Nostrand, 1962), pp. 46–47; italics in the text. "How one draws the line between unit and milieu also has practical as well as purely analytic consequences, depending on whether the focus is on *psychological* behavior or on achievement or accomplishment as measured in terms of *capabilities.*" *The Ecological Perspective on Human Affairs, With Special Reference to International Politics* (Princeton, N.J.: Princeton University Press, 1965), p. 41; italics in the text.

For a perceptive examination of these two levels of analysis and their methodological implications, see J. David Singer, "The Level-of-Analysis Problem in International Relations," *World Politics*, Oct. 1961, pp. 77–92. A "three-level" analysis is presented by Kenneth N. Waltz, *Man, the State, and War* (New York: Columbia University Press, 1959); and a "six-level" set of variables is proposed by Robert C. North *et al.*, *Content Analysis: A Handbook with Applications for the Study of International Crisis* (Evanston, Ill.: Northwestern University Press, 1963), pp. 5–7. See also Arnold Wolfers, *Discord and Collaboration* (Baltimore, Md.: Johns Hopkins Press, 1962), Chapter 3; George Liska, "Continuity and Change in International Systems," *World Politics*, Oct. 1963, pp. 118–36; Odd Ramsoy, *Social Groups as System and Subsystem* (New York: Free Press of Glencoe, 1963); Raymond Aron, *Introduction à la philosophie de l'histoire* (Paris: Gallimard, 1948), esp. pp. 227ff.

For admirable studies that combine both systemic and subsystemic perspectives, see Richard N. Rosecrance, *Action and Reaction in World Politics* (Boston: Little, Brown, 1963), and Adda B. Bozeman, *Politics and Culture in International History* (Princeton, N.J.: Princeton University Press, 1960).

4. See Wolfers, pp. 3–24; and Wolfram F. Hanrieder, "Actor Objectives and International Systems," *Journal of Politics*, Feb. 1965, pp. 109–32.

5. For a full treatment of this issue and a critical review of the relevant literature, see James N. Rosenau, "Pre-theories and Theories of Foreign Policy," in R. Barry Farrell, ed., *Approaches to Comparative and International Politics* (Evanston, Ill.: Northwestern University Press, 1966), pp. 27–92.

6. See Philip E. Mosely, "Research on Foreign Policy," Brookings Dedication Lectures, *Research for Public Policy* (Washington, D.C.: The Brookings Institution, 1961), pp. 43–72; Robert C. Good, "State-Building as a Determinant of Foreign Policy in the New States," in Laurence W. Martin, ed., *Neutralism and Nonalignment* (New York: Praeger, 1962), pp. 3–12; Fred W. Riggs, "The Theory of Developing Politics," *World Politics*, Oct. 1963, pp. 147–71.

7. See Ernst B. Haas's *Beyond the Nation-State*, his *The Uniting of Europe* (Stanford: Stanford University Press, 1959), his *Consensus Formation in the Council of Europe* (Berkeley: University of California Press, 1960), and his "Regionalism, Functionalism, and Universal International Organization," *World Politics*, Jan. 1956, pp. 238–63. See also Leon Lindberg, *The Political Dynamics of European Economic Integration* (Stanford: Stanford University Press, 1963); Amitai Etzioni, "The Dialectics of Supranational Unification," *American Political Science Review*, LVI (Dec. 1962), 927–35, and "The Epigenesis of Political Communities at the International Level," *American Journal of Sociology*, LXVIII (Jan. 1963), 407–21; Karl Deutsch *et al.*, *Political Community and the North Atlantic Area* (Princeton, N.J.: Princeton University Press, 1957).

8. See Leonard Binder, "The Middle East as a Subordinate International System," *World Politics*, Apr. 1958, pp. 408–29; Michael Brecher, "International Relations and Asian Studies: The Subordinate State System of Southern Asia," *World Politics*, Jan. 1963, pp. 213–35; George Modelski,

"International Relations and Area Studies: The Case of South-East Asia," *International Relations,* Apr. 1961, pp. 143–55; and *The Communist International System* (Princeton, N.J.: Center of International Studies, Princeton University, Research Monograph no. 9, 1960); Thomas Hodgkin, "The New West-African State System," *University of Toronto Quarterly,* Oct. 1961, pp. 74–82; Richard L. Walker, *The Multi-State System of Ancient China* (Hamden, Conn.: Shoe String Press, 1953).

9. John H. Herz, *International Politics in the Atomic Age* (New York: Columbia University Press, 1959) esp. Chapter 6; see also Edward Hallett Carr, *Nationalism and After* (London: Macmillan, 1945).

10. See Rosenau (*op. cit.* n. 5), pp. 63–65.

11. James N. Rosenau, ed., *International Politics and Foreign Policy* (New York: Free Press of Glencoe, 1961); esp. the Introduction and Part 1.

12. In addition to the studies already mentioned, see the following: Fred W. Riggs, "International Relations as a Prismatic System," *World Politics,* Oct. 1961, pp. 144–81; Chadwick F. Alger, "Comparison of Intranational and International Politics," *American Political Science Review,* LVII (1963), 406–19; Roger D. Masters, "World Politics as a Primitive Political System," *World Politics,* July 1964, pp. 595–619; Bruce M. Russett, "Toward a Model of Competitive International Politics," *Journal of Politics,* May 1963, pp. 226–47; Rudolph J. Rummel, "Dimensions of Conflict Behavior within and between Nations," *General Systems,* VIII (1963), 1–50; Michael Haas, "Some Societal Correlates of International Political Behavior" (Ph.D. Dissertation, Stanford University, 1964); Raymond Tanter, "Dimensions of Conflict Behavior Within and Between Nations, 1958–1960," *Journal of Conflict Resolution,* X (1966), 41–64; William H. Riker, *The Theory of Political Coalitions* (New Haven, Conn.: Yale University Press, 1962), esp. Chapter 9; James N. Rosenau, ed., *International Aspects of Civil Strife* (Princeton, N.J.: Princeton University Press, 1964); Bruce M. Russett, *Trends in World Politics* (New York: Macmillan, 1965), esp. Chapter 4; Otto Klineberg, "Intergroup Relations and International Relations," in Muzafer Sherif, ed., *Intergroup Relations and Leadership: Approaches and Research in Industrial, Ethnic, Cultural, and Political Areas* (New York: Wiley, 1962), pp. 174–76; Raymond W. Mack and Richard C. Snyder, "The Analysis of Social Conflict—Toward an Overview and Synthesis," *Journal of Conflict Resolution,* I (1957), 212–48; J. David Singer in his concluding remarks in Singer, ed., *Human Behavior and International Politics* (Chicago: Rand McNally, 1965), pp. 453–57.

13. Kurt Schumacher, "Die Staatsgewalt geht von den Besatzungsmächten aus" (SPD pamphlet, n.d.), p. 3.

Chapter one

1. For extensive treatments, see John F. Golay, *The Founding of the Federal Republic of Germany* (Chicago: University of Chicago Press, 1958); Peter H. Merkl, *The Origin of the West German Republic* (New York: Oxford University Press, 1963); Alfred Grosser, *The Colossus Again* (New York: Praeger, 1955); Norbert Toennies, *Der Staat aus dem Nichts*

(Stuttgart: Constantin, 1954); Kurt Zentner, *Aufstieg aus dem Nichts, 1945–1953* (Cologne: Kiepenheuer & Witsch, 1953), 2 vols. On Western occupation policy, see Lucius D. Clay, *Decision in Germany* (Garden City, N.Y.: Doubleday, 1950); W. Friedmann, *The Allied Military Government of Germany* (London: Stevens & Sons, 1947); Edward H. Litchfield *et al.*, *Governing Postwar Germany* (Ithaca, N.Y.: Cornell University Press, 1953): Harold Zink, *American Military Government in Germany* (New York: Macmillan, 1947); Harold Zink, *The United States in Germany* (New York: Van Nostrand, 1957); James K. Pollock and James H. Meisel, *Germany under Occupation: Illustrative Materials and Documents* (Ann Arbor, Mich.: Wahr, 1947). For developments in the Soviet-occupied zone, see J. P. Nettl, *The Eastern Zone and Soviet Policy in Germany, 1945–1950* (London: Oxford University Press, 1951); Horst Duhnke, *Stalinismus in Deutschland, die Geschichte der sowjetischen Besatzungszone* (Cologne: Verlag für Politik und Wirtschaft, 1955).

2. Friedmann, *Allied Military*, p. 270.

3. Grosser, *The Colossus Again*, Chapter 2. For a biting attack on the denazification program, see the novel *The Questionnaire*, by Ernst von Salomon (Garden City, N.Y.: Doubleday, 1955).

4. Clay, *Decision in Germany*, Chapter 22; Richard Hiscocks, *Democracy in Germany* (New York: Oxford University Press, 1957), pp. 38–49.

5. Clay, Chapter 22.

6. Edgar McInnis, "The Search for a Settlement," in Edgar McInnis, Richard Hiscocks, and Robert Spencer, *The Shaping of Postwar Germany* (New York: Praeger, 1960), p. 63; Duhnke, *Stalinismus, passim.*

7. U.S. Senate Committee on Foreign Relations, *Documents on Germany, 1944–1961* (Washington, D.C., 1961), p. 42.

8. Zink, *U.S. in Germany*, Chapters 16–19; Clay, *Decision*, Chapters 10, 11, and 14; for an extensive statistical presentation, see *Germany Reports* (Press and Information Office of the Federal Republic of Germany, 1955), pp. 281–92.

9. Henry C. Wallich, *Mainsprings of the German Revival* (New Haven, Conn.: Yale University Press, 1955), pp. 230–35.

10. See Nicholas Balabkins, *Germany Under Direct Controls, Economic Aspects of Industrial Disarmament, 1945–1948* (New Brunswick, N.J.: Rutgers University Press, 1964).

11. For the best material on the Saar, see Jacques Freymond, *The Saar Conflict, 1945–1955* (New York: Praeger, 1960); F. Roy Willis, *The French in Germany, 1945–1949* (Stanford: Stanford University Press, 1962); Per Fischer, *Die Saar zwischen Deutschland und Frankreich* (Frankfurt a. M.: Metzner, 1959).

12. As quoted by Freymond, p. 16.

13. U.S. Senate, *Documents on Germany*, pp. 35–42; James F. Byrnes, *Speaking Frankly* (New York: Harper, 1947), pp. 170–95; Clay, *Decision*, pp. 132–33; Freymond, p. 22 and pp. 34–35; Fischer, pp. 47–54; Ernst Deuerlein, *Die Einheit Deutschlands* (Frankfurt a. M.: Metzner, 1957), pp. 133–34.

14. Fischer, pp. 57–58; American reservations about French policy persisted, however; see U.S. Department of State, "The Present Status of the Saar," *Documents and State Papers,* I, no. 7 (Oct. 1948), pp. 435–50.

15. Deuerlein, pp. 22–97; Dwight D. Eisenhower, *Crusade in Europe* (Garden City, N.Y.: Doubleday, 1948), pp. 218, 431; Philip E. Mosely, "The Dismemberment of Germany," *Foreign Affairs,* XXVIII, no. 3 (1950), pp. 487–98.

16. Winston Churchill, *The Hinge of Fate* (Boston: Houghton Mifflin, 1950), pp. 710–11, and *Closing the Ring* (Boston: Houghton Mifflin, 1951), pp. 401–2, 406; Deuerlein, *Einheit,* pp. 93–102; U.S. Senate, *Documents on Germany,* pp. 12, 24–35.

17. *Documents on Germany,* pp. 14–15, 18.

18. *Ibid.,* pp. 43–51; Clay, *Decision,* Chapters 7, 8, and 9; Zink, *U.S. in Germany,* Chapters 6 and 7; Deuerlein, *Einheit,* pp. 138–47.

19. Clay, pp. 355–63.

20. *Ibid.,* Chapter 19.

21. For full accounts of the Oder-Neisse settlement, see Wolfgang Wagner, *Die Entstehung der Oder-Neisse Linie* (Stuttgart: Brentano, 1953); Elizabeth Wiskemann, *Germany's Eastern Neighbours* (New York: Oxford University Press, 1956); esp. Chapter 9; Zoltan M. Szaz, *Germany's Eastern Frontiers* (Chicago: Regnery, 1960); Chapters 5, 6, and 8.

Chapter two

1. For concise historical treatments, see John Lukacs, *A History of the Cold War* (Garden City, N.Y.: Doubleday, 1961); Kenneth Ingram, *History of the Cold War* (London: Darwen Finlayson, 1955); Evan Luard, ed., *The Cold War: A Re-appraisal* (New York: Praeger, 1964); John Spanier, *American Foreign Policy Since World War II* (New York: Praeger, 1960), esp. Chapters 2 and 3.

More tightly structured, "systemic" accounts are presented in Morton A. Kaplan, *System and Process in International Politics* (New York: Wiley, 1957), esp. pp. 36–43, 117–20; Richard N. Rosecrance, *Action and Reaction in World Politics* (Boston: Little, Brown, 1963), esp. Chapter 10, pp. 261–67; Morton A. Kaplan, "Bipolarity in a Revolutionary Age," in Kaplan, ed., *The Revolution in World Politics* (New York: Wiley, 1962), Chapter 12.

2. See Daniel Bell, "Ten Theories in Search of Reality: The Prediction of Soviet Behavior," a chapter in his *The End of Ideology* (New York: Crowell-Collier, 1961), pp. 315–53.

3. For some speculations on Soviet intentions, see Cyril E. Black and Frederick J. Yeager, "The USSR and NATO," in Klaus Knorr, ed., *NATO and American Security* (Princeton, N.J.: Princeton University Press, 1959), Chapter 3; John Strachey, *On the Prevention of War* (New York: St Martin's Press, 1963), Chapter 14; H. S. Dinerstein, *War and the Soviet Union* (New York: Praeger, 1962).

4. See Raymond Dennett and Robert K. Turner, eds., *Documents on American Foreign Relations,* XII (Princeton, N.J.: Princeton University Press, 1951), Chapter 14.

5. Beate Ruhm von Oppen, ed., *Documents on Germany under Occupation, 1945–1954* (London: Oxford University Press, 1955), p. 440.

6. See Lord Ismay, *NATO, The First Five Years* (Bosch-Utrecht, n.d.).

7. Roger Hilsman, "NATO: The Developing Strategic Context," in Knorr (*op. cit.* n. 3), esp. pp. 14–15.

8. Ismay, p. 47.

9. See Alastair Buchan and Philip Windsor, *Arms and Stability in Europe* (New York: Praeger, 1963), p. 34.

10. F. W. Mulley, *The Politics of Western Defense* (New York: Praeger, 1962), esp. p. 122.

11. *Department of State Bulletin,* XXXII, no. 810 (Jan. 3, 1955), p. 10.

12. Hilsman (*op. cit.* n. 7), pp. 24–26.

13. See Gordon A. Craig, "NATO and the New German Army," in William W. Kaufmann, ed., *Military Policy and National Security* (Princeton, N. J.: Princeton University Press, 1956), pp. 219, 224–25.

14. Buchan and Windsor, p. 38.

15. See Edgar S. Furniss, Jr., *France, Troubled Ally* (New York: Harper, 1960); and Daniel Lerner and Raymond Aron, eds., *France Defeats EDC* (New York: Praeger, 1957). For a full account of the entire complex of Franco-German relations, see F. Roy Willis, *France, Germany, and the New Europe* (Stanford: Stanford University Press, 1965).

16. James P. Warburg, *Germany, Key to Peace* (Cambridge, Mass.: Harvard University Press, 1953), p. 184.

17. Oppen, *Documents on Germany,* pp. 562–63.

18. Edgar McInnis, Richard Hiscocks, and Robert Spencer, *The Shaping of Postwar Germany* (New York: Praeger, 1960), p. 133.

19. For the best general account, see Henry C. Wallich, *Mainsprings of the German Revival* (New Haven, Conn.: Yale University Press, 1955); also Horst Mendershausen, *Two Postwar Recoveries of the German Economy* (Amsterdam: North-Holland, 1954).

20. Wallich, p. 17. See also Frederick G. Reuss, *Fiscal Policy for Growth Without Inflation: The German Experiment* (Baltimore: Johns Hopkins Press, 1964).

21. Oppen, *Documents on Germany,* p. 519.

22. For a full account of the ECSC, see Ernst B. Haas, *The Uniting of Europe* (Stanford: Stanford University Press, 1958).

23. See William Diebold, Jr., *The Schuman Plan* (New York: Praeger, 1959); M. Margaret Ball, *NATO and the European Union Movement* (New York: Praeger, 1959), esp. pp. 23–24; and Karl W. Deutsch and Lewis J. Edinger, *Germany Rejoins the Powers* (Stanford: Stanford University Press, 1959), Chapter 11.

24. For a full treatment, see Jacques Freymond, *The Saar Conflict, 1945–1955* (New York: Praeger, 1960).

25. Freymond, pp. 67–68; Eugene Davidson, *The Death and Life of Germany* (New York: Knopf, 1959), p. 292; Bundestag, *Sitzungsprotokoll der 144. Sitzung,* p. 5669.

26. Oppen, *Documents on Germany,* p. 609; Ball, *NATO,* p. 382.

27. Davidson, p. 364.
28. Freymond, *Saar Conflict*, pp. 195–201.
29. Oppen, pp. 522–27.
30. U.S. Senate Committee on Foreign Relations, *Documents on Germany, 1944–1961* (Washington, D.C., 1961), p. 87.
31. *Ibid.*, p. 88.
32. See Wilhelm Cornides, *Die Weltmächte und Deutschland* (Tübingen: Wunderlich, 1957), pp. 253–54.
33. Buchan and Windsor, *Arms and Stability*, p. 35.
34. U.S. Senate, *Documents on Germany*, pp. 117–23.
35. Buchan and Windsor, pp. 38–39.
36. *Keesing's Contemporary Archives*, X (London, 1956), p. 14169.
37. See Paul Sethe, *Zwischen Bonn und Moskau* (Frankfurt a. M.: Scheffler, 1956), pp. 104–6.
38. *Keesing's Contemporary Archives*, X, 14059.
39. Buchan and Windsor, *Arms and Stability*, p. 43; see also Donald Watt, "Germany," in Luard (*op. cit.* n. 1), pp. 118–19.

Chapter three

1. Jacques Freymond, *The Saar Conflict, 1945-1955* (New York: Praeger, 1960), p. 311.
2. See Kenneth N. Waltz, "The Stability of a Bipolar World," in *Daedalus*, Summer 1964, pp. 881–909.
3. See Paul Sethe, *Zwischen Bonn und Moskau* (Frankfurt a. M.: Scheffler, 1956), pp. 122–34.

Chapter four

1. For some penetrating studies, on which I have relied heavily, see Fritz René Allemann, *Bonn ist nicht Weimar* (Cologne: Krepenheuer und Witsch, 1956); Ludwig Bergstraesser, *Geschichte der politischen Parteien in Deutschland* (Munich: G. Olzog, 1960); Rupert Breitling, *Die Verbände in der Bundesrepublik* (Meisenheim: Hain, 1955); Ralf Dahrendorf, *Soziale Klassen und Klassenkonflikt* (Stuttgart: Ferdinand Eiche Verlag, 1957); Ossip K. Flechtheim, *Die Deutschen Parteien seit 1945* (Berlin: C. Heymann, 1955); F. A. Heydte and K. Sacherl, *Soziologie der deutschen Parteien* (Munich: Isar Verlag, 1955); Hans Speier, *German Rearmament and Atomic War* (Evanston, Ill.: Row, Peterson, 1957); Gerald Freund, *Germany Between Two Worlds* (New York: Harcourt, Brace, 1961); Karl W. Deutsch and Lewis J. Edinger, *Germany Rejoins the Powers* (Stanford: Stanford University Press, 1959); Hans Speier and W. Phillips Davison, eds., *West German Leadership and Foreign Policy* (Evanston, Ill.: Row, Peterson, 1957); Alfred Grosser, *The Colossus Again* (New York: Praeger, 1955); Klaus Bölling, *Republic in Suspense* (New York: Praeger, 1964); Wolfgang Hirsch-Weber, *Gewerkschaften in der Politik* (Cologne: Westdeutscher Verlag, 1959); Arnold J. Heidenheimer, *Adenauer and the CDU* (The Hague: Nijhoff, 1961); Douglas A. Chal-

mers, *The Social Democratic Party of Germany* (New Haven, Conn.: Yale University Press, 1964); Rudolf Wildenmann, *Macht und Konsens als Problem der Innen- und Aussenpolitik* (Frankfurt a. M.: Athenäum Verlag, 1963); Peter H. Merkl, *Germany: Yesterday and Tomorrow* (New York: Oxford University Press, 1965); Gerald Braunthal, *The Federation of German Industry in Politics* (Ithaca, N.Y.: Cornell University Press, 1965).

2. See Samuel L. Wahrhaftig, "The Development of German Foreign Policy Institutions," in Speier and Davison (*op. cit.* n. 1), pp. 7-56.

3. See *Journey to America: Collected Speeches, Statements, Press, Radio, and TV Interviews by Dr. Konrad Adenauer* (Press Office, German Diplomatic Mission, Washington, D.C., 1953), *passim*; Edgar Alexander, *Adenauer and the New Germany* (New York: Farrar, Straus, 1957), Chapter 6.

4. *Deutschland im Wiederaufbau, 1954* (Bonn: Presse und Informationsamt der Bundesregierung, 1955), esp. p. 11; also, *Journey to America*, p. 157.

5. Speier, *German Rearmament*, p. 158.

6. For excellent treatments of the factors affecting internal party cohesion, see Heinz Markmann, *Das Abstimmungsverfahren der Parteifraktionen in deutschen Parlamenten* (Meisenheim: Hain, 1955); Rudolf Wildenmann, *Partei und Fraktion* (Meisenheim: Hain, 1955); Dolf Sternberger, *Lebende Verfassung, Studien über Koalition und Opposition* (Meisenheim: Hain, 1956); Heydte and Sacherl, *Soziologie der deutschen Parteien*, esp. Chapters 12, 16, 17, 19.

7. The results of the 1949 and 1953 elections were as follows:

	1949		*1953*	
	Percentage of Votes	*Bundestag Seats*	*Percentage of Votes*	*Bundestag Seats*
CDU/CSU	31.0%	139	45.2%	243
SPD	29.2	131	28.8	151
FDP	11.9	52	9.5	48
DP	4.0	17	3.2	15
BHE	—	—	5.9	27
Bavarian Party	4.2	17	1.7	—
Extreme Right	1.8	5	1.1	—
KPD	5.7	15	2.2	—
Neutralists	—	—	1.1	—
Others	12.2	26	1.3	3
Total	*100.0*	*402*	*100.0*	*487*
Total votes cast	31,287,600		33,120,900	
Percentage of electorate voting	*78.5*		*86.0*	

The Cabinet formed after the 1949 election consisted of 9 members of the CDU (including the Chancellor), 3 from the FDP, and 2 from the DP;

the 1953 Cabinet consisted of 13 members of the CDU/CSU (including the Chancellor), 4 from the FDP, 2 from the DP, and 2 from the BHE-Refugee Party. See Alfred Grosser, *The Federal Republic of Germany—A Concise History* (New York: Praeger, 1963), p. 50.

8. Speier, *German Rearmament,* p. 74; Max Gustav Lange, "Die FDP—Versuch einer Erneuerung des Liberalismus," in Lange *et al., Parteien in der Bundesrepublik* (Stuttgart: Institut für Politische Wissenschaft, Ring Verlag, 1955), p. 345.

9. Lange, p. 348; Speier, pp. 163–64.

10. Henry L. Bretton, "The German Social Democratic Party and the International Situation," *American Political Science Review,* XLVII (1953), 984.

11. Grosser, *The Colossus Again,* p. 194.

12. The term "preventive nationalism" is Grosser's (*The Colossus Again,* p. 194). See also V. Stanley Vardys, "Germany's Postwar Socialism: Nationalism and Kurt Schumacher (1945–52)," *Review of Politics,* Apr. 1965, pp. 240–44. For a discussion of the development of the SPD's nationalism during the exile years, see Lewis J. Edinger, *German Exile Politics* (Berkeley: University of California Press, 1956); and Erich Matthias, *Die deutsche Sozialdemokratie und der Osten, 1914–1945* (Tübingen: Stapelmann, 1954).

13. Speier, *German Rearmament,* p. 156.

14. Bretton (*op. cit.* n. 10), p. 393; see also "The West German Political Parties and Rearmament," *The World Today,* IX, no. 2 (London: Royal Institute of International Affairs, 1953), p. 61.

15. See *Das Programm der Opposition: Einheit, Freiheit und Frieden für ganz Deutschland* (Bonn: SPD, 1954).

16. Arnold Heidenheimer, "Bonn Dispatch: The German Opposition," *New Republic,* Oct. 25, 1954, p. 17.

17. Lewis J. Edinger, *West German Rearmament* (Maxwell Air Force Base, Ala.: Documentary Research Div., Research Studies Inst., Air University, 1955), p. 136; C. G. D. Onslow, "West German Rearmament," *World Politics,* July 1951, p. 474; see also the three volumes of documents about the struggle to amend the Basic Law: *Der Kampf um den Wehrbeitrag* (Munich: Isar Verlag, 1952, 1953, 1958), in the series "Veröffentlichungen des Instituts für Staatslehre und Politik e. V. in Mainz."

18. *EMNID-Informationen,* VII, no. 1 (Jan. 1, 1953); Erich P. Neumann and Elisabeth Noelle, *Antworten* (Allensbach am Bodensee: Verlag für Demoskopie, 1954), p. 132.

19. See Gordon A. Craig, "NATO and the New German Army" in William W. Kaufmann, ed., *Military Policy and National Security* (Princeton, N.J.: Princeton University Press, 1956), pp. 194–232.

20. Otto Kirchheimer, "West German Trade Unions: Their Domestic and Foreign Policies," in Speier and Davison (*op. cit.* n. 1), esp. pp. 171–78; see also Wolfgang Hirsch-Weber, *Gewerkschaften*; Clark Kerr, "The Trade Union Movement and the Redistribution of Power in Postwar Germany," *Quarterly Journal of Economics,* LXVIII, no. 4 (1954), 535–64.

21. For the text of the Manifesto and the list of signatories, see *Rettet Einheit, Freiheit, Frieden! Gegen Kommunismus und Nationalismus!* (Frankfurt a. M.: Reithmüller, 1955).

22. See Gabriel Almond, "The Politics of German Business," in Speier and Davison (*op. cit.* n. 1), pp. 195–241.

23. Speier, *German Rearmament,* Part I.

24. *Ibid.*, p. 55.

25. *Ibid.*, pp. 75–82.

26. *Ibid.*, p. 80; as early as October 1952, a prominent FDP member, Dr. Karl Pfleiderer, had proposed that a neutral zone be established between East and West Germany from which all NATO and Soviet troops would be withdrawn, and which would serve as the basis for negotiations over reunification.

27. See Chapter 2, pp. 49–50; and *Deutschland im Wiederaufbau, 1954,* p. 5.

28. See Grosser, *The Colossus Again,* Chapter 6.

29. See Rudolf Holzgräber, "Die DP, Partei eines neuen Konservatismus?" in Lange (*op. cit.* n. 8), p. 442.

30. Bretton (*op. cit.* n. 10), *passim.*

31. Carlo Schmid, "Germany and Europe," *International Affairs,* XXVII, no. 3 (1951), pp. 310–11; Fritz Erler, *The Struggle for German Reunification* (SPD pamphlet, 1956), p. 18.

32. See Lange (*op. cit.* n. 8), pp. 303–29; Wilhelm Mommsen, *Deutsche Parteiprogramme* (Munich: Isar Verlag, 1960), pp. 696–98, 711; Holzgräber (*op. cit.* n. 29), pp. 445–47; Klaus Schütz, "Die Sozialdemokratie im Nachkriegsdeutschland," in Lange (*op. cit.* n. 8), p. 347; *SPD Action Program, 1952* (SPD pamphlet), pp. 17–25; Ludwig Erhard, *Prosperity Through Competition* (London: Thames and Huston, 1958).

For an excellent treatment of Germany's postwar recovery, see Henry C. Wallich, *Mainsprings of the German Revival* (New Haven, Conn.: Yale University Press, 1955); also André Piettre, *L'Economie allemande contemporaine 1945–1952* (Paris: Génin, 1952); Frederick G. Reuss, *Fiscal Policy for Growth Without Inflation, The German Experiment* (Baltimore: Johns Hopkins Press, 1964); Karel Holbik and Henry Myers, *Postwar Trade in Divided Germany: The Internal and International Issues* (Baltimore: Johns Hopkins Press, 1964).

33. For a full account, see Ernst B. Haas, *The Uniting of Europe* (Stanford: Stanford University Press, 1958); see also *Journey to America,* pp. 33, 149–50.

34. Haas, pp. 129–31; Lange (*op. cit.* n. 8), pp. 346–47; Deutsch and Edinger, *Germany Rejoins the Powers,* Chapter 11.

35. Haas, p. 130.

36. *Handelsblatt,* Dec. 19, 1951, p. 1; Haas, *Uniting of Europe,* p. 163.

37. Haas, pp. 129–30.

38. Deutsch and Edinger, pp. 156–57.

39. See Arthur M. Ross, "Prosperity and Labor Relations in Europe: The Case of West Germany" *The Quarterly Journal of Economics,* LXXXVI,

no. 3 (1962), pp. 331–59; Haas, *Uniting of Europe,* pp. 219–25; Bretton (*op. cit.* n. 10), p. 990.

40. Schmid (*op. cit.* n. 31), p. 307; Kurt Schumacher, *Deutschlands Forderung* (SPD pamphlet), pp. 13–14; Kurt Schumacher, *50 Jahre mit gebundenen Händen? Die Entscheidung über Kohle und Stahl* (SPD pamphlet); *Frankreich und der Schumanplan* (SPD pamphlet); *Der Schumanplan führt nicht nach Europa!* (SPD pamphlet); Haas, pp. 136–38.

41. *Der Schumanplan führt nicht nach Europa!* (SPD pamphlet), p. 69.

42. Haas, *Uniting of Europe,* p. 138.

43. Georg Droege, "Die Saarfrage und das politische Deutschland: die Stellung der bundesdeutschen Parteien zur Saarfrage" in Klaus Altmeier, Jakob Szliska, Werner Veauthier, and Peter Weiant, *Das Saarland* (Saarbrücken: Verlag "Die Mitte," 1958).

44. *Ibid.,* p. 144.

45. *Ibid.,* p. 145; see also Jacques Freymond, *The Saar Conflict, 1945–1955* (New York: Praeger, 1960), p. 78.

46. This appeared to be a well-founded expectation. In July 1951, 76 per cent of respondents in a German public-opinion survey felt that Germany should not acquiesce in the loss of the Saar. In January 1952, over 70 per cent were unwilling to give up the Saar even if this precluded establishing friendly relations with France. Reactions to the Europeanization of the Saar were not much more positive; it was not desired even if France were willing to contribute part of her own territory to this creation. By June 1954, "the attitude of the West German population toward the Saar question had stabilized itself. Two thirds wanted an Anschluss; only one third preferred other solutions that were being discussed in the political arena." With respect to the desirability of an overall rapprochement with France, a poll in February 1952 resulted in the following answers to the question "Do you consider Adenauer's attempts to arrive at a good relationship with France right or wrong?": 52 per cent thought it would be right; 15 per cent considered it right with reservations; 14 per cent called it wrong; and 19 per cent were undecided or unable to say. Neumann and Noelle, *Antworten,* pp. 127, 128, 130, 160; see also Freymond, *The Saar Conflict,* p. 279.

47. For the SPD's counterargument, see *Götterdämmerung beim Schumanplan* (SPD pamphlet), pp. 8–9.

48. Freymond, p. 117; Droege (*op. cit.* n. 43), p. 148.

49. Lange (*op. cit.* n. 8), p. 347; Freymond, p. 239.

50. *Deutschland im Wiederaufbau, 1954,* pp. 8–9.

51. Freymond, *The Saar Conflict,* p. 179; Droege (*op. cit.* n. 43), pp. 148–49; on the passive attitude of German business interests, and the lukewarm reception of French Saar policy even among French business interests, see Freymond, pp. 243–45.

52. Freymond, pp. 239–41.

53. *Journey to America,* pp. 155–56, 163.

54. *Deutschland im Wiederaufbau, 1954,* pp. 12–13.

55. See, for example, Erler (*op. cit.* n. 31), pp. 6–9.

56. Onslow (*op. cit.* n. 17), p. 474; Bretton (*op. cit.* n. 10), p. 994.
57. Erler, pp. 8–9.
58. According to public-opinion polls, during the early 1950's West Germans were increasingly preoccupied with the issue of reunification. By July 1953, 38 per cent of respondents considered the restoration of German unity the most important question confronting West German foreign policy, as compared with 18 per cent in October 1951. The lack of agreement among the political parties on the proper order of priority of the Federal Republic's major foreign policy goals was also reflected in public-opinion surveys. Confronted with the question "which is more important, security vis-à-vis the Russians or the unity of Germany," approximately half of the respondents opted for security, roughly one third for unity, the rest were undecided. A breakdown by party preference of responses to this question presented the following pattern:

More important:	*Parties of Voters*		
	CDU	*FDP*	*SPD*
Security vis-à-vis Russia	59%	55%	41%
Unity of Germany	33	33	45
Undecided, don't know	8	12	14

(Note the approximate "balance" within the SPD voter group on this order of priority, which underlines the dilemma faced even by the followers of the "reunification" party. The SPD group also shows the highest percentage of those undecided.)

The security-reunification dilemma is also reflected in responses to a somewhat similar question, put to West German respondents in July 1953: "Perhaps the Russians demand that in the future Germany shall not have an army or enter alliances with other countries. Should we accept these demands if they lead to reunification?"

	No, not accept	*Yes, accept*	*Don't know*
Total	44%	29%	27%
Men	50	33	17
Women	39	26	35

In 1954, in response to an almost identical question, the breakdown by party voters was as follows. Again, note particularly the SPD voter group.

	Total	*CDU*	*SPD*	*FDP*
No, not accept	45%	57%	34%	60%
Yes, accept	21	14	36	24
Undecided	34	29	30	16

Figures come from Neumann and Noelle, *Antworten*, pp. 119–23; Elisabeth Noelle, *Auskunft über die Parteien, Ergebnisse der Umfrage-Forschung in Deutschland* (Allensbach am Bodensee: Verlag für Demoskopie, 1955), p. 28.
59. Freund, *Germany Between Two Worlds*, p. 95.

60. Kirchheimer (*op. cit.* n. 20), pp. 174–76, 179–85.
61. Almond (*op. cit.* n. 22), pp. 195–241.
62. See the discussion in the *Handelsblatt,* Nov. 23, 1951, p. 3; Wolfgang F. Stolper, *Germany Between East and West* (Washington, D.C.: National Planning Association, 1960).
63. *Handelsblatt,* Nov. 23, 1951, p. 3.

Chapter five

1. George Liska, *Nations in Alliance* (Baltimore: Johns Hopkins Press, 1962), p. 162.
2. See Ernst B. Haas, "Regionalism, Functionalism, and Universal International Organization," *World Politics,* Jan. 1956, pp. 238–63; Wolfram F. Hanrieder, "International Organizations and International Systems," *Journal of Conflict Resolution,* X (1966), 297–313.
3. Wolfram F. Hanrieder, "The International System: Bipolar or Multi-Bloc?" *Journal of Conflict Resolution,* IX (1965), 299–308. For an application of the concept of "heterosymmetrical multipolarity" to a future international system, see Ernst B. Haas, *Beyond the Nation-State* (Stanford: Stanford University Press, 1964), pp. 483–97.
4. Henry A. Kissinger, *The Necessity for Choice* (Garden City, N.Y.: Doubleday, 1962), p. 12.
5. Robert E. Osgood, "Stabilizing the Military Environment," *American Political Science Review,* LV (1961), 27; italics in the text.
6. *Ibid.,* p. 29; italics in the text.
7. On this point, see John H. Herz, *International Politics in the Atomic Age* (New York: Columbia University Press, 1962), p. 175. Paradoxically, Russian technological advances contributed to intra-Soviet-bloc pressures as well; the schism between Communist China and the Soviet Union over the most effective strategy vis-à-vis the Western powers is at least in part the result of the increased capabilities of the Soviet Union.
8. For a perceptive account, see George Lichtheim, *The New Europe* (New York: Praeger, 1963).
9. See Walter Laqueur and Leopold Labedz, eds., *Polycentrism* (New York: Praeger, 1962); Alexander Dallin, ed., *Dissensions in International Communism* (New York: Columbia University Press, 1963); Zbigniew K. Brzezinski, *The Soviet Bloc* (Cambridge, Mass.: Harvard University Press, 1960), and his *Alternative to Partition* (New York: McGraw-Hill, 1965).
10. See Hans Speier, *German Rearmament and Atomic War* (Evanston, Ill.: Row, Peterson, 1957), pp. 169–89; and Robert E. Osgood, "NATO: Problems of Security and Collaboration," *American Political Science Review,* LIV (1960), 126.
11. *The Washington Post,* Jan. 26, 1955, as quoted by Speier, p. 14.
12. Osgood, "NATO" (*op. cit.* n. 10), pp. 118–20; for a perceptive analytical distinction between deterrence and defense, see Glenn H. Snyder, *Deterrence and Defense* (Princeton, N.J.: Princeton University Press, 1961); see also John Strachey, *On the Prevention of War* (New York: St Martin's Press, 1963), esp. Chapters 4 and 6.

13. Strachey, p. 93.

14. *Ibid., passim.*

15. For an American defense of this doctrine, see Robert Strausz-Hupé, James E. Dougherty, and William R. Kintner, *Building the Atlantic World* (New York: Harper, 1963).

16. See Robert E. Osgood, *NATO: The Entangling Alliance* (Chicago: University of Chicago Press, 1962), p. 109. Of course when both sides deploy tactical nuclear weapons, neither side can afford to concentrate conventional forces. See Malcolm W. Hoag, "Rationalizing NATO Strategy," *World Politics*, Oct. 1964, pp. 121–42.

17. Speier, *German Rearmament*, p. 210, also pp. 197–212.

18. Gerald Freund, *Germany Between Two Worlds* (New York: Harcourt, Brace, 1961), pp. 148–49.

19. Speier, *German Rearmament*, p. 220; Osgood, *Entangling Alliance*, p. 254.

20. Osgood, *Alliance*, pp. 253, 221–22.

21. *Ibid.*, p. 255; Freund, p. 154.

22. Freund, pp. 152–55.

23. Osgood, *Alliance*, pp. 253–55.

24. As quoted in Karl W. Deutsch and Lewis T. Edinger, *Germany Rejoins the Powers* (Stanford: Stanford University Press, 1959), p. 221.

25. Osgood, *Alliance*, pp. 221–22.

26. *Ibid.*, p. 226.

27. *Ibid.*, pp. 230–32.

28. James E. Dougherty, "European Deterrence and Atlantic Unity," in *Orbis*, VI, no. 3 (1962), p. 381, n. 15; Osgood, *Alliance*, p. 234.

29. Raymond Aron, *The Great Debate* (Garden City, N.Y.: Doubleday, 1965), p. 79; italics in the text. See also Charles B. Marshall, "Détente: Effects on the Alliance"; Alfons Dalma, "The Risks of a Détente Policy to Central Europe"; and James E. King, Jr., "Toward Stability in Central Europe"; all in Arnold Wolfers, ed., *Changing East-West Relations and the Unity of the West* (Baltimore: Johns Hopkins Press, 1964).

30. Henry A. Kissinger, "The Unsolved Problems of European Defense," in *Foreign Affairs*, XL, no. 4 (1962), p. 524.

31. See Samuel P. Huntington, *The Common Defense* (New York: Columbia University Press, 1961), p. 86.

32. Hoag (*op. cit.* n. 16), p. 347.

33. Laurence W. Martin, "The Future of the Alliance: A Pragmatic Approach," in Wolfers (*op. cit.* n. 29), p. 227.

34. The *New York Times*, May 10 and May 18, 1961.

35. Dougherty (*op. cit.* n. 28), p. 381, n. 15.

36. The *New York Times*, Oct. 17, 1962.

37. Alastair Buchan and Philip Windsor, *Arms and Stability in Europe* (New York: Praeger, 1963), esp. pp. 192–201.

38. The *New York Times*, Dec. 12, 15, and 18, 1962; Coral Bell, *The Debatable Alliance* (New York: Oxford University Press, 1964), p. 91; Dalma (*op. cit.* n. 29), *passim.*

39. Hoag (*op. cit.* n. 16), p. 130.

40. Buchan and Windsor, p. 12; see also Herman Kahn, *On Escalation: Metaphors and Scenarios* (New York: Praeger, 1965), esp. Chapter 6 and pp. 194–95.

41. For a persuasive presentation of this perspective see Dalma (*op. cit.* n. 29), esp. pp. 107–8.

42. *Economic Conditions in the Federal Republic of Germany*, EC (56), Oct. 1956 (Paris: OEEC), pp. 5–12.

43. The economy's rate of growth had slowed down and the real gross national product increased by only 5 per cent in 1957, as compared to an increase of 6.4 per cent in 1956 and almost 12 per cent in 1955. *Economic Conditions in Member and Associated Countries of the OEEC: Federal Republic of Germany,* EC (58) 9, Oct. 1958 (Paris: OEEC), p. 5; see also U. W. Kitzinger, *The Politics and Economics of European Integration* (New York: Praeger, 1963), esp. p. 18.

44. In February 1959, a DM 20.00 tax per ton was imposed on ECSC imports, except for a duty-free contingent; also in May 1959, a tax of 25.00 DM per ton was imposed on heavy fuel oil. *Economic Conditions in Member and Associated Countries of the OEEC: Federal Republic of Germany* EC (59) 25, Jan. 1960 (Paris: OEEC), p. 9; and (same title) EC (60) 25 (Paris, OEEC) p. 7.

45. OEEC Report, EC (60) 25, pp. 19–24.

46. Vacla E. Mares, "Key to Europe: West Germany," *Current History,* Mar. 1962, pp. 148–53; Heinrich Bechtoldt, "Germany and the Common Market," *India Quarterly,* XVI, no. 3 (1960), pp. 249–58.

47. Kitzinger, *Politics and Economics,* pp. 120–43; see also Emile Benoit, *Europe at Sixes and Sevens* (New York: Columbia University Press, 1961), p. 86; Isaiah Frank, *The European Common Market, An Analysis of Commercial Policy* (New York: Praeger, 1961).

48. Bechtoldt (*op. cit.* n. 46), p. 251, suggests that "after the Soviet ultimatum of 28 November 1958, De Gaulle . . . proved himself so reliable, even on the question of Berlin, that Dr. Adenauer was compelled to let the continuation of the close political cooperation with France outweigh his disappointment over the shelving of the negotiations regarding the Great Free Trade Zone."

49. Benoit, *Europe,* pp. 92–95; see also Randall Hinshaw, *The European Community and American Trade* (New York: Praeger, 1964), *passim.*

50. Benoit, pp. 86–87.

51. Bechtoldt (*op. cit.* n. 46), pp. 256–57.

52. Kitzinger, *Politics and Economics,* pp. 140–41.

53. Benoit, *Europe,* pp. 89–91; Herbert Nicholas, *Britain and the U.S.A.* (Baltimore: Johns Hopkins Press, 1963), Chapter 10.

54. Hinshaw, *European Community,* Chapter 4; William Diebold, Jr., "Economic Aspects of an Atlantic Community," in Francis O. Wilcox and H. Field Haviland, Jr., eds., *The Atlantic Community* (New York: Praeger, 1963), pp. 145–64; Lichtheim, *New Europe,* pp. 51–59.

55. Hinshaw, Chapter 6; Kitzinger, *Politics and Economics,* pp. 219-27;

for an account that minimizes the importance of the Nassau decision, see Robert Kleiman, *Atlantic Crisis* (New York: Norton, 1964), esp. Chapter 3.

56. *The Bulletin* (Bonn: Press and Information Office of the German Federal Government), Nov. 29, 1960; Jan. 17, Feb. 21, Mar. 28, and May 16, 1961. In Sept. 1962, the Government published figures of aid granted by the Federal Republic between 1950 and 1962. The total sum amounts to 19.2 billion DM. Of this, 15.2 billion DM were for bilateral and 4 billion DM were for multilateral aid. The bilateral payments were made up as follows (the first figure being public aid, the second private aid): Africa, 204 million DM, 777 million DM; Latin America, 577 million DM, 3.385 billion DM; Asia, 1.727 billion DM, 1.623 billion DM; Europe, 1.174 billion DM, 1.415 billion DM; not specifiable: 391 million DM, 979 million DM. Restitution granted on the basis of agreements amounted to 2.964 billion DM. Further restitution to the value of 3 billion DM, which was granted to individual persons in the developing countries, is not included in the survey. Multilateral aid was made up of the following contributions: United Nations Technical Aid, 78 million DM; United Nations Special Organizations, 45 million DM; EEC Development Funds, 508 million DM. Credits to the value of 2.625 billion and 266 million DM were made available to the World Bank. See *Bulletin*, Oct. 9, 1962, pp. 3–4.

57. See Fritz R. Allemann, *Zwischen Stabilität und Krise* (Munich: Piper, 1963), pp. 57–69, 70–80, 289–309.

58. Donald Watt, "Germany" in Evan Luard, ed., *The Cold War: A Reappraisal* (New York: Praeger, 1964), p. 118.

59. Buchan and Windsor, *Arms and Stability*, p. 53.

60. See Gerard Braunthal, "An Agreement with the Russians," in James B. Christoph, ed., *Cases in Comparative Politics* (Boston: Little, Brown, 1965), pp. 256–87.

61. U.S. Senate Committee on Foreign Relations, *Documents on Germany, 1944–1961* (Washington, D.C.: 1961), p. 207.

62. *Deutschland im Wiederaufbau, 1956* (Bonn: Presse und Informationsamt der Bundesregierung, 1957), p. 47.

63. *Ibid.*, p. 48.

64. For a discussion of the strategic and political implications of disengagement, see Osgood, *Entangling Alliance*, Chapter 10.

65. Buchan and Windsor, *Arms and Stability*, p. 35.

66. *Ibid.*, p. 43.

67. Werner Erfurt, *Moscow's Policy in Germany* (Esslingen: Bechtle, n.d.), p. 85.

68. Buchan and Windsor, pp. 48–49.

69. For two interesting accounts of the Berlin situation, see Jean Edward Smith, *The Defense of Berlin* (Baltimore: Johns Hopkins Press, 1963); and John Mander, *Berlin, Hostage for the West* (Baltimore: Johns Hopkins Press, 1962).

70. Freund, *Germany Between Two Worlds*, p. 220.

71. Allemann, *Stabilität und Krise*, pp. 136–63.

72. *Documents on Germany*, p. 460.
73. *Ibid.*, p. 575.
74. Allemann, pp. 153–63.
75. *Documents on Germany*, p. 589.
76. Freund, *Germany*, p. 206 and p. 206, n. 15.
77. See Philip Windsor, "Berlin," in Luard (*op. cit.* n. 58), pp. 120–39; Allemann, *Stabilität und Krise*, pp. 195–212.
78. Allemann, p. 217.
79. *Ibid.*, p. 236; Windsor (*op. cit.* n. 77), p. 137.
80. For a discussion of the "Second Rapallo" question, see Allemann, *Stabilität und Krise*, pp. 277–88; Osgood, *Entangling Alliance*, p. 328; and Freund, *Germany*, pp. 204–5.
81. *Bulletin*, June 30, 1962, p. 2

Chapter six

Raymond Aron summarizes the problem by suggesting that "the greater the stability[deriving from parity] at the level of ultimate weapons, the more uncertain it becomes at the level of conventional ones. The more the gap between limited wars and conventional arms on the one hand and nuclear arms on the other is stressed in both word and deed, the less reason there is to fear escalation. The less reason to fear escalation, the greater the probability of limited conflict. Hence the tensions among allies, some of whom are mainly afraid of all-out war while others worry just as much about limited ones." *The Great Debate* (Garden City, N.Y.: Doubleday, 1965), p. 215.

2. See Coral Bell, *The Debatable Alliance* (New York: Oxford University Press, 1964), p. 66.
3. *Ibid.*, p. 84.
4. See Malcolm W. Hoag, "Rationalizing NATO Strategy," *World Politics*, Oct. 1964, p. 133; Henry A. Kissinger, *Nuclear Weapons and Foreign Policy* (New York: Doubleday, 1957), pp. 228–91; Alastair Buchan and Philip Windsor, *Arms and Stability in Europe* (New York: Praeger, 1963), pp. 39–40.
5. Walter Lippmann, *Western Unity and the Common Market* (Boston: Little, Brown, 1962), p. 32.

Chapter seven

1. See Gordon A. Craig, "Germany and NATO: The Rearmament Debate, 1950–1958," in Klaus Knorr, ed., *NATO and American Security* (Princeton, N. J.: Princeton University Press, 1959), esp. p. 241; Hans Speier, *German Rearmament and Atomic War* (Evanston, Ill.: Row, Peterson, 1957), pp. 133–39; *Bundestag Debates*, June 28, 1955, p. 5232; Dec. 2, 1955, p. 6162; Dec. 7, 1955, pp. 6211–13.
2. Speier, pp. 194–205.
3. *News from Germany*, XI, no. 7, July 1957, and no. 8, Aug. 1957, (Bonn: Executive Committee of the SPD).

4. The results of the 1957 elections were as follows:

	Percentage of Votes	*Bundestag Seats*
CDU/CSU	50.2%	270
SPD	31.8	169
FDP	7.7	41
DP	3.4	17
BHE	4.6	—
Extreme Right	1.0	—
Others	1.3	—
Total	*100.0*	*497*
Total votes cast	35,400,900	
Percentage of electorate voting	87.8	

The Cabinet established consisted of 16 members of the CDU/CSU (including the chancellor) and 2 members of the German Party.

5. *News from Germany*, XI, no. 12 (Dec. 1957), pp. 2–4.

6. Craig (*op. cit.* n. 1), pp. 244–45.

7. *News from Germany*, XII, no. 4 (Apr. 1958), pp. 1–4.

8. *Keesing's Contemporary Archives*, XI (London, 1958), 16143–44.

9. "Das Nein zum nuklearen Selbstmord: der Kreuzzug des Gewissens" (Bonn: Arbeitsausschuss "Kampf dem Atomtod," 1958).

10. *Umfragen 1957* (Frankfurt: DIVO-Institut, 1958), p. 18. By August 1962, 50 per cent of the respondents rejected atomic arms for the Bundeswehr and 28 per cent declared themselves in favor. *DIVO-Pressedienst* (Frankfurt), Aug. 11, 1962; *Umfragen*, II, 45.

11. *Die Welt*, as quoted in *Bulletin*, July 8, 1958 (Bonn: Press and Information Office of the German Federal Government), p. 2.

12. Fritz R. Allemann, *Zwischen Stabilität und Krise* (Munich: Piper, 1963), pp. 57–80; Gerald Braunthal, "The Succession Crisis of 1959," in James B. Christoph, ed., *Cases in Comparative Politics* (Boston: Little, Brown, 1965), pp. 209–40; Peter H. Merkl, "Equilibrium, Structure of Interests, and Leadership: Adenauer's Survival as Chancellor," *American Political Science Review*, LVI (1962), 634–50.

13. The results of the 1961 elections were as follows:

	Percentage of Votes	*Bundestag Seats*
CDU/CSU	45.4	242
SPD	36.2	190
FDP	12.8	67
DP / BHE *	2.8	—
Extreme Right	0.8	—
Neutralists	1.9	—
Total	*100.0*	*499*
Total votes cast	37,440,715	
Percentage of electorate voting	87.7	

* The DP and the BHE merged in April 1961 to form the All-German Party (GDP).

The Cabinet established consisted of 16 members of the CDU/CSU (including the chancellor) and 6 members of the FDP.

14. For a full account of the background, see Douglas A. Chalmers, *The Social Democratic Party of Germany* (New Haven, Conn.: Yale University Press, 1964), esp. Chapter 3; Peter H. Merkl, *Germany: Yesterday and Tomorrow* (New York: Oxford University Press, 1965), Chapter 9.

15. *News from Germany*, XII, no. 12 (Dec. 1958), p. 3.

16. *Ibid.*, XIII, no. 12 (Dec. 1959), p. 1.

17. *Ibid.*, XIV, no. 1 (Jan. 1960), p. 1.

18. *Ibid.*, pp. 2–7. See also XIV, no. 6 (June 1960), p. 1; XIV, no. 8 (Aug. 1960), pp. 1–5.

19. *Ibid.*, XIV, no. 12 (Dec. 1960), pp. 2–3.

20. *Ibid.*, XV–XVI, nos. 12–1 (Dec. 1961–Jan. 1962), p. 2.

21. *Ibid.*, XVI, no. 3 (Mar. 1962), p. 3; XVI, no. 5 (May 1962), p. 4; XVI, nos. 6–7 (June–July 1962), p. 2.

22. Raymond Aron, *The Great Debate* (Garden City, N.Y.: Doubleday, 1965), p. 90.

23. Fritz Erler, "Partner oder Rivalen," in Hans-Adolf Jacobsen and Otto Stenzl, eds., *Deutschland und die Welt* (Munich: Deutscher Taschenbuch Verlag, 1964), pp. 414–25, esp. pp. 420 and 424.

24. The *New York Times*, Mar. 13, 1962, p. 17; *Christian Science Monitor*, June 27, 1962.

25. *DIVO-Pressedienst* (Frankfurt), Apr. 1 and Aug. 11, 1962.

26. Jacobsen and Stenzl, *Deutschland*, p. 386.

27. Kurt Becker, "The Development of Domestic Politics," in Walter Stahl, ed., *The Politics of Postwar Germany* (New York: Praeger, 1963), pp. 57–63.

28. *Die Debatte* (SPD periodical), no. 23 (June 1957), p. 4; *News from Germany*, XI, no. 12 (Dec. 1957), pp. 3–4.

29. *News from Germany*, XII, nos. 6–7 (June–July 1958), pp. 6–8; *Die Debatte*, no. 31 (May 1958), pp. 9–10.

30. *News from Germany*, XIII, no. 10 (Sept. 1959), pp. 2–3.

31. *Ibid.*, XV, no. 3 (Mar. 1961), pp. 2–4. For an SPD critique of the CDU's People's Shares program, particularly with respect to Volkswagen shares, see *News from Germany*, XV, no. 7 (July 1961), p. 2.

32. *Die Debatte*, no. 19 (Mar. 1957), *passim.*

33. *Ibid.*

34. Gerald Freund, *Germany Between Two Worlds* (New York: Harcourt, Brace, 1961), p. 117.

35. U. W. Kitzinger, *The Politics and Economics of European Integration* (New York: Praeger, 1963), p. 125; Leon Lindberg, *The Political Dynamics of European Economic Integration* (Stanford: Stanford University Press, 1963).

36. *News from Germany*, XIII, no. 12 (Dec. 1959), p. 3.

37. *Ibid.*, XV, no. 2 (Feb. 1960), pp. 1–2; see also Rüdiger Altmann, *Das deutsche Risiko* (Stuttgart: Seewald, 1962), p. 111; Don D. Humphrey, *The United States and the Common Market* (New York: Praeger, 1964).

38. *News from Germany,* XIV, no. 7 (July 1960), p. 2; XV, no. 1 (Jan. 1961), p. 3; XVI, no. 2 (Feb. 1962), pp. 3–4.
39. *Ibid.,* XII, no. 1 (Jan. 1958), pp. 1–2; XII, no. 2 (Feb. 1958), pp. 1–2; XII, no. 3 (Mar. 1958), pp. 1–2.
40. Craig (*op. cit.* n. 1), p. 255; *Keesing's Contemporary Archives,* XI, p. 16143; for a concise summary of developments within the FDP since 1956, see pp. 15757–58. See also *Bulletin,* VI, no. 13 (Apr. 1, 1958), p. 1.
41. *Die Debatte,* no. 29, Mar. 1958, *passim*; *News from Germany,* XII, nos. 6–7 (June–July 1958), pp. 3–5; XII, no. 10 (Oct. 1958), pp. 5–7; XII, no. 11 (Nov. 1958), p. 1.
42. *Ibid.,* XIII, no. 2 (Feb. 1959), p. 1.
43. Allemann, *Stabilität und Krise,* pp. 148–52.
44. The *New York Times,* Mar. 14, 1960, p. 1; this was disputed by the FDP, however—see the *New York Times,* Mar. 16, 1960, p. 2.
45. *News from Germany,* XIV, no. 6 (June 1960), p. 4; XV, no. 6 (June 1961), p. 2. The SPD's military expert put forth a modified and sophisticated proposal for some measure of disengagement as late as 1961; see Helmut Schmidt,*Verteidigung oder Vergeltung* (Stuttgart: Seewald, 1961).
46. *News from Germany,* XV, no. 7 (July 1961), p. 2; see also John W. Keller, *Germany, The Wall and Berlin: Internal Politics During An International Crisis* (New York: Vantage, 1964), *passim.*
47. *News from Germany,* XV–XVI, nos. 12–1 (Dec. 1961–Jan. 1962), p. 1.
48. See Gerard Braunthal, "The Free Democratic Party in West German Politics," in *Western Political Quarterly,* XIII, no. 2 (1960), pp. 332–48; the *New York Times,* Sept. 19, 1961, Mar. 13, 1962; the *Christian Science Monitor,* June 27, 1962.
49. Thomas Dehler, "Politik für Deutschland," in Jacobsen and Stenzl (*op. cit.* n. 23), p. 222.

Conclusion

1. James N. Rosenau, "Pre-theories and Theories of Foreign Policy," in R. Barry Farrell, ed., *Approaches to Comparative and International Politics* (Evanston, Ill.: Northwestern University Press, 1966), p. 65; italics in the text.
2. *Ibid.,* p. 66.
3. See John H. Herz, *International Politics in the Atomic Age* (New York: Columbia University Press, 1959).
4. Wolfram F. Hanrieder, "Actor Objectives and International Systems," *Journal of Politics,* Feb. 1965, pp. 109–35.
5. This possibility is explored more fully in my "Compatibility and Consensus: A Proposal for the Conceptual Linkage of External and Internal Dimensions of Foreign Policy," *American Political Science Review,* LXI (Sept. 1967).
6. See Zbigniew K. Brzezinski, *Alternative to Partition* (New York: McGraw-Hill, 1965), esp. pp. 124–25; Gordon A. Craig, *From Bismarck to Adenauer: Aspects of German Statecraft* (Baltimore: Johns Hopkins Press,

1958); Fritz R. Allemann, *Zwischen Stabilität und Krise* (Munich: Piper Verlag, 1963), pp. 229–40 and 277–88.

7. See Peter H. Merkl, *Germany: Yesterday and Tomorrow* (New York: Oxford University Press, 1965), p. 230.

8. Allemann, *Stabilität und Krise*, p. 63. This phenomenon may also account for the electoral success of the Free Democrats in 1961. Although the Socialists had also gained, it was primarily the FDP that profited from the apparent disenchantment with the Chancellor's overall policy program.

9. See O. K. Flechtheim, "Die Institutionalisierung der Parteien in der Bundesrepublik," *Zeitschrift für Politik*, Feb. 1960, p. 103; on the "end of ideology" see the following, reflecting a wide spectrum of political opinion: Ernst Fraenkel, *Deutschland und die Westlichen Demokratien* (Stuttgart: W. Kohlhammer, 1964); Otto Heinrich von der Gablentz, *Die versäumte Reform* (Cologne: Westdeutscher Verlag, 1960); Hans-Georg von Studnitz, *Bismarck in Bonn* (Stuttgart: Seewald, 1964); Erich Müller-Gangloff, *Mit der Teilung leben* (Munich: List Verlag, 1965); Günter Gaus, *Bonn ohne Regierung?* (Munich: Piper Verlag, 1965); Werner von Lojewski, *Bonn am Wendepunkt* (Munich: Bechtle, 1965). For an assessment of some of the critical reaction to the "de-ideologization" of West German politics, see H. P. Secher, "Current Ideological Emphasis in the Federal Republic" (Paper presented to the 1964 Meeting of the American Political Science Association); see also Gabriel A. Almond and Sidney Verba, *The Civic Culture* (Boston: Little, Brown, 1965), pp. 312–13.

10. See Seymour M. Lipset, "The Changing Class Structure and Contemporary European Politics," *Daedalus*, Winter 1964, pp. 283–84; Ralf Dahrendorf, "Demokratie und Sozialstruktur in Deutschland," *European Journal of Sociology*, Jan. 1960, pp. 86–121; for a theoretical treatment of the consequences of rationalization in the quest for support at the polls, see Anthony Downs, *An Economic Theory of Democracy* (New York: Harper, 1957).

Index